KATE!

ALSO BY CHRISTOPHER ANDERSEN

The King: The Life of Charles III

Brothers and Wives: Inside the Private Lives of William, Kate, Harry, and Meghan

Game of Crowns: Elizabeth, Camilla, Kate, and the Throne

The Good Son: JFK Jr. and the Mother He Loved

These Few Precious Days: The Final Year of Jack with Jackie

Mick: The Wild Life and Mad Genius of Jagger

William and Kate: A Royal Love Story

Barack and Michelle: Portrait of an American Marriage

Somewhere in Heaven: The Remarkable Love Story of Dana and Christopher Reeve

After Diana: William, Harry, Charles and the Royal House of Windsor

Barbra: The Way She Is

American Evita: Hillary Clinton's Path to Power

Sweet Caroline: Last Child of Camelot

George and Laura: Portrait of an American Marriage

Diana's Boys: William and Harry and the Mother They Loved

The Day John Died

Bill and Hillary: The Marriage

The Day Diana Died

Jackie After Jack: Portrait of the Lady

An Affair to Remember: The Remarkable Love Story of Katharine Hepburn and Spencer Tracy

Jack and Jackie: Portrait of an American Marriage

Citizen Jane: The Turbulent Life of Jane Fonda

The Best of Everything (with John Marion)

Young Kate: The Remarkable Hepburns and the Childhood That Shaped an American Legend

The Serpent's Tooth

Father

The Book of People

The Name Game

KATE!

THE COURAGE, GRACE, AND POWER OF THE WOMAN WHO WILL BE QUEEN

CHRISTOPHER ANDERSEN

GALLERY BOOKS
New York Amsterdam/Antwerp London
Toronto Sydney/Melbourne New Delhi

Gallery Books
An Imprint of Simon & Schuster, LLC
1230 Avenue of the Americas
New York, NY 10020

First Gallery Books hardcover edition May 2026

GALLERY BOOKS and colophon are registered trademarks of Simon & Schuster, LLC

INTERIOR DESIGN BY KARLA SCHWEER

Grateful acknowledgment is made to the following for permission to use the photographs in this book.

Shutterstock: 1, 2, 3, 4, 6, 7, 8, 9, 10, 11, 12, 13, 14, 15, 16, 17, 18, 19, 20, 21, 22, 23, 24, 25, 26, 27, 28, 29, 30, 31, 32, 33, 34, 35, 36, 37, 38, 39, 42, 43, 44, 45, 46, 47, 48

Zuma Press: 5, 40, 41

Manufactured in the United States of America

10 9 8 7 6 5 4 3 2 1

Library of Congress Control Number: 2025950873

ISBN 978-1-6680-8697-1
ISBN 978-1-6680-8699-5 (ebook)

For my Andersens, my Browers,
and my Andersen Browers

It's a roller coaster.

—Kate, on her cancer journey

CONTENTS

Be who God meant you to be,
and you will set the world on fire.

—the Bishop of London to William and Kate in his wedding sermon

Kate is the biggest star of them all.
She's an incredible woman and no one else compares.
She is the future of the monarchy.

—Dickie Arbiter, longtime spokesperson for Queen Elizabeth II

You find out that both your wife and your father have cancer. It was awful, absolutely awful. It's the lowest I've ever seen him.

—Jason Knauf, former aide to William and Kate

1

How Do We Tell Them?

What Do We Say?

A statement from Kensington Palace
Published 17 January 2024

Her Royal Highness the Princess of Wales was admitted to hospital yesterday for planned abdominal surgery. The surgery was successful and it is expected that she will remain in hospital for ten to fourteen days, before returning home to continue her recovery. Based on the current medical advice, she is unlikely to return to public duties until after Easter.

The Princess of Wales appreciates the interest this statement will generate. She hopes that the public will understand her desire to maintain as much normality for her children as possible; and her wish that her personal medical information remains private.

Kensington Palace will, therefore, only provide updates on Her Royal Highness' progress when there is significant new information to share.

The Princess of Wales wishes to apologize to all those concerned for the fact that she has to postpone her upcoming engagements. She looks forward to reinstating as many as possible, as soon as possible.

ELEVEN DAYS LATER

May I come in?" Kate looked up from her bed at the prestigious London Clinic to see the familiar face of her father-in-law, followed by white-coated medical personnel as he ambled into her hospital room wearing his favorite Turnbull & Asser robe, blue-striped pajamas, and the black velvet Crockett & Jones slippers with the Lion Rampant design he brought with him from Windsor. The seventy-five-year-old monarch had just undergone treatment for an enlarged prostate—the kind of minor surgical intervention commonly experienced by many men his age. That he came to see her and not vice versa is significant; after all, both were ostensibly having surgical procedures of a similarly routine sort—he for his prostate, Kate to treat the abdominal pain she had been experiencing for weeks. Under normal circumstances, protocol would dictate that the Princess of Wales make the trek to the elevator and down the hall to visit His Majesty. But these were not normal circumstances. Kate could tell instantly from the King's kindly but baleful basset hound expression—the look he so often employed to convey concern and sympathy—that he knew what the outside world didn't.

From the moment she arrived at the London Clinic, the Princess was secure in the knowledge that here she would get the very best care the medical world had to offer. Officially opened in 1932 by the Duke and Duchess of York, who would later become King George VI and Queen

Elizabeth (later the Queen Mother), over the years the London Clinic would count among its many famous patients Dwight Eisenhower, John F. Kennedy, Princess Margaret, Prince Philip, Elizabeth Taylor, and several British prime ministers.

The London Clinic's vaunted reputation aside, the procedure on the Princess of Wales was not, in fact, being conducted by one of its doctors—or even indeed by any British physician. The same team of Italian surgeons who had performed abdominal surgery on Pope Francis I the previous July had been secretly flown in from Rome's equally renowned Gemelli Hospital to operate on Kate. When she emerged from the anesthesia, Kate was told that the operation had been a complete success. Prince William was all smiles when he visited his wife the next morning, understandably relieved to learn that the procedure had gone, as a senior member of the hospital staff put it, "swimmingly." Seventy-two hours later, however, the news—and the mood—changed quickly. Sitting in a high-backed chair that had been positioned next to her room's floor-to-ceiling windows, Kate was taken aback when three of her physicians suddenly appeared looking pale and grim faced. Laboratory test results had just come back indicating that all was not as it seemed: cancerous cells had been detected, and an immediate course of what they would call "preventive therapy" would have to be undertaken immediately.

Cancer. Just hearing the word sent Kate into an emotional tailspin. "It was as if the bottom of my world suddenly fell out," she told a friend. "It felt like I had literally been kicked in the stomach." Indeed, for a moment others in the room thought the Princess might collapse. Were they certain it was cancer? she asked. Could the lab have made a mistake? Precisely what kind of cancer Kate had been diagnosed with was never made public, but there were several possibilities: ovarian, uterine, or colon cancer, hypothesized Giampaolo Tortora, director of the cancer center at the Gemelli Hospital. It was well known that, during her pregnancies, Kate had suffered from hyperemesis gravidarum (HG)—morning sickness so severe it required her to be hospitalized—and that later gallbladder issues were not uncommon among HG patients. Studies also showed that women like

Kate who suffered from HG were at greater risk for several cancers, most notably bladder cancer.

William's reaction to the stunning news was understandably one of complete disbelief. "That's impossible!" the Prince of Wales replied when Kate called Adelaide Cottage to tell him the devastating news. "They told you the surgery was a complete success, that everything was fine." But what had not been visible to the doctors was evident to the pathologists who, given the singular importance of their patient, consulted the clinic's chief pathologist before delivering their double- and triple-checked findings. The Prince of Wales had cleared his calendar for two full weeks so he could be with George, Charlotte, and Louis while their mother recovered at the hospital. Now he rushed to his wife's bedside and embraced her tearfully.

"We'll get through this," they reassured each other, but what about the children? Kate did not want to frighten them, and if news got out that their mother had been diagnosed with cancer the swirl of press around their school and the inevitable questions from their classmates would almost certainly leave them afraid and confused. They needed to be told by Mummy and "Pops"—their nickname for William, along with "Papa"—in the way a child might understand, and be given the time to process it all in the comforting surroundings of home. They would wait until the children were home for Easter break in late March to make a public announcement, but until then, William and Kate both agreed that her cancer diagnosis would be top secret. From the beginning, it was clear this would be a daunting task: it was later discovered that, while she was still at the clinic, several hospital staff members were caught trying to access the princess's private medical records.

At this moment, however, Kate was in her hospital bed gazing directly into the rapidly welling-up eyes of the King. William had shared the news of Kate's cancer with his father, and the King was there to lend his cherished daughter-in-law moral support. King Charles did not mention that he had just been dealt a gut punch of his own. The King's supposedly routine prostate procedure revealed something that took the entire medical team by surprise: it appeared that malignant cells were present in Charles's abdomen as well.

Before entering the hospital, His Majesty had hoped to raise awareness of men's health issues by issuing a statement describing his planned prostate surgery. It was a bold move, ripping away the veil of secrecy that traditionally surrounds the health issues of senior royals—a practice so deeply ingrained that, when Charles's grandfather King George VI was diagnosed with advanced lung cancer, the news was kept from the patient himself. Charles's own desire for newfound transparency aside, he wanted to make sure his doctors' suspicions were proven accurate by lab tests before springing the news on his unsuspecting subjects—or on the beautiful young mother of three who faced a daunting health crisis of her own. To be told one has cancer when they are three-quarters of a century old is one thing. But the King found it difficult to believe that the vibrant woman who had only recently celebrated her forty-second birthday must now be confronted with her own mortality. He did not speak the word "cancer," instead telling her she looked wonderful and that he was pleased she was on the road to complete recovery.

On January 29, Kate's trusted longtime personal assistant, Natasha Archer, drove up to the London Clinic's back entrance on Harley Street in her Range Rover and left for Adelaide Cottage with the princess hunkering out of sight in the back seat—all unbeknownst to the press. An hour later, a dapper and smiling King Charles and Queen Camilla—he bundled up in a blue double-breasted overcoat and she in a blue wool dress and boots—left via the hospital's main entrance on Devonshire Place and made their way to a waiting midnight blue Audi Q8 e-tron electric car. More than twenty photographers clicked and flashed away as the King waved to the waiting crowd of well-wishers—all in stark contrast to Kate's uncharacteristically cloak-and-dagger exit. The reason for all the stealth: while the King still looked robust and ruddy faced after only three days in the hospital, Kate had been there for two full weeks and the strain of it was etched on her face. Archer, who started working for the royal family in 2007 and three years later became Kate's personal assistant and unofficial stylist, got to work as soon as they arrived at Adelaide Cottage to restore the princess's healthful glow. When the kids rushed in from school screaming "Mummy's home! Mummy's home!," it quickly became clear to both Kate and William that they need not have fretted—Mummy hadn't changed a bit. She swept them up in her arms, just as she always did. They suspected nothing.

Ever since checking into the London Clinic, Kate had been eager to return to Adelaide Cottage—and with good reason. The property was conceived in 1831 as a sanctuary for William IV's wife, Adelaide of Saxe-Meiningen, who married King William one week after meeting him, fully aware that he had ten illegitimate children with a popular actress of the time, Dorothea Jordan. Instead of producing a legitimate heir, Queen Adelaide suffered several miscarriages, multiple stillbirths, and the deaths of two infant children—with a degree of dignity and fortitude that made her one of England's best-loved queen consorts.

Adelaide Cottage—just a fifteen-minute stroll south of Windsor Castle—was designed in the romantic, or "picturesque," style that was embraced by British architects in the mid-nineteenth century. With its pink stucco walls, peaked rooflines, and white gingerbread trim, Adelaide Lodge, as it was originally called, had a fairy-tale quality that William IV's successor, Queen Victoria, found irresistible. Throughout her sixty-three-year reign—second only in length to that of Charles's mother, Elizabeth II—Queen Victoria treated the cottage almost as if it were a child's playhouse, visiting it for breakfast or tea whenever the pressures of ruling what was then the world's greatest empire were simply too much. Victoria was so fond of the cottage that she had a special carriageway built leading there straight from Windsor Castle. When Dash, the King Charles spaniel Victoria would dress up in a scarlet jacket and blue trousers (she later described the dog as "my closest childhood companion"), died in 1840, she had him buried at Adelaide Cottage. More than 184 years later, George, Charlotte, and Louis would scamper through the cottage gardens past Dash's marble headstone with an inscription written by Victoria herself:

Here lies
DASH
The favourite spaniel of Her Majesty Queen Victoria
In his 10th year
His attachment was without selfishness
His playfulness without malice
His fidelity without deceit
READER
If you would be beloved and die regretted
Profit by the example of
DASH

After Victoria's death, Adelaide Cottage was used as a guesthouse for those lucky enough to be invited to Windsor Castle, and in the twentieth century it became a grace-and-favor property—one of the more than one hundred homes (the oldest being 10 Downing Street, official residence of the Prime Minister) bestowed rent-free on friends, family, and individuals out of gratitude for their service.

By the time William and Kate began casting about for a suitable home on the outskirts of central London, Adelaide Cottage had undergone several restorations, the most recent and extensive in 2015. Three years later, Queen Elizabeth offered Adelaide Cottage to brother Harry and his new wife Meghan as a wedding present. Instead, the Duke and Duchess of Sussex chose to undertake a major renovation of nearby Frogmore Cottage. That project would wind up costing more than $3 million—a sum that ignited a public outcry and forced the Sussexes to cover the cost themselves. Conversely, William and Kate were looking for a property that required no renovations at taxpayer expense. From the Waleses' standpoint, Adelaide Cottage was ideal: not only was it situated close to William's granny—the Queen—but it also was a short ride from Lambrook, the school all three children would be attending. Moreover, it offered another advantage: there are entrances to the Windsor Home Park, allowing the Waleses at least a fighting chance of eluding the paparazzi as they came and went.

With only four bedrooms—one for each of the children and one for their parents—the house itself is still modest by royal standards. But hints of grandeur remain nonetheless. There are two public reception areas: an opulently decorated formal living room with a marble Greco-Roman fireplace as its centerpiece, and a Grand Lounge featuring twenty-two-foot-high ceilings; Renaissance era tapestries; and an even more impressive monumental stone fireplace. While William and Kate decorated all the bedrooms to suit more modern tastes, the master bedroom—where the couple sleeps with the family dog at their feet—has always had a decidedly nautical theme: the high ceiling was covered with gilded dolphins and walls draped with rope ornaments from the *Royal George*, the famous yacht launched by George III in 1817. Intended for entertaining, the green-and-white formal Georgian dining room with barrel-vaulted ceiling contrasted sharply with the exposed beams, farmhouse sink, and wooden countertops in Kate's small country kitchen—the beating heart of the Wales household. Not that anyone was likely to forget that, for all its homey warmth, Adelaide Cottage was every inch a royal residence. Over the main entrance was a plaque carved with the intertwined letters *AR*, for Adelaide Regina.

Kate had only been home a matter of days when a phone call from William upended her world once again. "What? How is that possible?" Kate gasped. "No, it cannot be!" But it was: William's father had just called him with the news that test results confirmed the monarch was also suffering from cancer. The King was beginning treatments at home immediately; and although he would tell his immediate family what kind of cancer he was battling, he was less than forthcoming about the prognosis. The fact that Charles had not been diagnosed with prostate cancer—one of the more treatable cancers if caught early enough—was worrisome in and of itself. Queen Camilla, who had been at Charles's side when he was admitted to the hospital and visited him every day, fought back tears when doctors first told her of their suspicions.

For the moment, King Charles also wanted to delay going public just a few days more while he informed Prince Harry, Princess Anne, Prince Andrew, and Prince Edward. Coming in the midst of Harry and Meghan's highly public feud with the rest of the royal family, the King's seemingly out-of-the-blue call took Harry by surprise. Ever since Megxit, the Sussexes' noisy departure from royal life, Harry had focused on building a new life for himself; his wife; and their young children, Archie and Lilibet, in California. He and his father had not spoken in nearly three years. Stunned by the news, Harry told the King he would be on the first plane to London. When later asked about Charles's medical outlook by a television reporter, Harry did not offer the customary words of reassurance. "That stays," he said, "between me and him."

On February 5, 2024, just one week after King Charles had waved to photographers as he left the London Clinic, Buckingham Palace issued a cautiously worded statement:

> *During The King's recent hospital procedure for benign prostate enlargement, a separate issue of concern was noted. Subsequent diagnostic tests have identified a form of cancer.*
>
> *His Majesty has today commenced a schedule of regular treatments, during which time he has been advised by doctors to postpone public-facing duties. Throughout this period, His Majesty will continue to undertake State business and official paperwork as usual.*
>
> *The King is grateful to his medical team for their swift intervention, which was made possible thanks to his recent hospital procedure. He remains wholly positive about his treatment and looks forward to returning to full public duty as soon as possible.*
>
> *His Majesty has chosen to share his diagnosis to prevent speculation and in the hope it may assist public understanding for all those around the world who are affected by cancer.*

The maelstrom of tabloid headlines that ensued was decidedly less matter-of-fact. "King's Cancer Shock" screamed the front page of the *Mirror*, while the *Sun* blared "King: I Have Cancer" and the more buttoned-down *Times* opted for the simpler but no less attention-grabbing "The King Has Cancer." Despite the Palace's efforts to downplay the King's condition, there was no escaping the fact that it constituted a particularly cruel twist of fate. After waiting far longer than any other heir in British history to finally ascend to the throne—he was nearly seventy-four years old when he succeeded Elizabeth II, compared to Queen Victoria's son Edward VII becoming monarch at fifty-nine—Charles had only been king for seventeen months and already faced the brutal fact that his own reign might be cut short.

Quickly, media attention turned to Harry's arrival in London the day after the announcement and whether this visit with his father might signal a thaw in their relationship. There was conjecture that this moment might even lead to a truce with the once-beloved brother Harry had savaged in his memoir *Spare* one year earlier. But after just forty-five minutes with his father, Harry headed for Heathrow Airport and the eleven-hour, forty-minute flight home—without meeting William or any other member of the royal family. "Look, I love my family," Harry later recalled. "The fact that I was able to get on a plane and go and see him and spend any time with, I'm grateful for that." Asked by a journalist if his father's illness could have a "reunifying effect" on the royal family, Harry answered, "Absolutely. Yeah, I'm sure. . . ."

What the King did not share with Harry was the terrible secret of Kate's cancer diagnosis or the crushing weight of despair and responsibility that now rested on William's shoulders. If the Prince of Wales was still angry over what he views as his brother's betrayal, he was scarcely in the mood to make amends with Harry now that he alone was coping with the cancer diagnoses of both his father and his wife. When told that Harry wanted to meet with him, William's reply, delivered in front of several Kensington Palace staff members, was succinct: "Tell Harry to bugger off."

No one was more aware than Kate of the crushing burden now carried by her husband. William was always more emotionally fragile than Kate, given to bouts of depression and the occasional purple-veined rage. He had spoken openly about the psychological impact of his mother Diana's death in a car crash when he was only fifteen years old—and the post-traumatic stress syndrome that he and Harry coped with to this day. Nor did William's two years as an air ambulance helicopter pilot help matters. Spending twelve-hour days airlifting the victims of car crashes, falls, heart attacks, workplace accidents, and suicides to hospital emergency rooms had taken its toll. "When you're exposed to so much death, it impacts how you see the world," he later tried to explain. "You're exposed to such high levels of sadness, trauma, death that impacts your own life—and your family life. It's always there, and you're drawn into it. . . . You see the world as a much more depressed, darker, blacker place. . . . It leaves you with a very negative feeling where you think death is just around the corner everywhere I go. It's quite a burden to carry. I could feel it brewing up inside me, and I could feel it was going to be a problem."

William had always done such a superb job of concealing his innermost feelings from the public. Unlike his father, the king, whose fits of pique were legendary, William was all easygoing charm: handsome, fit, confident, engaging—everything a prince should be. Kate knew better. William had once spiraled into such a well of despair that she was deeply concerned that he, like his mother Diana might seriously consider taking his own life. William was sufficiently self-aware to do something about his own psychological issues. He sought counseling, continued to speak out about the growing epidemic of suicide—the leading killer of men under forty-five in the United Kingdom—and together with Kate and Harry launched the mental health charity Heads Together in 2016.

As worried as she was about William, Kate focused even more on hiding the truth of her diagnosis from their children, at least for now. To accomplish this, she knew William must bury his feelings, as he had done so effectively in the past, and create the illusion that all was well on the home front—that Kate was on the road to recovery from her surgery and his only added responsibility now was to fill in for the ailing king.

By late February, while William stepped in to perform investitures and accept the credentials of visiting diplomats—normally tasks performed by the monarch—no one noticed that Kate was quietly sneaking away to begin her twice-monthly treatments at London's Royal Marsden Hospital, founded in 1851 as the first hospital in the world dedicated to the study and treatment of cancer. If Kate had been spotted there, the press intrusion would have been unbearable. Fortunately, at that moment Britain's usually unrelenting tabloid press was still unaware of her shocking diagnosis and was satisfied that Kate was simply at home recuperating from abdominal surgery.

With the coast relatively clear, Kate left Adelaide Cottage hunkered down in the back seat of a black Range Rover with her assistant at the wheel and made the fifty-minute drive to the Royal Marsden Hospital on Fulham Road in London's Chelsea district. To avoid being detected, the Princess of Wales was ushered into the hospital through a back entrance on Dovehouse Street—the same entrance used by Princess Diana when she wanted to make unpublicized visits to children she had befriended in the pediatric care unit. It was no small miracle that, as Kate arrived at the hospital to begin her chemotherapy, one of the city's distinctive red, tourist-crammed double-deckers passed just a few doors away—and no one seemed to notice.

She would make this journey every two or three weeks for the next six months, allowing time between each chemo session to recover. The use of the word "preventive" is misleading. The treatments, also known as adjuvant therapy, are designed to destroy any microscopic cancer cells left after surgery; the cancer isn't being prevented, since it's already there. While a patient might normally be seated in a room with others during the hour-long infusion sessions, Kate was hustled down a vacant corridor to a private room where an oncology nurse administered an IV infusion. Occasionally, the need for blood tests to monitor her progress meant she would be required to stay longer—instead of one hour, two, or in rare cases even three. By way of further thwarting nosy reporters, there was no evidence of the princess ever having been there—no dates and times of Kate's visits, no entries in the normal patient logs.

It was one thing to keep the press in the dark, but the children were another matter. After the first chemo session, Kate began to suffer side effects that persisted on and off for months: nausea, vomiting, loss of appetite leading to weight loss, even peripheral neuropathy—nerve damage that results in a tingling in the hands and feet. In Kate's case, all of these were mild and fleeting. Nor did Kate require a "cold cap" to lower the temperature of the scalp—a means of combatting hair loss from the damaging effects of chemo. Kate's iconic tresses, a major component of the trendsetting royal's look and style, remained mercifully intact.

To more reliably deliver their cocktail of cancer-fighting drugs, doctors implanted a chemo port-a-cath in Kate's upper chest. She felt pressure but little pain. She would soon come to regard this small device as a lifeline.

Still, side effects would persist, and one in particular left Kate reeling: fatigue. This was the hardest thing to conceal from the children, who were used to their energetic, athletic mother kicking a ball around with them on the lawn or tussling with them indoors. In truth, there were moments when she was simply so "wrung out," as she told a friend, that she could barely stand up, much less play with the children.

Mummy was even absenting herself from their usual take-no-prisoners card games and marathon board games, instead retiring to her room for naps that wound up lasting for hours. Charlotte and Louis ("Lou Lou" to his doting siblings) grudgingly accepted the explanation their father offered them—that Mummy was still recuperating from her operation. Prince George, nicknamed "PG" by his sister and little brother, was older and innately more skeptical than either of his siblings—and that made him harder to convince. Kate was careful to put on more of an act around her eldest son, summoning all her strength to look like her old, upbeat, effervescent self. Once the children were off to school, she would collapse on the sofa.

Unsurprisingly, Kate leaned most heavily during this period on her mother. Carole Middleton was always there for her eldest child, and equally for Kate's sister, Pippa, and brother, James—no more so than during times of illness. During Kate's stay at the London Clinic, William, understandably preoccupied with filling in for his ailing father, was wary of luring the paparazzi to the hospital but visited every day anyway. Carole was a different story. Over the years, she had mastered the art of eluding the press, and was able to duck in and out of the clinic to visit her daughter as many as two or three times a day without being detected. Now Carole would get behind the wheel of her Audi 4X4 each morning and drive forty-three minutes from Bucklebury Manor, the Middleton family residence in Berkshire, to Adelaide Cottage.

Notwithstanding the Waleses' insistence on no longer having any live-in servants, the children's longtime nanny, Maria Teresa Borrallo, had also been recruited to help out. When her services were required at Adelaide Cottage, Borrallo stayed at one of the nearby properties on the Windsor estate. From her early days as George's nanny, she was often photographed outfitted in a short-sleeved brown dress, white gloves, and bowler hat—the distinctive uniform worn by graduates of Norland College, the prestigious school for English nannies. Many of the qualifications Borrallo brought to the job—a mastery of the Korean martial art of tae kwon do, and defensive driving skills in the event of a paparazzi chase or, worse, a kidnapping attempt—were above and beyond anything that might have been required of royal nannies in the past.

Still, there was no way of protecting against conspiracy theories that spread like wildfire across the social media landscape. The day after Kate checked out of the London Clinic, Kensington Palace was forced to dismiss as "total nonsense" a report on Spanish television that Kate had been in a coma immediately following surgery and taken two weeks to regain consciousness. "It's fundamentally, totally made up," said a Palace spokesman, "and I'll use polite English here: It's absolutely not the case."

As much as William wanted to be at Kate's side as she battled cancer, they both knew his absence from the public eye would only fuel more rumors. So, alternating with his aunt Princess Anne and his uncle Prince Edward, he continued as a stand-in for the King. Sadly, William's earnest attempt at drawing attention away from his seriously ill wife had little effect. By the time he walked the red carpet solo at the BAFTAs (British Academy of Film and Television Awards)—an event William and Kate always attended together—on February 18, 2024, the internet was awash in wild conspiracy theories. The frenzy grew even more intense ten days later, when at the last minute William backed out of a Windsor Castle memorial service for his godfather King Constantine of Greece "for personal reasons." Among the flurry of memes, jokes, and baseless theories populating social media:

that Kate was recovering from plastic surgery, that she was growing out her bangs, that she was hanging out with American actor Pete Davidson, that she was about to reveal her true identity on the reality show *The Masked Singer*, that she was in the throes of a complete nervous breakdown—or that she and William were getting a divorce. The princess-in-a-coma storyline suddenly made a comeback, along with the macabre suggestion that Kate had in fact died and that the Palace, fearing repercussions, was searching for a body double to replace her.

Incredibly, British intelligence was alarmed to discover that the Russians were in part to blame. Social media accounts linked to a prominent Russian disinformation campaign called Doppelgänger capitalized on "Kategate," as the phenomenon came to be known, exploiting the increased traffic to spread Russian propaganda aimed principally at Ukraine. ("It's about destabilization," security expert Martin Innes later explained. "It's about undermining trust in institutions: government, monarchy, media—everything.") To make matters worse, the bizarre stories about the princess were supercharged by artificial intelligence—specifically, by bots posting, retweeting, and sharing misinformation on the internet. "It feeds off itself," observed Paddy Harverson, Kate and William's former official spokesperson. "It's a sort of permanent doom loop. And it's the worst I've ever seen."

On the first sunny Monday in March, Carole Middleton picked Kate up at Adelaide Cottage and drove the princess to Royal Marsden Hospital for her chemotherapy session. When a photo of the two women—Carole Middleton behind the wheel wearing a black coat and a grim expression, and Kate looking equally serious behind oversized sunglasses—appeared on TMZ in the United States, media outlets did not hesitate to point out that this was the first time Kate had been seen in seventy days.

It was a single grainy image, but enough to finally convince Kensington Palace that something had to be done to reassure the public without disclosing anything about Kate's cancer battle—at least not until the children were out of school for Easter break and removed from the line of fire. "We were very clear from the outset," read a new official statement, "that the Princess of Wales was out until after Easter and Kensington Palace would only be providing updates when something was significant." They added that Kate was "making good progress."

For the moment, at least, the explanation seemed to have satisfied the majority of Britons: in a YouGov Poll, more than half the respondents felt they were getting the "right" amount of information about Kate's condition. Still, it would take only one misstep to send conspiracy theorists back to their keyboards. Kate had always marked Mother's Day by releasing a photo of her with the children, and she realized the gossipmongers would have a field day if she failed to release a heartwarming image this year. On the previous UK Mother's Day, in 2023, the princess and all three offspring were photographed sitting in a tree. This time, Kate posed for her husband sitting on a wicker chair in jeans and a black sweater, her broadly smiling brood gathered around her. "Thank you for your kind wishes and continued support," the princess wrote in her Instagram post. It was meant to be an informal family shot, but in the end it only succeeded in igniting a new firestorm of controversy.

Within hours of the photo's release, the Associated Press yanked it from distribution, claiming that the image had been manipulated. The giveaway: "The odd alignment of Princess Charlotte's left hand with the sleeve of her sweater."

Soon, experts detected no fewer than sixteen tweaks to the image. Kate rushed to clean up this unexpected mess. "Like many amateur photographers," she explained on social media, "I do occasionally experiment with editing. I wanted to express my apologies for any confusion the family photo we shared yesterday caused."

With Kate still out of sight and the one official photo of her exposed as something less than wholly authentic, the rumor getting the most traction centered on the state of the royal marriage. To make matters worse, Kate is not wearing her famous sapphire-and-diamond engagement ring—the one that had belonged to her late mother-in-law, Princess Diana—in the controversial photo. Inevitably, much of the chatter revived nagging but baseless gossip that the Prince of Wales was engaged in a steamy affair with the royal couple's longtime friend and married mother of three Rose Hanbury,

Marchioness of Cholmondeley (pronounced "Chumley"). Hanbury, who went down this same road when rumors about a possible affair burbled to the surface in 2019, was stunned when on March 12, 2024, American television personality Stephen Colbert breathed oxygen into the rumor during his late-night monologue on CBS. "The kingdom has been all aflutter by the seeming disappearance of Kate Middleton," Colbert quipped. "Well, now internet sleuths are guessing that Kate's absence may be related to her husband, the future king of England, William, having an affair. So I think we all know who the alleged other woman is. Say it with me: the Marchioness of Cholmondeley—what a beautiful name!" Riffing on Hanbury's title, Colbert then went on to call her "the Marching Band of Chicanery" and "the Marcus Mumford of Chumbawamba."

Hanbury, whose own 106-room Houghton Hall estate is located just four miles down the road from William and Kate's country retreat, Anmer Hall, ordered her lawyers to write a letter to CBS threatening legal action. An on-air apology of sorts would be forthcoming, but only after news of Kate's true condition was finally made public. Understandably, Kate always felt personally humiliated by whispered rumors of adultery. Having them broadcast on a nationally televised show in the United States only magnified the growing sense of helplessness. She could not, after all, dignify the rumors by addressing them directly. As Easter break approached, Kate could only hope that George, Charlotte, and Louis had been sufficiently shielded from the weird social media chatter—and that somehow, miraculously, they were oblivious to all the hyperventilating about Mummy. What they soon would be facing was all too real. Easter break had arrived.

Telling the children—that would be the hardest thing of all. Harder than enduring the aftermath of an hours-long operation, harder than suffering the stabbing pains in her abdomen that had landed her on the operating table at the London Clinic in the first place, harder even than desperately trying to conceal the truth from a world that so easily feasted on conspiracy theories. Usually, this ritual of picking up the children was a high point of the day: a leisurely fourteen-minute drive from Adelaide Cottage in Windsor Park, down the narrow stretch of A322 that leads past the endless expanse of green lawns and ancient trees to Winkfield Row and Lambrook School.

There was even more reason to be upbeat today: the children were understandably excited by the prospect of two whole weeks without school. But this was also the moment when the family would have to pull together to confront some hard truths. As William drove their Portofino blue Range Rover SUV with his wife sitting ramrod straight at his side, they stared ahead in stony silence, dreading the task ahead.

For this one fleeting moment at least, the Prince and Princess of Wales were determined not to dampen the children's unfettered joy at having been sprung from school. With their ever-present royal protection detail of four Glock-armed officers right behind them, William and Kate pulled onto Lambrook's circular drive—for security reasons, they are the only parents allowed to drive right up to the front door rather than wait near the front gate—and bounded out of their car, arms outstretched, to greet the little princes and princess. With headmaster Jonathan Perry's wife, Jenny, rushing to keep up with them like a protective mother hen, the trio, all dressed in their identical navy blue school uniforms emblazoned with the interlocking letters *L* and *S* (for Lambrook School), scrambled to the waiting SUV, clambered into the back seat, and buckled up.

The chatter on the drive home would be familiar to any parent of school-age children—a patience-trying eruption of "Did *so*!" and "Did *NOT*!" rising exponentially until either Mummy or Pops spins around to lay down the law. For the most part, Louis remained silent while George and Charlotte bickered over whose turn it was to clean out the guinea pig cage—a messy task that often fell to Pops. "I have to spend my life cleaning out the guinea pig cage," the future king once complained to a group of farmers, "because the children keep forgetting to do it!"

How do we tell them? What do we say? We don't want to frighten them. . . . Like so many moments in royal life, this one had to be expertly choreographed. Kate and William sat the children down at the long farmhouse-style table in the kitchen for their daily after-school snack. Usually, they were offered something healthy—yogurt, carrots, or perhaps an apple. Instead, Mummy today served up their all-time favorite treat: chocolate brownies from Gail's Bakery in London.

While the children began to devour their brownies, Mummy gently talked about how much better she'd felt since coming home from the hospital in January, and how she looked forward to having fun with them over the next two weeks. Kate also explained why she sometimes still needed to rest—that when she was in the hospital, doctors found just a few of these tiny cancer cells, and to make sure they wouldn't come back, Mummy was taking some special medicine. It's the medicine, she told them, that sometimes made her tired.

Kate and William went on to say that they had hoped to keep everything in the family, but that was no longer possible. People wanted to know why Mummy had not been out and about with Pops, doing her usual job. When their parents asked if they had any questions, George, Charlotte, and Louis shook their heads. Much to their parents' relief, they did not appear traumatized—or even particularly surprised—by what they had been told.

Of course, all this would change once the world was made aware that Kate was being treated for cancer—something the Palace had explicitly said in the beginning was not the case—and the truth ricocheted around the world. Their children would not be able to escape the "Kate Has Cancer!" headlines, or the inevitable hysteria that followed. But the Prince and Princess of Wales did all they could to prepare them for the coming whirlwind.

Kate and William now agreed with their senior staff at Kensington Palace that the online frenzy and endless speculation had reached such a fever pitch that a public announcement was critical. Rather than have the Palace simply issue a statement similar to the King's announcement of his cancer diagnosis, Kate wanted to share the news in a personal video message. She insisted on writing the statement herself—"This must be in my words," she told her staff—and, rather than have the Palace press record the video, she wanted the BBC to send out a production crew. And not just any crew, but the crew that had covered her father-in-law's coronation. The BBC agreed, as long as it was clear that it would not edit the video—no one wanted another scandal like the one triggered by Kate's Mother's Day snapshot. The BBC also declined to have anything to do with the video's distribution. "We wanted to distance ourselves from any possible blowback," one crew member later said, "so we left everything up to the Princess."

Accordingly, Kate also chose the venue—a favorite bench in the middle of Windsor Castle's Moat Garden. On March 20, a sunny Wednesday, the Princess of Wales took her place against a backdrop of daffodils and cherry blossoms. She wore blue jeans and one of her most comforting and familiar articles of clothing—an $821 black-and-white-striped Erdem Lotus sweater. There was another reason Kate plucked this particular sweater out of her closet. Her dress size (UK women's size 6, US women's size 2) and her twenty-four-inch waist had always prompted unfounded rumors that, like Princess Diana, she suffered from an eating disorder. Now that she had lost fifteen pounds during chemo, the broad horizontal stripes would make Kate look heavier than her 110 pounds.

With William watching from behind the cameras, Kate, her hands folded demurely in her lap with her iconic sapphire-and-diamond engagement ring fully visible, did a brief rehearsal using a teleprompter. Then she took a deep breath, looked directly into the camera, and delivered a flawless two-minute-and-fifteen-second performance:

> *"I wanted to take this opportunity to say thank you, personally, for all the wonderful messages of support and for your understanding whilst I have been recovering from surgery.*
>
> *"It has been an incredibly tough couple of months for our entire family, but I've had a fantastic medical team who have taken great care of me, for which I am so grateful.*
>
> *"In January, I underwent major abdominal surgery in London; and at the time, it was thought that my condition was noncancerous. The surgery was successful. However, tests after the operation found cancer had been present. My medical team therefore advised that I should undergo a course of preventative chemotherapy, and I am now in the early stages of that treatment.*

"This of course came as a huge shock, and William and I have been doing everything we can to process and manage this privately for the sake of our young family.

"As you can imagine, this has taken time. It has taken me time to recover from major surgery in order to start my treatment. But, most importantly, it has taken us time to explain everything to George, Charlotte, and Louis in a way that is appropriate for them, and to reassure them that I am going to be okay.

"As I have said to them; I am well and getting stronger every day by focusing on the things that will help me heal in my mind, body, and spirits.

"Having William by my side is a great source of comfort and reassurance, too. As is the love, support, and kindness that has been shown by so many of you. It means so much to us both.

"We hope that you will understand that, as a family, we now need some time, space, and privacy while I complete my treatment. My work has always brought me a deep sense of joy and I look forward to being back when I am able, but for now I must focus on making a full recovery."

It is at the very end that Kate looks down and pauses for a thoughtful moment. "At this time," she concludes, "I am also thinking of all those whose lives have been affected by cancer. For everyone facing this disease, in whatever form, please do not lose faith or hope. You are not alone."

Two days later, the video was released to the media, sending shock waves around the globe. The King, whose own treatment for an undisclosed type of cancer was proving more grueling than expected, wept when he and Queen Camilla screened Kate's video in advance. His Majesty was the first to issue a statement saying he was "so proud of Catherine for her courage." Noting that he remained "in the closest of contact" with his "beloved daughter-in-law," King Charles promised that he and Camilla would continue to "offer our love and support to their whole family through this difficult time."

The Duke and Duchess of Sussex were among those taken completely by surprise; like the rest of the world, they knew nothing of Kate's diagnosis before the video's release. "We wish health and healing for Kate and the family," read their message, "and hope they are able to do so privately and in peace." Kate's brother, James, meanwhile, posted a childhood photo of himself and Kate on a hiking trip. "Over the years, we have climbed many mountains together," he said on the Instagram post. "As a family, we will climb this one with you, too."

Instantly, world leaders reacted to the shocking news. Noting that the Princess of Wales had for months been the subject of an internet feeding frenzy, Britain's Conservative prime minister, Rishi Sunak, praised Kate for showing "tremendous bravery" in the face of "intense scrutiny." Kate had been, he went on to say, "unfairly treated by certain sections of the media around the world and on social media." Sunak's successor as prime minister, Labor Party Leader Sir Keir Starmer, was heartened by the princess's optimism and "message of faith and hope." But he also remarked on the "added stress" Kate was subjected to by "lurid speculation" even as she coped with her cancer diagnosis.

Prayers and wishes poured in from abroad. Kate's "strength and resilience," intoned French President Emmanuel Macron, "inspire us all." US President Joe Biden, who had lost his son Beau to cancer and would soon be facing a cancer battle of his own, issued a statement saying he joined "millions around the world in praying" for Catherine's "full recovery." One international figure who remained silent was Pope Francis, still guarding the secret that he and Kate shared the same team of Italian surgeons.

As stunning as the King's cancer news was, it paled in comparison to the impact Kate's diagnosis had. Over the twenty-four-hour period following her dramatic announcement, there were 2.7 million posts about Kate on social media. The press, of course, went wild. "A Nation Touched by Kate's Courage" proclaimed the *Sunday Express*. "Kate: My Cancer Came as a Huge Shock" shouted the *Daily Express*. The *Daily Mail* blared "Cancer Shock," and the most widely read British tabloid, the *Sun*, told the princess in its front-page headline: "Kate, You Are Not Alone."

For just a few fleeting moments, Kate relished the fact that she had shared her own story on her own terms, and in her own words. But she also knew she had thrown the royal family into fresh turmoil—and that the monarchy was teetering. More than 5,460 miles away in her Montecito, California, mansion, another princess dabbed at tears as she tried to absorb the head-spinning news of her sister-in-law's cancer. For all the tension that has famously existed between them, Meghan told her friends that, as the mother of two young children herself, she could not stop thinking about George, Charlotte, and Louis. On the dining room table that served as Meghan's home office desk was the latest edition of *People* magazine. The cover of the issue, which sold out instantly, posed the most momentous question of all:

"Kate Has Cancer: What Happens Next?"

I had a very happy childhood. It was great fun.
I'm very lucky, I've come from a very strong family—
my parents were hugely dedicated to us.

—**Kate**

My childhood was complicated. . . . The drama and the stress when
you're small really affects you when you're older.

—**William**

2

"A Certain Aura"

An Ineffable Sadness

September 1998

Marlborough College, a Prep School in Berkshire

Oh my God. It's him!" And with that breathless announcement, a hundred of Britain's most-well-heeled young women and girls rushed to catch a glimpse of the future king of England as he took to the pitch as part of Eton's visiting field hockey team. Normally, as one might expect, they would be cheering for their own school's players—but not today. The Marlborough players, standouts in their eye-catching red-and-black-striped uniforms, were every bit as skillful as the blue-and-tan-clad Etonians. But this particular afternoon that was scarcely the point. In the six months since William and Harry (the Heir and the Spare) had visited Vancouver on a ski trip—an excursion during which Beatlemania-sized crowds of teenage girls showered the Heir with cries of "William, William, William!"—Charles and Diana's elder son was no longer taken aback by the tumult his mere presence often caused.

Not every young woman at Marlborough got swept up in the hysteria that afternoon. One sixteen-year-old brunette in particular—none other than the captain of the girls' field hockey team—hung back, watching the celebrated visitor discreetly but intently from the sidelines. This was the moment Kate Middleton caught her first in-the-flesh glimpse of Prince William, although it would be three years before he laid eyes on her.

None of Kate's classmates were surprised at Kate's reticence; she was, a school friend observed, "always much cooler than the rest of us. She was a lot of fun and always game for things like practical jokes and just being plain silly. But when something was really important to her, she could suddenly turn quite serious." And it was abundantly clear to everyone that when it came to William, Kate—until she turned fifteen she was almost exclusively called Catherine—could be quite serious, almost painfully so.

In contrast to her fellow female Marlburians who papered their dormitory room walls with posters of movie heartthrobs like Leonardo DiCaprio or boy bands of the era like NSYNC and Britain's own Take That, over her bed Kate hung a life-size color photo of William in jeans and a blue shirt. (Kate would eventually insist it was "the Levi's guy" in the photo, but her classmates maintained that the shirtless jeans model came later.) No one knew more about the Heir: Kate slavishly monitored his official schedule on the Buckingham Palace website and inhaled whatever was written about William in the press.

Kate was not alone in devoutly hoping to land her Prince Charming. Just as Carole Middleton and untold numbers of other young women around the world pined over the future Charles III a generation earlier, Kate clung to the belief that she might someday be the one. As storybook princes of the realm went, it was hard to imagine anyone who fit the bill more precisely than William of Wales. Far from being jug-eared and stuffy, William had all the Disney attributes: he was tall, blond, blue-eyed, intelligent, athletic, thoughtful, charming, and Hollywood handsome. Moreover, despite an inherent shyness, the boy possessed a natural charisma mixed with compassion—the oft-repeated "human touch" undoubtedly inherited from his mother, Diana.

Yet there was also an ineffable sadness about William that tugged at Kate's adolescent heartstrings. She remembered how, along with the rest of the planet, she had awoken on the morning of August 31, 1997, to learn that the Princess of Wales had been killed in a car crash with her lover, Dodi Fayed, while being pursued by paparazzi through the streets of Paris. Diana was only thirty-six at the time of her death, but for seventeen years she had dominated the news like no other woman before or since. Like Kate's entire generation, she grew up hearing Diana's name on a continual basis—as the beautiful wife of the future king, as the young mother of two spirited young boys, as a fashion and style avatar, as a humanitarian who hugged babies suffering from AIDS when no one else would and walked bravely through a minefield in Angola to illustrate the human suffering wrought by unexploded landmines.

Yet above all else, Diana was seen as the first truly relatable member of the royal family. As her marriage crumbled over Charles's scandalous, headline-making affair with his old flame Mrs. Camilla Parker Bowles, the Princess of Wales spoke openly of her own struggles with bulimia and suicidal depression. Such defiant openness vexed Charles and the faceless Palace operatives—Diana derisively called them the "Men in Gray"—who actually ran the monarchy.

By the time Diana committed the cardinal sin of secretly cooperating with journalist Andrew Morton to craft his 1992 bombshell tell-all *Diana: Her True Story*, she had already established her reputation as a rebel who had no intention of quietly acquiescing to her husband's adultery as generations of royal women had dutifully done before. Six months after the book's publication, Prime Minister John Major stood up in Parliament and announced the separation of the Prince and Princess of Wales. The deftly worded statement, crafted by Queen Elizabeth's top advisors, stressed that the decision was amicable, and that Charles and Diana "will both continue to participate fully in the upbringing of their children." The Queen and her husband Prince Philip, the statement continued, asked that "the intrusions into the privacy of the Prince and Princess may now cease. They believe that a degree of privacy and understanding is essential if Their

Royal Highnesses are to provide a happy and secure upbringing for their children."

Happy and secure? Certainly there were many happy moments for William and Harry. But secure? Far from it. Both children were caught in the crossfire during their parents' bitter and very public divorce wars. Not only did they often find themselves fleeing the room as their parents hurled insults and objects at each other but William and Harry also became hapless pawns in a nasty game of one-upmanship.

When it came to proving who was the better parent, Diana had the upper hand from the start. Charles, who had described his own mother as aloof and his father as a bully, had always seemed stiff and detached, even with his own children. One of the biggest setbacks to his image as a father: famously keeping a date to attend a performance of the opera *Tosca* at Covent Garden when William, then eight, was accidentally struck in the head with a golf club and needed emergency surgery for a fractured skull. "What Sort of Dad Are You?" was the inevitable headline on the front page of the *Sun*. In fairness, it was not reported in the press that right up until the moment William was wheeled into the operating room, both of his parents were with him in his hospital room offering words of encouragement. (This severe head injury, which required William to undergo a seventy-minute-long procedure, left him with a permanent scar above his left eye.)

Diana's childhood was no less dreadful than Charles's: when she was six, her mother ran off with her lover, leaving Diana to be raised by a series of cruel governesses—one of whom enjoyed striking her in the head with a wooden spoon whenever she spoke out of turn. Eager to break the cycle, Diana showered affection on her own offspring—albeit sometimes when cameras were present to record the event. In an effort to give them something approaching a normal childhood, she took William and Harry to amusement parks, go-kart tracks, and fast-food outlets (Kentucky Fried Chicken was her favorite). She insisted they not grow up with too strong a sense of entitlement; when the trio went to the movies, for instance, mother and sons paid for their tickets and stood in line with everybody else.

At the same time, Diana was determined that her boys know something about the very real problems of average people. From an early age, William and his brother accompanied their mother on her clandestine visits to homeless shelters, AIDS clinics, and orphanages. As someone who could connect with the man and woman on the street—and empathize with them for having to cope with problems never experienced behind palace walls—Diana had been unique within the royal family. Now she had company. Even as children, William and Harry were showing that they shared Diana's magic touch.

Yet at what cost? Eventually, although she could not have suspected it then, Kate's life and the lives of her own children would be impacted by the emotional turmoil Prince William endured as a schoolboy. When his mother fled to the bathroom in tears after a screaming match with Charles, it was ten-year-old William who slid tissues under the door and pleaded, "Don't cry, Mummy."

If things got too violent—Prince Charles had a penchant for slamming doors and throwing things—William would try and shield his terrified little brother from the mayhem. Such bedlam had been playing out even before William made his entrance: Kate's future husband was almost killed in utero when, after another bitter quarrel with Charles over his affair with Camilla, a very pregnant Diana threw herself down the stairs at Sandringham, the sovereign's privately owned twenty-thousand-acre estate two hours and twenty minutes north of London by car. Queen Elizabeth found her daughter-in-law on the marble floor of the main entrance and was, according to Diana, "physically shaking, absolutely horrified." Years later, the battling couple's protection detail voiced concerns that there were so many hunting rifles and other firearms available to Charles and Diana at the various royal residences. "I'm afraid," said one bodyguard in a memo, "that someone is going to get shot."

To make matters even worse for William, he was also being leaned on heavily by his mother for emotional support. At Ludgrove, the elite boarding school he and Harry attended thirty minutes outside London, William was outgoing and popular with his peers, a superb student who excelled at sports and seemed to possess his mother's innate charm. At the same time, his teachers observed that he was also prone to long silences, moodiness, and, like his mother, nail-biting anxiety.

As soon as William was capable of voicing an opinion, his mother was consulting him on matters that ran the gamut from her wardrobe and hair-style to what he really thought of the new prime minister and what causes to support. Diana called him "my deep thinker" and "a wise old man in child's clothing." She worried that "he's just like me. He's too sensitive. He feels everything too much." That didn't stop her from putting William in the bizarre position of having to offer her romantic advice. After all, she reasoned, at the age of ten, William was in reality an "old soul."

The one thing Diana did not consult her son about was the one thing that would, in the end, deal a final, fatal blow to her marriage. After BBC reporter Martin Bashir tricked her with forged bank statements and checks into believing that she was being spied upon by Charles's allies, the Princess of Wales did a wide-ranging interview with Bashir for the hugely popular news program *Panorama*. During the fifty-five-minute interview, Diana looked up from heavily mascaraed lashes and spoke in hushed tones about everything from her eating disorders and depression, her attempts at suicide, and what she said was a Palace conspiracy aimed at destroying her. She also discussed her affair with her sons' riding instructor James Hewitt ("Yes, I adored him, yes, I was in love with him") and her husband's affair with Camilla ("There were three of us in this marriage, so it was a bit crowded"). She added that no one in the royal family believed "they should relate to the world, the world of today. They want me and my children to behave as if we were still in Victorian England." Not that Diana was pressing for a divorce—quite the opposite. She stressed that she saw "a future ahead—a future for my husband, a future for myself, and a future for the monarchy."

Like the vast majority of the viewing public, the Middletons were sympathetic to the embattled princess. Polls showed that 75 percent of Britons approved of Diana's performance on *Panorama*, and for a brief time the princess basked in the glow of what was unquestionably a huge public relations victory. Euphoria soon turned to panic when Diana realized she had deeply offended the only person who really mattered: her mother-in-law, the Queen. Twenty days after the *Panorama* interview aired, Her Majesty wrote notes to Charles and Diana to obtain an "early divorce" that would be "in the best interests of the country."

Diana was devastated, for her children as much as herself. Knowing what it was like to come from a broken home, she told friends it was "the very last thing" she wanted for William and Harry. She would suffer another blow when the divorce settlement was reached on February 28, 1996. Although Charles was basically emptying his personal coffers to pay his soon-to-be ex-wife $22.5 million in cash—and she was being allowed to remain at Kensington Palace with an annual income of $600,000—Diana was stripped of her HRH status. William once again stepped up to bolster her spirits, insisting that not being referred to as "Her Royal Highness" was only a temporary setback. Once he became king, he promised to reinstate the honorific. In the meantime, he said, "I don't mind what you're called. You're still Mummy."

As a commoner from a working-class family with no connections to the aristocracy, Kate could only sympathize with William's plight from afar. His parents' turbulent marriage and bitter divorce would obviously leave deep psychological scars—doubts, frustrations, and fears William would eventually share with Kate—but for the time being he did a masterful job of concealing them.

William had flourished at Eton College, the uber-elite prep school founded in 1440 just a stone's throw from Windsor Castle on the banks of the Thames. With its Gothic turrets, redbrick chimneys, and mullioned windows, Eton provided a reassuringly familiar environment for William, who bunked with forty-nine other boys aged thirteen to eighteen at Manor House. The future monarch slept like everyone else in a seven-by-ten-foot room, albeit the only one with a private bathroom and a bodyguard in the room next door armed with a Heckler & Koch machine pistol.

The Duke of Wellington once famously observed that the Battle of Waterloo was "won on the playing fields of Eton"—a nod to the school's reputation for preparing young men to become wartime leaders but also to excel on the world stage. As first among equals, it was not altogether surprising that William would fit in perfectly among the other ruddy-faced, improbably tall sons of Britain's ruling class. His test scores ranked at or near the top of his class, and he excelled at rugby, rowing, and especially water polo—a sport that combined his father's passion for horses with his mother's love of swimming. Diana felt that William had picked water polo as a sport to pursue because "on some subconscious level it was a way of pleasing both Charles and myself."

There was also squash, judo, tennis, karate, golf, and the bizarre Eton wall game, so called because it involved one team storming a brick wall being defended by an opposing team. Caked with mud and virtually plastered to the wall in one seamless mass, the defending team makes it inevitable that no one will score a goal. The last time that happened was 1909. In the warmer months, students were divided into "wet bobs" (rowers) or "dry bobs" (cricketers). William was classified as a wet bob, although during the fall he was one of the school's star rugby and soccer players.

William was also required to master Eton's arcane lingo. A student who was summoned to see a "beak" had been ordered to report to a teacher in his office. Classes were "divs," the headmaster was "head man," top students were "tugs," and anyone who belonged to the small band of acknowledged student leaders known as "Pop" wore a brightly colored vest of his own design. Noting that William had "that Etonian look" as he dashed from class to class in the school's Mr. Chips getup of swallow-tail coat and striped trousers, British writer Sue Townshend chalked it up to the "burnished" look that set Britain's young aristocrats apart. "They are like angels, you know, and they float around the world."

To the outside world, William seemed to have adjusted well to his parents' divorce. No one was more pleased with her grandson's smooth transition to Eton life than Queen Elizabeth, who could keep an eye on her favorite grandson playing rugby from the window of her bedroom at Windsor Castle. While there were plenty of tall towheads scrambling for the ball, the initials on the back of his jersey made him easy to spot: *WOW*, for William of Wales.

Every Sunday at 3:50 p.m. the Heir, with his close protection team trailing not far behind, made the stroll over the short span of bridge linking Eton to the village of Windsor and up the hill to Granny's house—a journey on foot of no more than seven minutes. Once inside, he would proceed to the Oak Drawing Room, where the Queen would be waiting for him over a pot of her favorite Earl Grey tea. Like English matrons everywhere, Elizabeth II would be mother, pouring the tea while they discussed his progress in school, whether Eton was having a winning season, what his aristocratic friends and their families were up to, and—given her singular obsession with horses—how his riding was coming along. In keeping with his Windsor heritage, William gave the distinct impression he'd been born on horseback and since the age of ten had been playing polo with his father and grandfather Prince Philip.

Occasionally, the Queen would try to deftly sneak in a history lesson—giving him a peek at a letter from Disraeli to Queen Victoria, perhaps, or sharing some pearls of wisdom from her first and favorite prime minister, Winston Churchill. One subject Her Majesty studiously avoided was Princess Diana, whom she still viewed as an emotional powder keg capable of blowing the entire monarchy to smithereens.

What not even the Queen realized was that William was still being called upon to advise his mother on her love life. The Princess of Wales was now smitten with the only man she ever called her "soulmate"—pudgy, chain-smoking Pakistani heart surgeon Hasnat Khan. William watched as his mother donned jeans, a leather jacket, dark glasses, and a long black wig, then headed out in her own dark blue BMW 3 Series E36 coupe to pick up Khan at Royal Brompton Hospital. With Khan hidden in the back seat under a tartan plaid quilt, Diana smuggled her lover into Kensington Palace.

As had always been the case, William was spared few of the details concerning his mother's romantic escapades. "She spoke with him about things one's child really should never hear," Diana's friend Lady Elsa Bowker once observed. "In that sense it was probably not a healthy relationship." Aware that she might have to convert to Islam in order to marry Khan, Diana sought William's approval. "Mummy," he said, "you have to do what makes you happy." He was surprised when, without warning Khan's parents, she impulsively flew to Pakistan to ask if they could accept a non-Muslim as their daughter-in-law.

As it turned out, Khan's family said they would be delighted, but it scarcely mattered. Sadly for Diana, the chronically publicity-shy Khan had no intention of marrying the world's most celebrated woman. After one last window-rattling shouting match, Khan stormed off, leaving Diana in tears and William to console his shattered mother in the aftermath of another disastrous romance. Soon William was patiently listening to Mummy as she hatched another scheme, this time a plan to make Khan jealous by dating another Muslim. But when Diana unexpectedly found herself falling for her ersatz lover, wealthy Egyptian playboy Dodi Fayed, William eagerly promoted the affair. "Dr. Khan made you very unhappy, Mummy," William told her. "Dodi makes you laugh."

Kate was oblivious to such Machiavellian machinations, the building blocks of her future husband's complex, conflicted, and at times tortured psyche. She was certainly not alone. To the world at large, in the wake of his parents' breakup, William the teen heartthrob was doing just fine. No one was a bigger booster of William's potential star power than Mummy. "Isn't he superb?" Diana gushed to friends. "And he's so tall, too! The girls will be mad for him!" William was particularly mortified when she called him by one of her favorite nicknames: "DDG," for Drop Dead Gorgeous.

This could—and did—get worse. William was just shy of his fifteenth birthday when the UK teen magazine *Smash Hits* ran a centerfold pullout of His Royal Highness wearing a blue blazer. After the issue flew off the stands, the publication gave away 250,000 "I Love Willy" stickers. Seemingly overnight, a new and even more humiliating moniker was bestowed on William: "Dreamboat Willy."

For all the psychological ramifications of his unique childhood—not just emotional baggage but a truckload of hopes, dreams, doubts, fears, confusion, hyperbolic expectations, and mind-spinning chaos—William was holding it together in late summer of 1997. Or at least it seemed so to Kate. Although she was six months older than the prince and was going through the usual trials of adolescence, she already looked at William with a kind of reverence—not simply for his fame, good looks, and place in history but for his character. At fifteen, he had spent his entire life in the spotlight, coping with dysfunctional parents and a relentlessly intrusive press. Yet everything he had endured—all the psychological damage that had already been done during his childhood—was mere prelude to one earth-shattering event. . . .

September 6, 1997
A sunny Saturday in London

If she had admired William's quiet strength, she marveled at it now. Kate was perched alongside her mother and her younger sister, Pippa, on the Middleton family's floral print sofa in Berkshire, dabbing at tears as they watched live television coverage of Princess Diana's funeral—the single greatest collective outpouring of grief in the nation's history. Over the past week since Diana's shocking car-crash death in Paris, Great Britain and the world had gone through a kind of catharsis. While the nation looked to its sovereign for words of comfort, the Queen had remained silent, preferring not to interrupt her annual summer holiday at Balmoral Castle. Nor did she initially agree to lower the flag over Buckingham Palace to half-staff—a gesture traditionally made only upon the death of the monarch. In this instance, Her Majesty's subjects were in no mood to slavishly obey protocol. "Let the Flag Fly at Half-Mast" shouted the front page of the *Daily Mail*.

Public outrage was palpable—and would have been even more so had it been known that the Queen at first strongly opposed honoring Diana with an official funeral, or that one of the first calls she placed was to the British consul in Paris demanding to know if Diana had any royal jewels in her possession when she died. ("The Queen wants to know," an embassy official shouted at nonplussed hospital staff members in Paris, "where are the jewels? *Where are the jewels?*" As it happened, all the jewelry Diana had brought to Paris on that fateful trip belonged to her.)

For days, William's grandmother ignored headlines like "Show Us You Care" in the *Daily Express* and the *Sun*'s plaintive "Where Is the Queen When the Country Needs Her"; only after pressure from Charles and Prime Minister Tony Blair did the Queen grudgingly relent on all fronts.

In what would be a desperate last-ditch attempt to right her teetering throne, Her Majesty also agreed to address her people in a nationally televised speech that would ultimately be seen by tens of millions around the world. In what was a defining moment of her forty-five-year reign, the Queen paid tribute to Diana as "an exceptional and gifted human being."

Now a sea of floral tributes swelled at the wrought iron gates of all London's palaces, monuments, and government buildings, as well as at landmarks like Westminster Abbey, Parliament, and 10 Downing Street. Yet as Diana's funeral procession began to make its way through central London and streets clogged with more than a million and a half mourners, nothing touched hearts more than the simple bouquet of white rosebuds atop her flag-draped coffin with a block-printed note from Harry that read simply "MUMMY."

"How terribly, terribly sad," Kate's mother said as she watched the caisson drawn by six horses of the King's Troop Royal Horse Artillery pulling to a stop in front of Kensington Palace. There the cortege was joined by the Windsor and Spencer men: Prince Charles, Prince William, Prince Harry, Prince Philip, and Diana's brother Charles, the 9th Earl Spencer. From the outset, Spencer protested that it was "bizarre and cruel" to ask his nephews to walk behind their mother's body for four miles as it made its way to Westminster Abbey. He was told they asked to join the procession, but Spencer later discovered that was a lie. He would go on to remember the experience as "a feeling of high emotion around you of the most sad and confused sort, all hammering in on you. It was a tunnel of grief. . . . I still have nightmares about it. It was horrifying . . . the most harrowing experience of my life."

Still in shock over losing their mother in such a violent and senseless way, Diana's sons merely did as they were told. William coped by tilting his head down and employing the "Shy Di" gesture that his mother had made famous. Fixing his gaze on the pavement before him, the prince hid his eyes behind the shock of blond hair he kept at that length for just this purpose—"my security blanket," William conceded. Harry, meanwhile, clenched his fists so tightly his fingernails dug into his skin. For the entire thirty-eight-minute walk, William tried to reconcile "me being Prince William and having to do my bit versus the private William, who just wanted to go into a room and cry because he'd lost his mother." Just as disconcerting for William were the "hysterics" and "horrible screams" coming from strangers in the crowd. "I thought, 'You didn't even know her,'" William remembered. "'Why and how are you so upset?'"

As he always had, Harry turned to his older brother for support. He kept "a fraction of Will always in the corner of my vision" and drew "loads of strength from that." Most of all, Harry remembered "the sounds, the clinking bridles and clopping hooves of the six sweaty brown horses, the squeaking wheels of the gun carriage they were hauling . . ."

With no counseling and precious few words of comfort offered by the devoutly stiff-upper-lipped royal family—Harry would later remember that his grandfather Prince Philip looked "serene, as if this were merely another royal engagement"—it would be decades before Diana's sons could even begin to process how the loss of their mother and the subsequent "long and lonely walk," as William called it, had scarred them psychologically.

Watching as the drama unfolded before a worldwide audience of two and a half billion—one of the largest live events in TV history—Kate could still fantasize about marching down the aisle with her handsome prince. But there was an added element of pathos that now made the prospect somehow even more beguiling. The other, less romantic half of the equation came under the general heading of "Be careful what you wish for." Whoever the lucky girl wearing the glass slipper turned out to be, the demons William was dragging into adulthood would eventually become hers to deal with as well. Moreover, she would be joining a wildly unstable family that had repeatedly proven itself capable of devouring its own, not to mention a revered, thousand-year-old institution nonetheless rife with betrayal, deceit, corruption, and intrigue.

Now that a year had passed since Diana's death had rattled the world, Kate's mother was focusing with laser-like precision on finding an opening into the rarefied world of Britain's upper classes. Like other teenage girls in Britain in the 1960s and 1970s—including Camilla Shand and Diana Spencer—Carole Goldsmith taped photos of the then-callow Prince Charles on her bedroom wall alongside posters of pop stars like Paul McCartney, David Cassidy, Rod Stewart, and Queen. But unlike Lady Diana and Camilla—who was the granddaughter of a baron and the great-granddaughter of one of Edward VII's mistresses—Carole was not merely a commoner but decidedly working class with no social connections whatsoever.

Carole was seeing to it that Kate's flight path was now set on a more vertical trajectory. While she by no means neglected her two younger children—making certain they, too, ultimately found success—Carole would understandably soon be consumed with trying to help Kate exploit the almost unimaginable opportunities that would be presented to her. But for the moment, Carole was disappointed to hear that Kate had not managed to push her way to the front of the crowd of girls at Marlborough and introduce herself to the mud-splattered prince after his rugby match. After all, Kate's mother was a former flight attendant who pushed her way to the top as a canny entrepreneur, turning her skill at arranging children's parties into a multimillion-dollar mail-order business. But no matter. Carole was confident that the more diffident Catherine would eventually find a way.

She was certainly in the right place to forge alliances with the privileged few her own grandparents referred to as "nobs" and "aristos." Marlborough College, established in 1843 for the sons of Anglican clergy, is situated beside a Neolithic mound on the River Kennet near where a Norman castle once stood. Not as old or prestigious as Eton or that other citadel of British privilege, Harrow, Marlborough had much the same look: a brick, stone, and stucco hodgepodge of traditional styles including Gothic, Tudor, Georgian, and Victorian. It also boasted its share of esteemed alumni, including the artist William Morris, the poet Sir John Betjeman, pioneering aviator and solo sailor Sir Francis Chichester, and actor James Mason. Once it opened its doors to female students in 1968, donors opened their wallets and paid for a swimming pool, new tennis courts, and even an observatory.

In the future, Prince Andrew and his wife Sarah Ferguson, Duchess of York, would send their daughter Eugenie to Marlborough. In the meantime Kate would have plenty of lords and ladies, viscounts, earls, and marquises to rub shoulders with. Peers of the realm, meantime, could chat up the scions of Britain's newly minted millionaires—Kate's cohort.

How the Middletons clambered up the social ladder even to this level was something of a fairy tale in itself. Oddly enough, there was, in fact, a weak family link to royalty lurking in genealogical files. Prince William's Spencer side and Kate's paternal forebears, the Middletons, are descendants of seventeenth-century soldier and statesman Sir Thomas Fairfax. It is no small irony that Fairfax, known to his troops as "Black Tom" because of his dark coloring, commanded the parliamentary armies that defeated Charles I and led to the king's beheading. Years later, "Black Tom" Fairfax changed his mind and took up arms to restore Charles II to the throne. In the end, this skimpy but fascinating connection to Fairfax makes William and Kate fifteenth cousins. It would, by extension, also ultimately link Kate to all three of the British kings named Charles. Tracing her father's lineage, Kate also turned out to be a distant cousin to legendary actor Sir John Gielgud, film director Guy Ritchie (and for a time, via marriage, his ex-wife Madonna), and Peter Rabbit creator Beatrix Potter. There was also one startling connection to an American figure of some note: according to the New England Historic Genealogical Society, Kate is also a distant cousin—specifically, an eighth cousin eight times removed—of George Washington.

Certainly the hardscrabble family histories of both Kate's parents seemed light-years away from the burnished lives of the posh and privileged. Michael Middleton's ancestor Thomas Glassborow, Kate's great-great-great-great grandfather, was one of London's most notoriously cruel constables, rounding up petty criminals so they could be shipped off to penal colonies in Australia. His son Edward was the black sheep of the Glassborow clan, shackled and tossed into London's infamous Holloway Prison in 1881 for public drunkenness. Three years later, Thomas's cousin, Frank Lupton, who had built a textile manufacturing empire, died and left a fortune that in 2025 would be the equivalent of more than $50 million—only to have most of it squandered by his heirs.

A descendant of coal miners who labored under Dickensian conditions in northeastern England's sooty County Durham, Carole had heard the stories of deprivation, disease, and death that defined the lives of the working poor in nineteenth-century England. Carole's hard-drinking, chain-smoking grandmother Edith Goldsmith, widowed in the 1930s with six young children to care for, scraped by filling jars in a pickle factory.

Edith's son Ronald managed to find work painting houses—he later rebranded himself as a "craftsman decorator"—and when he married jewelry saleswoman Dorothy Harrison they moved into public housing in the London borough of Ealing. Dorothy's mother, Elizabeth "Lily" Harrison, had already taken a step up the social ladder—at least in her own mind. While her husband, Tom, returned from the mines each day covered in coal dust, Kate's great-grandmother Lily was known throughout the working-class Durham village of Spennymoor for her impeccable wardrobe. "Everything about Aunt Lily had to match—from her gloves to her lipstick," said her niece Shirley Beedle, who along with everyone else in the family began calling Kate's great-grandmother "the Duchess."

Not that the Duchess was reluctant to turn a profit. A skilled seamstress, she deftly copied Christian Dior's haute couture New Look and sold her knockoff dresses and evening gowns to her more fashion-conscious neighbors. Determined to move up in the world, Kate's great-grandmother pushed her husband to doff his miner's cap and retrain as a carpenter. (Carole Middleton's memories of her tenacious, upwardly mobile grandmother persist. "The Duchess was an amazing woman," she said in 2023. "Everybody loved the Duchess.")

Kate's grandmother Dorothy—Carole's mother—by all accounts suffered from a similar folie de grandeur, putting on airs and forcing her beleaguered spouse to finance her lavish tastes. "Lady Dorothy," as her neighbors referred to her, was a transformative figure in the Goldsmiths' lives, holding on to the belief that she and her only daughter, Carole, were a cut above. Dorothy often reminded people that she was a direct descendant of a baronet—Sir Thomas Conyers of Horden. She neglected to mention that Sir Thomas was apparently always dead broke and spent much of his adult life laboring in a grimy London workhouse. Since he had no male heirs, the baronetcy died with him in 1810.

No matter. The memory of Dorothy pushing her baby daughter through the narrow doorway of her council flat in the same top-of-the-line Silver Cross pram used by royal family governesses persisted among her neighbors for decades. (It turns out Kate's forebears were also distantly connected to Prince William's family through Sir Thomas's Bowes-Lyon cousins—a tidbit Dorothy would almost certainly have mentioned had she known. Elizabeth the Queen Mother was a Bowes-Lyon.)

In 1966, when Carole was eleven and her brother Gary not quite a year old, her parents borrowed the money for a deposit on an $8,000 (the equivalent of about $80,000 today) three-bedroom duplex at 20 Kingsbridge Road in the more prosperous Norwood Green section of Southall, West London. Carole wanted to be a teacher but was told her parents couldn't afford to send her to a teacher's college, so she dropped out of school at sixteen and landed a job at the Prudential insurance company in central London. "One of those massive offices with rows and rows of desks," she later recalled. "I hated it."

Carole returned to school, earned her diploma, and went to work as a trainee at John Lewis, the upscale UK department store chain, but decided being a sales assistant wasn't for her. "I said blow that, I'm not doing that for six months. It's really boring." From there, Carole learned shorthand—a skill she would retain well into the 2020s—and went to work at British European Airways (BEA) as a secretary. As willful as her mother, Dorothy, Carole decided she was also unhappy in that job. So she brushed up on her high school French—a requirement at the time for BEA employees seeking to interact with the public—and joined the airline's ground staff.

It was in 1974, shortly after BEA merged with British Overseas Airways (BOAC) to become British Airways, that Carole met Michael Middleton. He was six years her senior, wore a pilot's uniform, and, she remembered, "he was rather shy but very handsome." The son of World War II veterans—Royal Air Force fighter pilot Peter Middleton and Valerie Glassborow, who with her twin sister Mary was part of the crack team of code breakers at Bletchley Park who helped unlock the secrets of the Nazi's Enigma machine—Michael grew up comfortably in Leeds on the fringes of high society. His once-wealthy Lupton family relatives still owned large swaths of property in West Yorkshire. Michael attended the same private school his father and grandfather had—Clifton College—and earned a bachelor of science degree at the University of Surrey.

Michael fully intended to follow in his father's footsteps but discovered after six months of flight training that he actually had no appetite for piloting a plane. So instead he signed on as a British Airways dispatcher running operations on the ground—a highly paid position that carried with it the right to wear the same uniform as a British Airways pilot. By the time they began dating, Carole had made the opposite decision—to take to the friendly skies. As an air hostess, she donned a Hardy Amies–designed uniform: dark blue knee-length skirt and collared jacket with red piping, black stockings, white blouse with a white scarf, high heels, and a blue-and-red pillbox hat.

At a time when air travel was still largely for businessmen and the well-to-do, Carole epitomized the kind of attractive, charming, and capable young woman international airlines were looking for. In addition, her new career as a flight attendant afforded her both an opportunity to see the world and, Dorothy would periodically remind her daughter, land a rich husband.

On their first date, Carole tried to impress Michael with her cooking. Referring to a scene in the film *Bridget Jones's Diary* where the title character makes blue leek soup, Carole remembered preparing "mushroom risotto and it looked like grey porridge. It was Bridget Jones." Nevertheless, Carole and Michael's romance blossomed, and after three years of dating she moved into his cramped flat at 33 Arborfield Close in Slough, a gritty industrial neighborhood near their jobs at Heathrow. In 1979, they purchased a modest redbrick house with a faux-Tudor roofline and twin chimneys on Cock's Lane in Bradfield Southend, a village with a population of seven hundred in West Berkshire.

The following June, the couple wed at the twelfth-century church of St. James the Less in the even tinier hamlet of Dorney, Buckinghamshire. (St. James the Less had the dubious distinction of being stoned by locals while preaching the gospel in Palestine during the early days of Christianity. When that didn't do the trick, he was beaten to death with a club.)

The nuptials were attended by scores of Middletons who had made the trip down from Yorkshire, but only two Goldsmith relatives, not counting the parents of the bride. Dorothy, determined not to be looked down upon by her daughter's well-bred in-laws, controlled the guest list and excluded the dozens of Goldsmiths she felt were unsuitable. Carole, wearing a white, floor-length, shoulder-baring Bardot dress with balloon sleeves, walked down the aisle on her father Ronald's arm. (Forty-one years later, her son James's bride, Alizée Thevenet, would borrow the dress to wear at her wedding in France. "It was amazing to give such a beautiful dress a second lease on life," Alizée said.)

After the brief Anglican ceremony, the happy couple left the church in a horse-drawn carriage and headed for a bonfire dinner that the bride had also organized. The main course, chosen by Carole: chili con carne. "It was," she said, "all very low-key."

It would have been impossible for them to imagine it, but the Middletons were about to affix the date January 9, 1982, in the annals of British history. At 9:03 that evening, Carole gave birth to a green-eyed girl at the Royal Berkshire Hospital in Reading. (The hospital was a pet project of the last king named William, William IV.) On June 20, 1982, Catherine Elizabeth Middleton was baptized at the now-defunct Church of St. Andrew in Bradfield, a fourteenth-century stone structure situated near the picturesque if unfortunately named villages of Tutts Clump and Rotten Row.

The day after Catherine's christening, in yet another bizarre nod to their future entanglement with royalty, the Middletons toasted their own second wedding anniversary—and the birth of the future king, William Arthur Philip Louis. The nation rejoiced with pealing cathedral bells, booming cannons, and public fountains bathed in blue lights to celebrate the birth of a princeling. No one outside the monarchy's inner sanctum sanctorum—certainly not Michael and Carole Middleton—was aware that, just six months earlier, a pregnant Diana was so desperately unhappy she tried to kill herself. "We were all so naive back then," Carole would tell a friend years later. "Totally without a clue. Everything looked so perfect."

It wasn't long before the Middletons were welcoming another daughter; Philippa Charlotte—called Pippa from the very beginning—arrived in September 1983. The following May, the Middletons, who had always talked about living abroad, picked up and moved the family to Jordan, where Michael ran British Airways operations in the capital city of Amman. Two-year-old Kate attended the English-language Assahera nursery school with one hundred other children from Jordan, Japan, the United States, Britain, India, and Indonesia. Before breaking up into classes of twelve, the children would spend the first part of their morning learning Arabic by reading passages from the Quran. They would also sit in a circle singing "Eensy Weensy Spider" in both English and Arabic. The school's founder, Sahera al Nabulsi, dressed up as Santa Claus at Christmas, and a drummer was brought in to perform for the children at the end of Ramadan. "The idea," she said, "was to reinforce concepts like respect and love."

Kate would retain many of the Arabic phrases she learned in Jordan over the family's three years there. She also remembered that period fondly, including the time the family visited the Roman ruins at Jerash and she scampered over the toppled columns with her sister, Pippa. Carole and Michael also held on to happy memories of their stint in the Holy Land. "The parties at the British Embassy," Carole said, "were amazing." Socializing with diplomats and foreign leaders aside, these were impressionable years in the life of a young child. Decades later, Kate would acknowledge that the sights, sounds, and smells of Jordan remained with her—that at such a formative age, the exposure to another culture that was "so different and so fascinating" is "the kind of thing that stays with you, becomes part of who you are."

Eventually, it was Carole who insisted the family move back to their little house on Cock's Lane in West Berkshire. "I wasn't convinced I wanted to be an expat mum," she said. Kate was four and a half and Pippa almost three when the family returned to the United Kingdom. Carole, now thirty-two, was expecting her third child. "I thought, 'Oooh, bills to pay.' But I got married at twenty-five, had Catherine at twenty-six. I had the strongest feeling that I hadn't achieved anything."

Once the Middletons were back on home turf, Carole wasted no time signing up both her daughters for the preschool adjacent to nearby St. Peter's Church—a gray, shingle-clad building for children two and a half to five years old. While Kate and Pippa, both dressed in the St. Peter's uniform of green sweater and pants, sang songs, sat in reading circles, and finger-painted with the other children, Carole won over the other mothers by volunteering to carpool and pitch in as a tireless volunteer at school events.

Carole may not have been an accomplished cook, as evidenced by her soggy risotto, but she was an expert at putting together candy-and-trinket-filled goody bags for the endless round of children's birthday parties that are the bane of every young parent's existence. Before long, other mothers in the neighborhood were gladly paying Carole for her colorful goody bags—and she was turning a handsome profit. Soon Carole encountered problems of her own trying to find supplies for Kate's fifth birthday party. "All I could find," she recalled, "were basic clown plates. I realized there was a gap in the market, so I decided to design my own." She took prototypes of paper plates, party hats, and favors to several retailers in one of London's most famous shopping districts, High Street, but was rebuffed.

It did not take long for Carole, urged on by her retail-savvy mother, to seize the moment. Right after the birth of Kate's brother, James William, Carole began assembling a line of party supplies at the kitchen table. Within a couple of months, she leased storage space several miles from her home and announced the startup of her own mail-order business aimed at making party organizing "a little easier" for mothers everywhere.

From the beginning, Party Pieces was a family affair. Kate appeared on the cover of the company's first catalogue, blowing out the candles on a birthday cake. Pippa soon joined her in posing for ads and other promotional material. In one early black-and-white photo, a smiling Carole looks directly into the camera while Kate blows a noisemaker into her face and Pippa looks on. "My children inspired my business," Carole would later explain, "and have been involved from the start."

Kate in particular became the early face of Party Pieces, modeling for the company's flyers in rhinestone tiaras and glittery fairy princess costumes. "All little girls like pretending to be princesses," one of the other Bradfield Southend mothers commented, "but looking back, it does seem as if, even then, Catherine looked especially comfortable playing the part." Already showing signs of artistic talent, Kate also came up with designs for invitations and other party-related products like place mats and napkins.

Straight out of the gate, Party Pieces was an enormous success. Much like the indoor fireworks that the company also supplied for revelers, the Middletons' family income skyrocketed. Michael left his position at British Airways to join his wife's team, and by the time Kate turned seven and had joined the local Brownie troop, Carole was driving her the six miles to and from St. Andrew's, a tony elementary school set on fifty-four wooded acres outside the village of Pangbourne. Annual tuition for St. Andrew's, which catered to boys and girls ages three to thirteen, was $20,000, roughly equivalent to $50,000 in 2025.

Throughout her childhood, Kate often turned to her paternal grandmother for emotional support in much the same way Prince Charles relied on the Queen Mother for "hugs and cuddles." Kate would later recall that it was her World War II code-breaking "Granny Val" who spent hours with the Middleton children, "baking cookies and making pies, helping us with our arts and crafts, doing all the wonderful things grannies do." While her mother zeroed in on building her fledgling business, Kate "actually learned a lot about parenting from my grandmother."

A stellar student who excelled at sports, young Kate was also a standout at the visual and performing arts. It came as no surprise when, at age ten, Kate was cast in the lead of a school production of Alan Jay Lerner and Frederick Loewe's *My Fair Lady*. "She played her role with passion and a steely conviction," recalled Andrew Alexander, who acted opposite her as Henry Higgins. Even though he, too, was only ten at the time, Alexander remembered Kate as being both "enchanting" and "intimidating."

Ostensibly, nothing in Kate's childhood was more foreshadowing than the snippets of dialogue she uttered during her last performance at St. Andrew's, this time playing the heroine, Maria Marten, in the Victorian-era potboiler *Murder in the Red Barn.* The entire play was recorded by a proud parent for posterity, and some of thirteen-year-old Kate's lines seem eerily prophetic. Early on, a psychic tells her a "rich, handsome man" will marry her and take her away to London. Later, the man in question proposes marriage. "Yes," Kate answers, "it's all I've ever longed for! Yes, oh yes, dear *William*!"

Fortunately, the similarities between the play and Kate's future end there. It is difficult to conceive of a more inappropriately gruesome, reality-based melodrama to be picked for a school production. *Murder in the Red Barn* is based on one of the most infamous crimes in nineteenth-century England, the 1827 murder of the trusting Maria Marten by the man with whom she had an out-of-wedlock child, William Corder. After a sensational trial, more than seven thousand citizens showed up to witness Corder's execution by hanging, then filed by his body after it was slit down the middle—one of the charming practices in England under the Murder Act of 1752 and the Anatomy Act of 1832, both of which made the bodies of executed murderers available for dissection and public display.

If Carole and Michael Middleton had any objections to *Murder in the Red Barn*'s macabre subject matter, they did not voice them. They had their hands full with the sudden explosion of their business—all the result of Carole's shrewd decision to launch a Party Pieces website in the early 1990s, when the internet was still in its infancy. Soon, the company expanded to thirty full-time employees, all filling thousands of orders every week at Party Pieces' new headquarters in rural Ashampstead Common in west Berkshire. Appropriately enough, Carole took over what had been Childs Court Farm, a group of dilapidated barns, cattle pens, grain sheds, and a hayloft technically located in Yattendon—the village where Yattendon Castle once stood. It was at Yattendon Castle where Queen Anne

Boleyn dropped a handkerchief during a dance that was retrieved by her friend Henry Norreys, setting in motion rumors that would eventually lead Henry VIII to behead both Boleyn and Norreys.

Now that Party Pieces was grossing $3 million a year, the Middletons could easily afford to move up—and they did, purchasing Oak Acre, a red-brick house with Georgian-style windows, five fireplaces, six bedrooms, and a solarium—all hidden behind hedgerows on one and a half acres in Berkshire's Bucklebury. Right outside Kate's bedroom window was St. Mary the Virgin, an imposing stone twelfth-century church dating back to Edward the Confessor. Steps away is the River Pang, a tributary of the Thames thought to have inspired Kenneth Grahame's *The Wind in the Willows*. (As if the setting for Kate's early upbringing wasn't enchanted enough, Bucklebury is also the main town of the Buckland Hobbits in the works of J. R. R. Tolkien.)

While Prince Charles and Princess Diana hovered over their eldest son as he enrolled at Eton in 1995—an event made all the more memorable when the future head of the Church of England asked his parents what he should put in the space marked "Religion"—Kate started classes at Downe House, a posh boarding school for girls aged eleven to eighteen that had originally been housed in the former home of Charles Darwin. Until now, Kate had flourished in a coeducational environmental. Unaccustomed to the cliques and cattiness that were an inescapable part of life at upper-class unisex schools in England, the newcomer whose family fortune was founded on paper plates and party hats was quickly targeted by Downe House's reigning mean girls. Nor did it help that Kate, who lived just ten minutes away, was one of only thirty day students in a student body of nearly six hundred.

Aside from being classified as nouveau riche—many of the students at Downe House were offspring of the landed gentry and a few actually had titles—Kate suffered from being, in the words of one teacher, "a very sweet, friendly girl." Such qualities were alien to the overindulged daughters of Great Britain's elite and within days of her arrival, Kate found herself being ostracized by the other girls. Spiteful rumors about Kate and her up-by-the-bootstraps family began circulating, and she became the target of pranks and even physical abuse. Among other things, her books were stolen, she was ganged up on during field hockey practice, and she was tripped and shoved on the way to and from class. Kate had hoped to use her natural athletic ability to join a school team and make new friends. Field hockey was her chosen sport at the time, but Downe House only offered lacrosse, a very different sport. Kate went ahead and tried out for lacrosse, but failed to make the team after what she later described as a "humiliating" performance. To make matters worse, she was booed as she left the field.

Kate's experience as the victim of bullying during her time at Downe House would leave a lasting impression. "I was fortunate to go through that, in a way," she later explained. "Otherwise, I might never have understood how terribly toxic and damaging bullying can be—for the bully as well as the victim."

Having never seen Kate this unhappy—so miserable, in fact, that she now suffered from anxiety-induced eczema—Michael and Carole removed her from Downe House and for the remainder of her high school education enrolled her instead in another exclusive boarding school, Marlborough College. For someone parachuted into a coed environment more than halfway through the school year, there would still be an awkward period of adjustment. Over her first dinner in Norwood Hall, the main dining hall at Marlborough, Kate wondered why the boys seated at a distant table were staring in her direction, then chuckling as they scribbled down notes. New girls, Kate was informed, were rated on a scale from 1 to 10. When they held up their ratings, Kate had scored only 1s and 2s.

Not surprisingly, such slights, coupled with homesickness, chipped away at Kate's self-confidence. Almost overnight, the popular, high-spirited, outgoing girl, who excelled at sports and starred in school plays, had become diffident, timid, and unsure of herself. By the time Pippa joined her in 1997, Kate had managed to forge two or three friendships, but still refrained from widening her social circle.

Pippa, by contrast, fit in right away. Still, her arrival did nothing to bring Kate out of her shell. While Pippa blossomed, her big sister largely kept to herself, studying alone in her room or in the school's tomb-quiet Memorial Library. Over the summer of 1998, however, "something must have clicked," as her classmate and friend Gemma Williamson put it. Enlisting style and makeup advice from her mother, Kate underwent a Galatea-like transformation. When she stepped into her first class that fall, "Kate came back an absolute beauty. It happened quite suddenly."

Instantly, soft-spoken Kate went from wallflower to someone who was "extremely popular. Good at tennis, swimming, running, maths, and science . . . Everything looked good on her because she had such a perfect body." Kate's metamorphosis meant that she was no longer an outsider, but that didn't mean she had forgotten how miserable it felt to be one. She took it upon herself to socialize with everyone, eschewing the idea of joining one clique or another. Able to spot those who had been unfairly ostracized, Kate went out of her way to befriend them. Even as a teenager, this empathetic streak was evident to all who knew her. Williamson described her as "kindhearted" and "very special," adding, "I've never known anyone quite like her. I think a lot of people who got to really know her feel that way."

Now that she was turning heads, lissome, chestnut-maned Kate went out on dates and engaged in the inevitable "snogging [necking] sessions," but refrained from anything more serious. She not only gave the impression to Williamson that she intended to "save herself for someone special" but that Prince William was that someone. Kate "read absolutely everything about him," claimed Williamson, who described her as being "besotted" with the future king. "It meant that, at least at the time, no other boy really had a chance."

When it came to gathering intelligence on her Prince Charming, Kate didn't have to rely solely on what she read in the papers. Her close friend and roommate Jessica Hay would ultimately end up dating William's cousin and Eton College mentor Nicholas Knatchbull. (Knatchbull was the great-grandson of Charles's beloved great-uncle Lord Louis Mountbatten.) She provided Kate with an information pipeline straight from the source. After several encounters with William at Eton and Broadlands, the Mountbatten family estate, Hay reported to Kate that, among other things, William was shy, polite, and had a "wonderful" sense of humor. "Kate would just sigh when I told her things like that," Hay remembered.

There was one habit of William's that Hay found disturbing, but, much to her astonishment, didn't seem to bother Kate at all. While William studiously avoided the drugs that were knocking down young aristocrats like so many dominoes, the young prince was seriously hooked on Marlboro Light cigarettes. As the daughter of chain smokers, Kate took the prince's nicotine addiction in stride. "It was just another thing that connected him to her," another friend said. "You know, it was familiar—the look, the smell, these can be comforting for children from a family of smokers." Besides, Kate bravely predicted that one day she would help him kick the habit.

Unlike most of the other girls at Marlborough, Kate never smoked cigarettes—or pot, for that matter—and refrained from consuming alcohol. "I never once saw her drunk," Hay said. Kate "had very high morals. She was always very levelheaded. You could always count on Kate to do the absolutely right thing."

Not that Kate didn't have a fun-loving side—make that backside. On a dare, Kate and Hay began throwing open their second-floor window and exposing their nude posteriors to the boys' dormitory across the way. The male students who had once held up cards that rated them from 1 to 10 were now asked to identify which derriere belonged to which girl. It didn't take long for Hay to tire of this naughty little game and quit, but not Kate. According to Hay, Kate "kind of got addicted to it." After exposing her bare bottom more than ninety times during the 2000–2001 school year, Kate earned the dubious sobriquet "Kate Middlebum."

Miss Middlebum's antics paled in comparison to William's. Scouring the broadsheets—Fleet Street tabloids—for any information about the man she not-so-secretly planned to marry, Kate actively worried that Will, as he now liked to be called, was falling under the influence of his drug-abusing, born-to-the-purple chums. Chief among them was Camilla Parker Bowles's son, Tom, who was frequently seen boozing it up with William at some of London's hottest clubs. In 1995, Tom was convicted of possessing the drug ecstasy and marijuana. Soon Nicky Knatchbull and Lord Frederick Windsor, yet another of William's cousins, were owning up to the fact they were snorting cocaine at many of the nightspots they frequented with the future sovereign.

Will, always accompanied by at least two royal protection officers who went to great lengths to remain invisible, drew the line at taking illicit drugs. Not that he wasn't, on an increasingly regular basis, partying with attractive young women into the early morning hours and getting, in his own words, "very seriously, seriously drunk." Kate was less interested in the clubs William was frequenting—trendy venues of the time like MiMo, K Bar, and Chinawhite—than she was in the young women he was rumored to be seeing.

After early schoolboy crushes on Camilla's niece Emma Parker Bowles, and on the unfortunately cocaine-addicted royal family friend Tara Palmer-Tomkinson, William had been linked to several highborn young ladies—three of whom were invited to join him aboard Greek shipping magnate John Latsis's four-hundred-foot superyacht *Alexander* when Charles and his sons embarked on a ten-day cruise of the Aegean in July 1999: Davina Duckworth-Chad, Emilia "Mili" d'Erlanger, and Mary Forestier-Walker. Devonshire beauty Mili d'Erlanger, Kate's Marlborough classmate and a close friend, was the niece of the tenth Viscount Exmouth and her family had ties to both the Spencer and Mountbatten-Windsor sides of William and Harry's family tree. She was also a member in good standing of the so-called Glosse Posse that socialized with William and Harry at Highgrove, Prince Charles's estate north of London in Gloucestershire (hence the shorthand term "glosse"). D'Erlanger reassured Kate that she had nothing to worry about; none of the girls, with the possible exception of the stunningly beautiful Duckworth-Chad, a distant cousin of both Princess Diana and the writer Virginia Woolf, whose two-thousand-acre Georgian estate, Pynkney Hall, was a stone's throw from Sandringham.

Mili d'Erlanger would go on to become one of Kate's closest confidantes. But for the moment, Mili seemed more rival than pal. When news got back to Kate that Mili had begun keeping company with Will at York House, the residence at St. James's Palace in London where he and Harry had their own suite of rooms, Kate's expression grew uncharacteristically somber. What neither Kate nor Mili knew at the time was that their Prince Charming was smitten with his cousin, Nicholas Knatchbull's sister Alexandra, a dark-eyed brunette with more than a passing resemblance to Kate.

Alexandra did not attempt to hide her feelings for William—and vice versa. "Desperately in love—absolutely potty for each other" is the way one acquaintance put it.

Kate paid close attention to a carefully circumscribed eighteenth-birthday interview veteran royal correspondent Peter Archer was allowed to do with the prince. She paid particularly close attention to what William had to say about dating. Archer asked how he decided a particular girl was someone he'd like to get to know better. He cagily replied, "Trying to explain how might be counterproductive. I like to keep my private life private."

That spring of 2000, however, romance was not exactly front of mind for either Kate or William. Scholastically, both consistently ranked at or near the top of their respective classes. They were both involved in student government, and had set records in school sports—she in track and field for the high jump, he as a freestyle swimmer. Still, much hinged on the outcome of their all-important A levels—akin to taking finals and college entrance exams at the same time.

William skipped his own eighteenth birthday party at Windsor Castle—a long-planned bash hosted by his grandmother Queen Elizabeth that also celebrated the landmark birthdays of the Queen Mother (turning one hundred), Princess Margaret (seventy), Princess Anne (fifty), Prince Andrew (forty)—to study for his A levels. Unbeknownst to the prince, Kate was burning the midnight oil just fifty-eight miles away in her small but uncluttered room at Marlborough.

The all-night study sessions proved well worth it. William aced his exams, and Kate did even better, earning A levels in maths and art, and a B in English. Her fellow students also voted Kate the "Person Most Likely to be Loved by Everybody." Yet by the time she graduated at age eighteen, Kate had only dated two boys—Willem Marx, who later became a journalist covering the war in Iraq, and Harry Blakelock. Kate's relationship with Marx never progressed past the friendship stage, but despite her overarching crush on the Heir—and her friend Gemma Williamson's insistence that Kate "didn't need a guy to be happy"—she fell hard for Blakelock. The dashing captain of Marlborough's rugby team, Blakelock was seventeen and Kate sixteen when they started seeing each other. According to a mutual friend, Blakelock "seemed to have blown hot and cold with her when they were at school." After Blakelock graduated, "she was always talking about how she could get him back. She spoke about him all the time and he seemed to have messed her around quite a bit. She was totally hung up on him."

Now that she had graduated with honors, Kate had more weighty matters to consider—principally, where she would attend college. Carole Middleton made no secret of her desire to see all three of her children matriculate at one of the two most prestigious institutions in the United Kingdom—and, for that matter, the world. Oxford and Cambridge were the prime choices for anyone seeking to rise in British society—and for those who were already at the very top. The pressure on William to sign up either at Oxford or his father's alma mater, Cambridge, was "just tremendous, nonstop," he would later say.

Both William and Kate, not surprisingly, had minds of their own. She had been honing her picture-taking skills at Marlborough, but lacked the necessary confidence to pursue a career as a professional photographer. Instead, she considered becoming a curator of photography and contemporary art exhibits, perhaps at a museum or gallery. For an artistic curriculum, students flocked to the University of Edinburgh in Scotland. Carole accompanied Kate on a tour of the campus, and, acknowledging that Sir Walter Scott, Sir Arthur Conan Doyle, Alexander Graham Bell, and Charles Darwin were among its distinguished alumni—not to mention numerous viscounts, dukes, and members of foreign royal families—gave her consent. What put Edinburgh over the top had less to do with Edinburgh's illustrious past than its possibility-filled future. By early 2000, while Kate and Carole were weighing their options, there was widespread speculation in the press that William would be attending Edinburgh—speculation that, according to Kate's friends, Carole Middleton took note of.

In truth, Edinburgh was not even on William's radar. He was too busy making the case against Oxbridge, as the United Kingdom's two wealthiest, best-known, and most prestigious institutions of higher learning are jointly known. During his four years at Eton, William had grown fond of his housemaster, Andrew Gailey; indeed, Gailey watched over the prince like a surrogate father. Not surprisingly, William sought out Gailey's advice on what university to attend, and, equally unsurprisingly, Gailey sang the praises of his own alma mater, the University of St. Andrews in Scotland. Nevertheless, William might still have caved to the pressure and enrolled at Charles's alma mater, Cambridge's Trinity College, had he not consulted one more person on the matter—the woman he and Harry had always called, simply, "Granny."

Queen Elizabeth, who had always treasured her holidays spent at Balmoral Castle in the Highlands, had a soft spot in her heart for Scotland and for the Scots; Her Majesty never missed the caber-tossing competition at the Braemar Gathering Highland Games. Yet the nationalist movement in Scotland was gaining momentum, and there was a real concern that Scotland would soon hold a referendum on whether or not to secede from the United Kingdom entirely. No other heir to the British throne had ever attended a Scottish university. Sending William to St. Andrews would deliver a powerful message of support to Granny's Scottish subjects—and make it clear to his Palace handlers that the Heir was his own man.

William applied to St. Andrews and was accepted immediately. As determined as he had been to earn high marks on his final exams, it stretched credulity to think the future sovereign might ever receive a letter of rejection. Now that Kate had been accepted by Edinburgh, they could both focus on their upcoming gap year—the post–high school graduation hiatus ostensibly intended to provide some real-world exposure before succumbing to the rigors of college life.

William started off his gap year by quietly boarding a Royal Air Force plane bound for Belize on the Yucatán Peninsula. (It was shortly after he arrived that he learned about his A level grades over shortwave radio.) There, while training with a unit of the Welsh Guards in the steaming Central American jungle, he encountered crocodiles, black widow spiders, vampire bats, and pit vipers like the dreaded fer-de-lance ("spearhead" in French), responsible for more deaths in Central America and South America than any other reptile. "Incredibly hot, continuously soaking wet, and with nowhere to hide from potentially horrendous results," the adventure-loving prince later recalled. "It's a time I look back on fondly."

His next assignment: under the alias Brian Woods, he did field research as part of the Royal Geographic Society's marine observation program on Rodrigues Island in the Indian Ocean. Scuba diving and snorkeling for specimens, William quickly fell under the island's spell of luxuriant tropical forests, endless miles of white sand beaches, and cerulean blue waters.

"Brian Woods" was hoping to follow up his tropical idyll competing against some of his father's polo-playing pals in Argentina, but Palace officials thought otherwise. Instead, starting in October 2000, William signed up with the Raleigh International program to spend ten weeks with 110 other young volunteers—including recovering drug addicts and homeless teens—tutoring children, painting houses, digging ditches, scrubbing floors, and putting up fences in Tortel, a small village in the Chilean province of Patagonia. Tortel, surrounded by glaciers, is one of the most isolated villages in the region.

William's Patagonian sojourn wasn't all work. When his ten weeks were up, the prince got busy at a party "dirty dancing with a lot of girls and making a spectacle of himself," said fellow volunteer Kevin Mullen. According to Mullen, "the girls didn't seem to mind."

While William was working up a sweat at the bottom of the world, Kate was whiling away long, sunny afternoons in Florence—sipping cappuccino, gazing at Michelangelo's *David*, and strolling across the Ponte Vecchio. That fall, she and thirteen others had enrolled in a three-month-long Italian language course at the British Institute of Florence, a century-old international school housed in the city's historic Palazzo dello Strozzino.

Il British, as the institute was affectionately called by Florentines, offered far more than language classes. For the thousands of British gap year students it hosted each year, it offered a tantalizing taste of la dolce vita. Kate, who shared a two-bedroom walkup over a café with three other girls, once again made it clear to everyone that she was all about control. While drinking, drugs, and sex were part and parcel of the gap year experience in the city of the Medicis, Kate limited herself to a glass or two of wine with dinner. "Everybody liked her straightaway," a fellow student recalled. "She was very sort of bubbly and friendly. She just wasn't interested in getting wasted."

Nor was she interested in having a summer fling with any of the Vespa-riding Italian boys who pursued her with wolf whistles and pinches. In truth, she was still preoccupied with old Marlburian Harry Blakelock. When her former paramour showed up in Florence as part of the study group and then debarked for Rome almost as suddenly, Kate was left reeling. "She was all about getting him back, but nothing happened," another student at the British Institute said. "I think it left her feeling confused and a little abandoned."

In late September, the Blakelock spell was finally broken when Kate, like the rest of the world, heard William's voice for the first time. In his damning memoir *Shadows of a Princess*, Diana's once-trusted private secretary Patrick Jephson described his former boss as neurotic, paranoid, and a "scheming liar." Feeling the need to speak up in his late mother's defense, William made the extraordinary decision to go before television cameras and denounce Jephson's book.

Dressed in a beige pullover and jeans, William stood by his father outside Highgrove and told reporters that he and Harry had read excerpts of *Shadows* and were both "horrified" at the way Jephson had "betrayed" and "exploited" their mother. Since an embargo on press coverage of the princes had been in effect since Diana's death three years earlier, the general public was surprised to hear the eighteen-year-old speak in a calm, slightly nasal, distinctively "plummy" voice brimming with confidence.

William did not confine himself to talking about Jephson's problematic memoir. He spoke about how his gap year was progressing and mentioned how he was looking forward to starting his university studies in Scotland the following year. It had already been more than a month since William's plans to attend St. Andrews had been announced, and applications soared 44 percent over the previous year—nearly all from women. As it turned out, Mili d'Erlanger—Kate's Marlborough pal with the William connection—was among them.

That November 2000, Kate's parents flew to Florence, and Carole wasted no time trying to talk their daughter into switching from Edinburgh to St. Andrews. Kate resisted at first, but, after repeated entreaties by her mother, relented by Christmas.

Kate went a step further and signed up for the same South American charity youth program William was attending. Although Raleigh International expedition leader Malcolm Sutherland called it "absolutely crazy," the fact that Kate then journeyed to the remote outpost in Chile where William had been doing charity work—missing him by just days—hardly seems coincidental. While William came into the program "with a profile—we knew who he was," Kate was "just like the rest of us."

Hewing to a similarly demanding regimen, Kate trekked through the wilderness, worked with marine scientists on an inflatable boat, and helped put the roof on a new firehouse. "She was definitely one of the fitter and stronger members of her group," said Sutherland, who added that Kate "kept to herself mostly." Described as "easygoing and popular" by another group leader, Rachel Humphreys, Kate stood out as someone special even then. There was, Humphreys said, "a certain aura" surrounding her. "She was always very in control of herself and impeccably behaved."

Once she was back in the United Kingdom in the spring of 2001, Kate embraced yet another gap year challenge: joining the crews of several seventy-two-foot sailing vessels training for the Clipper Round the World Race in the Solent, a strait between the Isle of Wight and mainland Great Britain. Paid just $8 an hour, Kate swabbed decks and served lunch to clients from corporations like Volkswagen, Barclays Bank, and Nokia.

Kate's boss at the time, yachtsman Sir Chay Blythe, was impressed with Kate's work ethic. "We had other girls, mainly students, who were a pain in the ass, complaining about this and that. But Kate was not one of them," Sir Chay recalled. He was also impressed by the fact that she "got on with her job and refused to let herself be distracted by all the male attention." Indeed, said Sir Chay, "most of the talk about her concerned her very tight shorts."

Promptly nicknamed "Beautiful Kate," the future princess spent most of the summer fending off advances and was soon regarded, said one male crew member, as "something of a prude." Inevitably, she became the target of teasing and practical jokes. On one occasion, Kate was supposed to demonstrate the proper use of life jackets for a group of corporate guests. When she unrolled the life jacket, a dozen condoms tumbled out and onto the deck. Everyone laughed, but not Kate. She was, said one of the crewmen who staged the prank, "horribly embarrassed and went bright, bright pink. It may have been rather cruel. She didn't find it at all funny."

As it happened, Kate did not resist the advances of all her fellow crew members. At one point, she began dating Ian Henry, another seasonal deckhand who was headed for Oxford that fall. Their relationship quickly evolved into a casual romance—serious enough for the couple to go sailing together again months later, and for Henry then to be invited to join Kate and the rest of the Middletons on their vacation on Barbados.

While Kate and Ian Henry were getting to know each other, William was pursuing a steamy affair of his own 4,200 miles away at the foot of Mount Kenya in East Africa. From March to mid-July, the Heir was working as a hired hand at the 53,000-acre Lewa Wildlife Conservancy, a wildlife preserve and arguably the world's largest rhino sanctuary.

Between mending fences and working alongside antipoaching rangers, William made time to strike up a romance with Jessica Craig, the nineteen-year-old daughter of conservancy owner Ian Craig. Just days before William was scheduled to leave, he and "Jecca" climbed into a conservancy Land Rover and churned up billowing clouds of yellow dust as they drove to the foot of Mount Kenya with the prince's security detail in hot pursuit. Stopping beneath an acacia tree, they got out and embraced. Then William bent down on one knee and, while William's gape-mouthed bodyguards looked on from a discreet distance, staged what they would later call a "mock proposal." Ten years later, William would ask for the hand of another stunning young woman near the same spot—only this time in earnest.

Leaving Jecca behind, William returned home to hone his polo skills competing on the Beaufort Polo Club grounds near Highgrove. Instead, he found himself beguiled yet again—this time by Arabella "Bella" Musgrave, whose father, Major Nicholas Musgrave, was manager of the rival Cirencester Park Polo Club. It did not take long for Bella to correctly decide that William, who still carried a torch for Jecca Craig, had a roving eye and abruptly dump him. Taken by surprise, William was described by one of his polo buddies as being "completely crushed." Over a period of several months, he would repeatedly try to win Bella back—but not at the expense of ignoring other opportunities for romance that arose on a more or less daily basis.

William didn't have to look far. As was the case with Bella, the Gloucestershire polo clubs surrounding Highgrove provided a veritable cornucopia of attractive and exceedingly willing young ladies. One whose name was more than a mouthful: Isabella Amaryllis Charlotte Anstruther-Gough-Calthorpe. "Bellie" Calthorpe was the granddaughter of both a baronet and an earl, and a direct descendant of Charles II via one of the king's fifteen official mistresses. (Calthorpe went on to become a model, actress, and socialite. In 2013 she married William's doppelgänger, billionaire Richard Branson's son, Sam. Her half sister Cressida Bonas would later become Prince Harry's girlfriend.)

For a time, William divided his attention between Bellie Calthorpe and his friend since early childhood Rose Farquhar, whose father, Ian Farquhar, had been a close chum of Charles and Camilla and a Master of the Beaufort Hunt. (Farquhar, an aspiring singer, would later perform on the TV reality show *The Voice UK*.) Also drifting in and out of William's orbit was Olivia Hunt, an English and history student at Edinburgh who had gotten acquainted with William through their mutual pals the Van Cutsems; Hugh van Cutsem had known Charles, then the Prince of Wales, at Cambridge, and Hugh's sons Edward, Hugh Jr., and Nicholas had been friends with both William and Harry their entire lives. (For a decade, the Van Cutsems rented Anmer Hall—the sprawling Georgian manor house on the grounds of Sandringham that would eventually become William and Kate's country residence—from Queen Elizabeth.)

Pulling to the head of the pack for a time was someone with no royal connections at all. While William had reportedly conducted a series of email exchanges with model Lauren Bush, then-President George W.'s niece, back when he was at Eton, he was now dating Beaufort Polo Club staffer Amanda Bush (no relation). The animated Amanda was known as Tigger or Tig to her friends, after Winnie-the-Pooh's bouncy sidekick.

As the summer wound down, Kate made the kinds of preparations any first-year college student would: sorting out roommate possibilities, deciding what to pack and which meal plan to sign up for, what student organizations to join. Not surprisingly, she was, like everyone else, oblivious to the complexities of William's precollege planning. Best known as the birthplace of golf—Mary, Queen of Scots was said to have played it there as early as 1567—St. Andrews was a blustery, remote village perched on a promontory overlooking the turbulent waters of the North Sea. Yet even at this quaint, mist-shrouded spot where the streets had names like Greyfriars Garden and Doubledykes Road, precautions had to be taken to ensure the safety of the heir to the throne.

Both Kate and William would be staying, as would the other first-year students, in a fifteen-by-fifteen-foot room at St. Salvatore's Hall ("Sallies"), but with some major differences. While Kate roomed with New Jersey native Laura Warshauer—Warshauer would go on to pursue a singing career under the name Gigi Rowe—William's insistence on having a roommate was denied. So, too, was his request for a room without a bath, so he could experience student life to the fullest by standing in line to use the communal shower facilities like everybody else.

Instead William, who from the start had turned down an offer to live at the cushy residence of the university's vice-chancellor, Dr. Brian Lang, was assigned a private room with an en suite bath installed specifically to accommodate the prince. William's security detail, now given the formidable task of shielding their charge without impinging on his social life as a college student, occupied an adjacent, similarly outfitted room.

Before his arrival, MI5, the United Kingdom's domestic intelligence agency, scoured William's dormitory room for listening devices. Their concerns were not ill founded. Not only were British tabloids eavesdropping on royal conversations, but there were credible threats to William's life surfacing on the internet—namely from Scottish separatists and an IRA splinter group that had set off a bomb in 1998, killing twenty-nine people in the village of Omagh.

Kate's parents drove her up to St. Andrews, where she was among the 262 students who arrived on September 2, 2001, with lamps, bedding, and laptops in tow. Like other first-year students, Kate was shown around campus by a student guide (a designated "big sister" for the girls, a "big brother" for the boys), and after a day spent trudging up and down dormitory stairs and hallways and meeting with faculty advisors, the students and their parents gathered for a cookout on the main lawn. By the time she joined in the traditional Scottish reel that capped off the day, Kate had already begun several friendships that would last decades.

It was the sort of bonding experience that St. Andrews's first-year student number 263 yearned for but wasn't there to experience. Much to the disappointment of Carole Middleton, in particular, Prince William was nowhere to be seen. Buckingham Palace and the university agreed that William's arrival at the school on opening day would be too disruptive for the rest of the student body. "It would have been a media frenzy," William agreed, "and that's not fair on the other students. Plus," he added with a nod to St. Andrews's party school reputation, "I would probably end up in a gutter completely wrecked, and the people I met that week wouldn't end up being my friends anyway."

Scotland had new security concerns as well, stemming from intercepted emails that included a map showing where a shooter might be positioned within "extremely accurate range" of the prince. If there were doubts in anyone's mind that terrorism was a valid concern, they evaporated on September 11, when four hijacked airliners slammed into New York's World Trade Center, the Pentagon in Washington, and a field in Shanksville, Pennsylvania, killing nearly three thousand people. Gathered with scores of other students around the television in St. Salvatore's main common room just before 3 p.m. UK time, Kate joined in the collective gasp of horror as the first of the WTC's twin towers collapsed. The normally self-contained

Kate, along with Laura Warshauer and dozens of other first-year students from the United States, was openly weeping by the time the second tower collapsed about thirty minutes later.

Watching the unfolding tragedy with the Queen and the rest of the royal family winding up their summer vacation at Balmoral, William and Harry got on their phones to friends in the United States. The brothers had felt a strong connection to America ever since their mother first took them to Disney World in 1993, and in the months before her death Princess Diana was hatching a plan to divide her life between London and California. (In fact, Dodi Fayed went ahead and paid $7.4 million for the nine-thousand-square-foot Tuscan villa that replaced the Malibu beach house where Julie Andrews and her husband, director Blake Edwards, had lived for years.)

Now that the threat level had risen exponentially, William was being urged to live off campus in a residence that could be more easily protected. The answer from the prince was a resounding no. "I just want to go to university and have fun. I want to go there and be an ordinary student," he insisted to a BBC reporter, adding prophetically, "I mean, I'm only going to university. It's not like I'm getting married, although it feels that way sometimes." When told that some female students claimed to have already ordered their wedding dresses in anticipation of landing the prince, William replied with a sigh of resignation, "I suppose they're saying that tongue in cheek."

When he finally did show up on September 23, William was hoping for what the Palace called a "more subdued entry into college life." Instead, the media frenzy that he'd skipped orientation week to avoid was in full view. Prince Charles, shaken by the screaming crowd of four thousand that was there to greet them, nearly crashed into St. Andrews's narrow archway entrance. William climbed out of the car and ambled toward the mob to shake hands. The Prince of Wales was clearly more rattled than his son by the chaotic reception. "I almost turned around and fled," he admitted.

Just as she had three years earlier when William's Eton field hockey team played Marlborough's, Kate remained at the back of the pack "with the rest of us hiding like twelve-year-olds," said one undergraduate. If Kate was caught up in the excitement, "she never let on. At university, Kate was always part of things and at the same time apart from things, keeping a little distance." To be sure, Kate was a canny observer not only of the nineteen-year-old prince but of the young women who were, quite literally, throwing themselves at him.

William had always been wary of strangers' intentions, and that was not likely to change now that he was in Scotland—all of which he made clear in an interview just before entering St. Andrews. "People who try to take advantage of me and get a piece of me—I spot it quickly and go off them," he said, quickly adding in his customary, self-deprecating way that "it will get easier as time goes on. Everyone will get bored of me—which they do."

William wanted to make it clear that he wished to mix with those working-class students who attended what the British call "state schools" (public schools in the US) who made up over half of St. Andrews's student body. "It's not as if I'll choose my friends on the basis of where they are from or what they are," he explained. "It's about their character and who they are and whether we get on. I just hope I can meet people I get on with. I don't care about their backgrounds."

Nevertheless, the prince seldom strayed far from the loyal band of friends he arrived with—notably his old Etonian pals Oliver Chadwyck-Healey and Fergus Boyd. Kate, on the other hand, arrived at St. Andrews knowing at least a dozen fellow Marlburians—including William's sometime flame Mili d'Erlanger—and even one of the schoolmates who stood up to the mean girls bullying Kate at Downe House back when they were both just fourteen, Virginia Fraser. As the daughter of the 3rd Baron Strathalmond of Pumpherston and heiress to an oil fortune, Ginny Fraser had no difficulty being accepted into William's inner circle.

Kate was another matter. She had been poised and self-possessed as long as anyone could remember. "She is the kindest, most caring, down-to-earth, genuine person," recalled Laura Warshauer. "I remember the first time I met Kate, thinking, 'Wow.' She just had a lovely way about her." Warshauer was not alone in her assessment of the girl from Bucklebury; during her first week at St. Andrews—well before William arrived—Kate was voted "prettiest girl in the dorm."

"She's obviously stunning," Warshauer said. "But Kate doesn't act in any way like, 'Oh, I'm this gorgeous person.' Kate was just genuine. And I don't feel like she'll ever change." Her aura of self-confidence aside, Kate was still "terrified" at the thought of meeting the Nordic-handsome, athletic, six-foot-three-inch-tall prince. As she told Warshauer, "He takes your breath away."

The moment came when William, intent on breaking the ice with his dorm mates, invited the other students on his floor to drop by for a drink and "bring your friends." With his ever-alert bodyguards perking up in the next room, William propped his dorm room door open and greeted each visitor with an outreached hand and a disarming "I'm William."

The prince, well aware of the effect he had on others, employed various means for putting people at ease. At one point, he would invariably spill a drink on himself or the furniture, then make a self-conscious fuss over his mess. Although he would admit to always having had a clumsy streak, this gambit "always brought the tension level down a notch," said Fergus Boyd. "He hated making other people feel uncomfortable. So he never hesitated to poke a bit of fun at himself, if that's what it took."

The normally outgoing Kate hesitated at first, but was ultimately coaxed into taking the student prince up on his invitation. Standing slightly behind several other dorm residents, she had to be nudged to the front. What happened then would be etched in her mind for years. "I turned bright red and sort of scuttled off," she later recalled, "feeling very shy about meeting him."

Still, Kate slowly overcame her shyness and managed to forge a casual friendship with William based largely on their shared pangs of homesickness—and the gnawing realization that St. Andrews was simply too isolated. "Weekends at St. Andrews," he complained to journalist Peter Archer at the time, "are not particularly vibrant." Not that he would know. Nearly every Friday, the prince would get behind the wheel of his black four-door VW Golf—a gift from Prince Charles—and head off to party at clubs in Edinburgh. Something of a speed demon who enjoyed blaring Shaggy and Kylie Minogue out the windows as he raced down the A92, William allowed that his father would "go absolutely bananas if he saw me."

Edinburgh was only one "escape hatch from boredom" that William made ample use of during this period. Occasionally, he fled to his father's beloved Highgrove, where he could compete against his brother at the nearly adjacent Beaufort Polo Club and then while away evenings at Club H, the basement space at Highgrove that Charles turned into a hideaway for his sons, complete with video games, a state-of-the-art sound system, a dance floor, and a fully stocked bar.

Such restless moments notwithstanding, soon both Kate and William were in the throes of a college romance—but not with each other. Between trying to win back Bella Musgrave with weekend visits to Highgrove and keeping up a long-distance relationship with Jecca Craig over the phone, the prince was infatuated with Kate's old friend Carly Massy-Birch, the daughter of a Devon farmer. A creative writing student who was a year ahead of William and Kate, Carly met the prince when he was auditioning for the role of Zooey in a play based on J. D Salinger's classic novel about a disillusioned college student and the brother who tries to help her after she suffers a nervous breakdown, *Franny and Zooey*.

Stunningly attractive, Carly nonetheless clomped around campus in green Hunter boots and took pride in calling herself "a real country bumpkin"—all of which William found enormously appealing. During his first seven weeks at St. Andrews, "they could not be pried apart," a fellow Sallies resident observed. "They were totally gaga for each other."

Carly's parents knew that William and their daughter were intimately involved, and they wholeheartedly approved—but not simply for the obvious reasons. "He is such a good, good guy," said Mimi Massy-Birch, who understood that William had had only one serious girlfriend prior to Carly—reportedly Arabella Musgrave. "He *really* is . . . so down-to-earth. Very kind, very shy."

The cloak-and-dagger aspects of William's dating life—hunkering down in the backs of cars, darting in and out of alleyways and side streets to avoid the paparazzi, and all the while being watched over by royal protection officers—chipped away at their relationship. Even when Carly would cook him the occasional pasta dinner in their shared dormitory kitchen, the mere thought that William's bodyguards were on alert in the room next door made her feel "nervous and queasy." Being endlessly pursued, the "constant attention"—it all proved overwhelming for the self-proclaimed "country bumpkin." Carly knew that William was accustomed to life in a proverbial fishbowl, and that it would take "a very special sort of person" to handle the pressure.

Carly told William the reason she was breaking up with him—"It's all just too much for me"—right before late October's Raisin Weekend, one of St. Andrews's epically bacchanalian pub crawls where, theoretically, William could drown his sorrows in the company of some other fetching young coed. Instead, William, now adding heartbreak to a simmering case of homesickness, retreated to Highgrove to lick his wounds.

Kate, meanwhile, was in the throes of her own chaotic romance with twenty-two-year-old Rupert Finch, a tall (albeit at six feet, two inches slightly shorter than William) fourth-year student who also happened to be a standout player on the university's cricket team. Like Kate, "Finchie" was decidedly upper middle class, although, coincidentally enough, he did have one tangential connection to William. Finch's father, John, had made a considerable amount of money as a tenant farmer on Norfolk land owned by Diana's brother, Lord Spencer. Aside from what a fellow student of Finch's called the "obvious physical chemistry" between them, the two were drawn together by shared middle-class values. "They are both very popular, very hard-working, kind people," the classmate said. "There was no sense of entitlement whatsoever. They had a lot in common. You could easily see them making it as a couple, actually."

Kate and Finchie were still very much an item when, on March 27, 2002, she made the conscious decision to redefine herself in the eyes of her classmates. "Sweet" and "kind" were the words invariably used to describe her, and while there was never any question about her attractiveness, the young "Kate Middlebum" who once took such obvious pleasure in flashing her derriere at Marlborough College was now determined to shatter her porcelain doll image.

Toward that end, Kate agreed to walk the runway at St. Andrews University's annual Yves Saint Laurent–sponsored "Dont Walk" charity fashion show held at the Fairmont St. Andrews Bay hotel. While Rupert Finch might understandably have been reluctant to see his then-girlfriend essentially parading around in what might be considered scanty attire, Kate's other friends promised to be in the audience for moral support. Not the least of these was the Heir, who anted up two hundred pounds (at the time roughly $300) for one seat in the front row.

Ever the perfectionist, Kate rifled through dozens of garments before selecting a sheer lace dress worn over a bandeau bra and bikini panties. Keenly aware of what would appeal to this audience made up largely of young men, Kate refused a dresser's plea that she wear a black shirt over the barely there outfit. "I like it this way," Kate insisted. "It's much sexier." Indeed, the student designer of the piece, Charlotte Todd, had actually made it two years earlier for a project called "The Art of Seduction."

Kate took a deep breath, struck a model's standard expressionless pose, and strode down the runway to whistles and foot stomping. A cheering William leapt to his feet and led the applause when she returned in a white lace bra and panties—accompanied by his pal Fergus Boyd in black boxers.

"There were a lot of attractive girls modeling at the show," said classmate Ben Duncan. "But what she was wearing," he added, was "very daring." Duncan looked over to see William "sitting in the front row—his eyes were like stalks." Classmate Jules Knight, who had met and befriended both William and Kate while waiting outside the university's Buchanan Building for the start of their first class, was "blown away. We were all wowed. It was a turning point in people's perception of her."

William was suddenly interested in Kate, who up until this point he regarded as "quiet and reserved." But there was still the matter of her not-to-be-ignored twenty-two-year-old boyfriend. Told that Finch was about to graduate and move on to a trainee position at a London law firm, William wasted no time declaring his intentions. "Then," he told Boyd before heading off to Switzerland to ski with Harry and their father, "I think I'll have a go."

Just three days after the fashion show, the BBC halted programming to broadcast the news that the most beloved member of the royal family, the Queen Mother, had died at the age of 101 at Royal Lodge, her seventeenth-century, thirty-room manor house in Windsor Great Park. "Oh, William is going to be devastated," Kate told Carole Middleton over the phone from St. Andrews. "He adored her." William spoke often about his "Great Gran," who had hosted him at Balmoral Castle just before he arrived at St. Andrews. "If there are any good parties," the fun-loving Queen Mother told him, "invite me down." William told Kate he had no intention of honoring her request. "I said yes, but there was no way," he said. "I knew full well that if I invite her down she would dance me under the table."

Kate also knew that no one would be more upset over the Queen Mother's passing than Prince Charles, who relied on his grandmother for the affection and support that was never forthcoming from his distant, emotionally strangulated parents. In a nationally televised tribute, Charles would describe the Queen Mother as "quite simply the most magical grandmother you could possibly have and I was utterly devoted to her. Ever since I was a child, I adored her."

Now Kate, like millions of others, watched from afar as a somber William joined the rest of his family as well as more than a dozen crowned heads of Europe seated at his great-grandmother's funeral service inside Westminster Abbey. Witnessing her friend do the singular job he was born to do—and with a grace and dignity far beyond his nineteen years—Kate was suddenly hit with the realization that William's life was not his own, and never would be. "I felt so sorry for William," Kate told a St. Andrews classmate, adding that she was reminded of William walking behind his mother's coffin during Diana's funeral just five years earlier. "He can't even grieve in private."

Not that Kate, along with other members of his tight circle at St. Andrews, needed much reminding that William was in a category unto himself. The press, at this point, really wasn't a problem. Britain's watchdog Press Association faithfully abided by the hands-off policy regarding William and Harry following Diana's death, agreeing not to photograph or pursue the princes as long as they were attending school. But that didn't prevent the occasional hyperventilating tourist from leaping off a passing bus, cell phone in hand, hoping for a selfie with the future king.

Then there was the matter of security. More than once Kate watched as royal protection guards came running, guns drawn, because William had gone to the roof of St. Salvatore's for a smoke and inadvertently tripped the security sensors. Another time at St. Andrews, William was walking home from a bar with Kate and a group of friends when he noticed a bulge in Jules Knight's jacket pocket. William reached in, pulled out a pellet pistol, and laughed as he began waving it around—until he realized that his bodyguards who had been shadowing him were on the verge of shooting his friend. Knight, for his part, would never get over how unaffected William seemed to be. "I'm tempted to call him normal," Knight said, allowing that even William "would admit that he's not." Kate, meanwhile, "was like the rest of us, completely awed by the way he handled the pressure. We'd exchange these 'how does he do it?' glances all the time."

Nearly three-quarters of the way through their first term, Kate and William still harbored doubts about their choice of St. Andrews. After talking it over with their respective parents, they made a pact. If at the close of the school year they were still unconvinced, they would depart together for Edinburgh.

As it happened, Kate finished her first year at St. Andrews with an A minus average—and promptly went to work earning $8 an hour as a barmaid for a London event catering company called Snatch. "I was terrible at it," she later said, although her boss at the time, Rory Laing, remembered that she "took home plenty in tips—she's a pretty girl."

In contrast, William, who ended his first year with a B plus average, was presented by his father, Prince Charles, with a $32,000 gold-inlaid hunting rifle. "It's completely over the top—I feel sort of embarrassed by it," he told Kate, who throughout the summer would speak to him almost daily over the phone. "My father means well. I suppose he is just so thrilled that I stuck it out."

Once again, Kate watched from a distance as William went back to his royal duties—this time rejoining his fellow Windsors as they marked Granny's fiftieth year as monarch. The high point of Her Majesty's Golden Jubilee celebration, Kate and William would later agree, was the televised Party at the Palace pop concert staged on the Buckingham Palace grounds. Everyone was caught up in the excitement of performances by such megastars as Elton John, Paul McCartney, Tom Jones, Queen, Bryan Adams, Phil Collins, Eric Clapton, Steve Winwood, Annie Lennox, Rod Stewart, Ricky Martin, Beach Boy Brian Wilson, and Tony Bennett. But the seat in the royal box occupied by William—nestled between the Queen and Prince Charles—left no doubt as to who the real stars of the evening were.

Determined not to lose her cocktail waitress job, Kate kept her cell phone set on vibrate while she served her customers martinis and cosmopolitans. "When she'd duck out to return a call," Laing said, "no one had the slightest idea it was Prince William on the other end of the line. She never let on, never mentioned his name once."

For Kate, it was difficult enough trying to reconcile the gangling, unassuming teenager she knew at St. Andrews with the globally famous figure she saw on television and the front pages of newspapers. Kate confided to her sister, Pippa, that she found it all "so surreal" trying to convince herself that the William she knew and the future king were "the same person." Friend Jules Knight agreed that it was "all very weird," in part because William was more than a mere celebrity. "Will is such a great, down-to-earth sort of guy. But he also has a place in history. Kate was like the rest of us who were around him then. It was difficult at first trying to wrap our heads around it."

In the wake of her breakup with Rupert Finch and the dawning realization that she and William were on the precipice of something more than friendship, Kate consciously refrained from dating. "She felt something for Will straightaway," said Knight, "there's absolutely no doubt about that." However, that did not prevent the Heir from hitting the London party circuit with a vengeance. Despite the fact that he resisted being sucked into St. Andrews's notoriously over-the-top drinking culture, the prince was now spotted stumbling bleary-eyed out of nightspots like Purple and Boujis in South Kensington. The drinking, conceded Knight, "was nonstop."

Notwithstanding the press's pledge not to bother William while he pursued his studies in Scotland, several of the prince's encounters with other women were breathlessly reported in Britain's insatiable tabloids. Yet, when Diana's longtime bodyguard Ken Wharfe added his name to the list of former employees labeling the late Princess of Wales as scheming and mentally unstable in a tell-all memoir, Kate was the one person Will turned to. In stark contrast to most of the younger women William was cutting loose with at nightclubs or at house parties thrown by his aristocratic chums, Kate was "a superb listener," Knight said. "Kate is very compassionate, very kind."

By the time they returned to St. Andrews in the fall of 2002, William had made up his mind to move out of Sallies and into an off-campus apartment that would afford him more space and hopefully a measure of freedom. He asked Kate and two of their pals—the ever-accommodating Fergus Boyd and Olivia Bleasdale, the daughter of a Royal Artillery officer—if they'd be interested in sharing an apartment in town.

Initially, Kate was reluctant to lean on her parents for the additional money it would take to share in an off-campus rental. Nonsense, said Carole, who clearly saw the possibilities. William had his eye on a $2,200-per-month, furnished four-bedroom flat on the ground floor of 13A Hope Street, a classic Victorian terraced town house located just two blocks from the center of campus.

Unfortunately, the owner of 13A Hope Street was not keen on renting to male students. "We'd had an unfortunate experience with some boys in the flat once before and were determined not to have young men there again," Charlotte Smith said. "Broken furniture, broken windows—there was a lot of damage." She told the rental agent flatly "no boys," and was about to reject the prince's application when the agent replied, "What if I were to tell you that it was Prince William?"

Amazingly, Smith was still unconvinced. She reached out to her neighbors to make sure they wouldn't mind the presence of the prince and his ever-lurking team of bodyguards—they occupied the flat above—before finally agreeing to approve HRH's application. She then asked to meet with Boyd, Bleasdale, and Kate, but stopped short of demanding an interview with Will because "we thought his credit rating must be quite good." The prince insisted, however. "He was very friendly, very charming, a thoroughly nice man," recalled Smith, who was particularly impressed with the fact that he was "very gracious about the rent and didn't try to haggle." As for Kate: "I remember when she brought her brother, James, around to visit early on—he was fifteen and she was very patient and kind with him, explaining everything. They were such nice people, Kate especially." In the end, Smith would declare the foursome to be "ideal tenants. I wish they were all like William and Kate and their friends."

Coincidentally, William's old flame Carly Massy-Birch lived just across the street. She and William could wave to each other from their respective living room windows, much to Kate's chagrin.

It didn't take long for the tabloids to take note of Kate's presence in William's new house-sharing equation. The *Sun*'s headline was fairly typical: "William Shacks Up with Stunning Undies Model." Kate was embarrassed by the grainy amateur photos of her in barely there lingerie now being splashed across front pages around the globe, not to mention what the headlines implied.

When they moved into their new off-campus digs on St. Andrews's aptly named Hope Street, Kate and William were still merely friends. It took less than a few weeks, however, for all that to change. "It just sort of blossomed from there, really," William later recalled. "We just saw more of each other, hung out a bit more. . . ." By the time classes were well underway in late September, the Heir and the commoner were lovers.

As obvious as their chemistry seemed to Jules Knight and others, Fergus and Olivia were taken aback when they realized that William and Kate had fallen for each other. As awkward as it seemed to their roommates at first, William later said, "They came around quickly when they realized it was really nice and good fun. We had a really good giggle with them about the whole situation."

For the next two years, theirs was, in William's own words, "quite a cozy setup." The initial division of chores among the four roommates promptly "broke down into complete chaos," but that was fine with Kate. "We just," William explained, "attended to things in the usual haphazard way." In the part of the flat now occupied by William and Kate, that meant that William did much of the cooking—or attempted to, anyway.

It was not uncommon for the prince to tie on an apron and attempt to whip up paella or flambé something. "When I was trying to impress Kate, I was cooking these amazing fancy dinners, but," he added, "I would burn something, something would overspill, or something would catch on fire." Kate would monitor things from the hallway, and as the crescendo of crashing pans and cursing reached its zenith, she would, she later recalled, "wander in and try and save things." Kate was "always taking control of the situation," William concurred. "I was quite glad she was there at the time." More frequently, they ordered out—Italian from Pizza Express, Chinese from Ruby's, or southern fried chicken from P.M.'s Diner on Market Street.

Despite his party animal reputation in London, William was still wary of taking part in St. Andrews's alcohol-fueled nightlife. Kate, however, knew that her new boyfriend needed to let off steam. At her urging, they went along with their small coterie of pals to student haunts like the West Port Bar, Broons, the Gin House, and—for karaoke—a nondescript, hole-in-the-wall ground floor pub inside the St. Andrews Golf Hotel called Ma Bell's. In these settings, far from the prying eyes of Fleet Street and the more decadent crowd of young aristos who circled around William in London, Kate felt William was free to unwind without worrying about upsetting his Palace handlers. Even though she would nurse one glass of wine while he guzzled drink after drink on these evenings out, Kate "never nagged William, never. It was obvious she loved seeing him get out from under all the stuff he had to deal with and just have a good time."

Kate and William also clearly reveled in their newfound domestic bliss. They went grocery shopping together at local supermarkets like Tesco and Safeway, rode around town together on the 125 cc Kawasaki motorcycle his father had given him, and—with the exception of the two hours every Thursday night he devoted to training as captain of St. Andrews's water polo team—spent evenings at home watching movies, listening to William's R&B CDs, or playing chess with their roommates.

Operating inside what Jules Knight called the "safe bubble" provided by St. Andrews, Kate and William were able to "go for a drink and hold hands and no one batted an eyelid." But for the most part, they refrained from public displays of affection. Kate also went to extraordinary lengths not to let her own family in on the secret. Carole Middleton didn't need to be told. "She can read me like a book," Kate said of her mother, who unilaterally decided that the family needed a London pied-à-terre if the Middletons were suddenly to find themselves moving in royal circles. Toward that end, Carole spent $1.2 million on a three-bedroom flat with a fireplace, high ceilings, and French doors opening onto a balcony—all spread out over three floors in a stucco-fronted town house across from a bus stop in Chelsea.

Soon Kate was moving in royal circles, albeit among fifteen others invited to a shooting party at Sandringham. The ruse continued in Edinburgh and in London, where William and Kate went to high-profile restaurants and clubs, but always as part of a group. Invariably, they would depart at different times, then make their way separately back to Kate's new flat in Chelsea.

Kate understood why William was reluctant to risk exposure by taking her to Clarence House, the stucco-walled neoclassical mansion adjacent to St. James's Palace in London that had been occupied by the Queen Mother and was now home to Charles and his longtime mistress, Camilla Parker Bowles. Instead, William and Kate drove the two hours north from St. Andrews to Balmoral, the granite castle Queen Victoria and her husband, Prince Albert, had built in the heather-swathed Scottish Highlands alongside the River Dee.

More precisely, Kate was taken to Balmoral's next-door neighbor Birkhall, the late Queen Mother's six-thousand-acre estate on the banks of the River Muick. Even this was too grand for Kate, who asked if she and William could stay at Tam-Na-Ghar ("the House on the Mountain" in

Scottish Gaelic); Tam-Na-Ghar was a modest, three-bedroom cottage that the Queen Mother had given to William and Harry not long after their mother's death.

It was during this first visit to Balmoral, punctuated by long walks through the moors and angling for salmon and trout, that William briefed his girlfriend on how to win over the Prince of Wales. "Country pursuits are everything to my father," he told her. "My mother preferred the city. She would come here when she had to, but she couldn't wait to get back to London." Foxhunting, fishing, hunting, the sheer, pristine beauty of the Scottish countryside—these were the subjects she should stick to when conversing with Pa. After all, it was at Balmoral that a then-fourteen-year-old William shot his first stag and was "blooded"—a rite of passage in which the dead animal's blood is smeared on the triumphant hunter's face.

Kate had never hunted or fished for salmon before, but she gamely attempted both to impress her hosts. William's girlfriend, while also admitting she was no equestrian, did not hesitate to mount one of Queen Elizabeth's ponies for a ride on one of Balmoral's many trails—never letting on that she was allergic to horses.

Kate's enthusiasm paid off. "She is clearly a country girl," a senior aide to Prince Charles proclaimed, noting that this constituted "a huge advantage" when dealing with the Windsors. A Balmoral staffer went so far as to describe Miss Middleton as "a perfect fit." Kate later admitted that she had been "quite nervous about meeting William's father, but he was very, very welcoming, very friendly. It couldn't have gone easier really for me."

Kate's first meeting with William's famously mischievous brother went even more smoothly. Even before they became intimate, William took Kate into his confidence in January 2002 when newspapers trumpeted the news that the Spare had a drug problem severe enough for his father to take him to rehab. But the story wasn't true. "Sickened, horrified, and in shock," Harry called his brother to explain that he had been set up by their father and Camilla, and that the Prince of Wales's spin doctor, Mark Bolland, had concocted the whole thing. Harry told William that he was "heartbroken" over the fact that his own family had sacrificed him so that Charles could have his "shiny consolation prize. No more the unfaithful husband," Harry recalled of the scandal, "Pa would now be presented to the world as the harried single dad coping with a drug-addled child."

William was furious about the way Harry had been treated, and particularly angry at the role Camilla played in the plot. "At moments he was even angrier about the whole thing than I was," Harry said, "because he was privy to more details about the spin doctor and the backroom dealings."

At the time, the brothers felt powerless to do or say anything. All Kate could do was sympathize. When she did meet Harry the following year, they clicked. "I liked his new girlfriend," the Spare remembered. "She was carefree, sweet, kind. She'd done a gap year in Florence, knew about photography, art. And clothes. She loved clothes." Most of all, they shared a screwball, somewhat slapstick *Monty Python*ish sense of humor—often at William's expense.

Still, Harry was sworn to secrecy about their relationship; Kate and William were determined to keep up the subterfuge. When rumors of a romance began bubbling to the surface yet again, Michael Middleton, still very much in the dark, went so far as to issue a flat denial that there was anything romantic going on. "I can categorically confirm that they are no more than good friends," he told the press. "They are the best of pals. . . . There is nothing more to it than that." Kate's father went on to say that he and Carole were "very amused at the thought of being in-laws to Prince William, but I don't think it is going to happen."

Michael Middleton began to feel otherwise when William showed up unannounced at Oak Acre, their house in Bucklebury, to wish Kate a happy twenty-first birthday—and meet Kate's parents and siblings for the first time. By all accounts, they hit it off instantly. Having grown up inside the maelstrom of his parents' turbulent marriage, William was struck by what appeared to be the Middletons' unforced, genuinely happy upper-middle-class family life—particularly the good-natured way in which they routinely teased one another. "It's all very relaxed and cozy," he told his friend Guy Pelly, "but fun as well. They really take the mickey out of each other and nobody gets angry or hurt. They laugh *a lot*."

For the time being at least, William regarded the secret nature of his romance with Kate as no laughing matter. Just how serious the prince was about keeping their affair under wraps came into focus during a dinner party at 13A Hope Street. One of the hosts' favorite drinking games was Never Have I Ever, during which a player makes a statement of fact about themselves—"Never have I ever . . . gone to the moon," for example—and waits to see if someone in the room actually has. That person must then take a swig. Carly Massy-Birch happened to be one of the guests that evening, and when it was her turn to play, she allegedly blurted, "Never have I ever . . . dated two people in this room!"

Kate's eyes widened in disbelief. Everyone in the room knew William had dated Carly before becoming involved with Kate, but no one who wished to remain in the prince's good graces dared acknowledge it. Whether intentional or inadvertent, William was clearly irked that he and Kate were in a sense being outed. He shook his head and looked up at Carly. "I can't," he said, "believe you just said that."

Publicly, the Heir toed the party line about his dating life. "I don't have a steady girlfriend," he proclaimed in a BBC interview marking his twenty-first birthday. "If I fancy a girl and I really like her and she fancies me back, which is rare, I ask her out. But, at the same time, I don't want to put them in an awkward situation, because a lot of people don't quite understand what comes with knowing me, for one—and secondly, if they were my girlfriend, the excitement it would probably cause." He added: "There's been a lot of speculation about every single girl I'm with and it actually does quite irritate me after a while, more so because it's a complete pain for the girls. These poor girls . . . suddenly get thrown into the limelight and their parents get rung up and so on. . . . I'm used to it, but it's very difficult for them and I don't like that at all."

William's $800,000 Out of Africa birthday bash at Windsor Castle—the theme was Kate's idea—fueled even more speculation about the women in his life. Nobody seemed to notice that Kate, who was careful not to cozy up to her boyfriend, was wearing a skimpy animal-print costume to match the birthday boy's Tarzan loincloth. Instead, all eyes were on Jecca Craig, the girl William had "proposed" to during his gap-year sojourn in Africa. In part to divert attention from herself, Kate insisted that William invite Craig to the party as his guest of honor.

The ruse worked—perhaps too well. Soon Prince Charles was forced to issue a rare official denial "that there is or ever has been any romantic liaison between Prince William and Jessica Craig." Three months later, Kate, confident that the romance between William and Jecca Craig was indeed well in the past, did not protest when he departed for a month-long stay with the Craigs at their wildlife refuge in Kenya. Kate did, however, regret her decision when William returned home and was promptly stricken with stabbing pains in his stomach. After several days of trying to tough it out, William finally sought medical assistance at Kate's insistence. The verdict: the heir to the throne was suffering from a parasitic disease that, if left untreated, can be fatal.

Not long after, Kate suffered the loss of her maternal grandfather, Ronald Goldsmith, to multiple system atrophy, a degenerative disease. Eight years earlier, Goldsmith had been cleaning the rain gutters for an elderly woman in his village when he lost his balance and fell, shattering both heels. No one was home at the time, so he crawled to a neighboring house to call for an ambulance. He spent his final years in a wheelchair and at the time of his death was unaware that his granddaughter had been dating Prince William for more than a year.

To kick off their third year at St. Andrews, William and Kate decided to leave their Hope Street roommates and go it alone. Their new home was Balgove House, an ivy-covered cottage set within Strathtyrum, the four-hundred-acre private country estate owned by William's distant cousin Henry Cheape. "I do think I am a country boy at heart," William explained. "I do like space and freedom." All that space and freedom came at a price—$2.5 million, to be precise, spent primarily on installing elaborate surveillance systems, bombproof doors, and bulletproof windows, as well as providing space next door for a bolstered security force. Their main indulgence: a $400, eighteen-bottle wine fridge.

For the next six months Kate and her prince lived their lives much as they had before, ordering takeout, laughing as they tried to fend for themselves in their small kitchen, taking long sunset walks together, entertaining friends. Now that they were away from the town center, the young couple could enjoy their newfound sense of independence and let their guard down a bit—or so they thought.

During their spring break in late March 2004, paparazzi captured Kate and William cozying up to each other on the snowy slopes of Klosters, the Waleses' favorite Swiss ski resort. The *Sun* blasted the news all over its April 1 front page: "Finally, Wills Gets a Girl."

Prince Charles was livid that the Palace's hands-off agreement with Britain's tabloid press had been broken. St. James's Palace denounced the *Sun* and barred its photographers from covering both William and Harry. But there was no turning back for Kate. She had been catapulted into the spotlight, where she would remain forever.

Now more camera shy than ever, the prince and his commoner girlfriend stuck close to home. When they did venture out—to attend the school's annual May Ball or dress up as Rhett Butler and Scarlett O'Hara for a costume party—they remained on high alert.

Behind the scenes, Kate comforted Will when he lost his "Gran Fran"—Diana's mother, Frances Shand Kydd—to Parkinson's Disease at age sixty-eight. Kate shed more tears for her prince as she watched on television as he and Harry became emotional during the July 6, 2004, dedication of the Diana Memorial Fountain in Hyde Park.

There were also angry tears shed that summer, as William and Kate argued furiously about the prince's plan to visit Jecca Craig in Africa—yet again. Kate had no doubt that there was nothing to the rumors about William and Jecca, but she felt humiliated nonetheless. Ultimately, he backed down. Instead, he took Kate to Rodrigues, the island paradise in the Indian Ocean where he had spent part of his gap year.

As magical as their tropical excursion was, William was soon linked in the press with yet another stunningly attractive young woman—this time an American named Anna Sloan. William and Sloan, who met in 2001 while she was attending Edinburgh University, bonded over the tragic accidental deaths of their parents—Sloan's father was killed that year when his shotgun went off accidentally. Now William was accepting Sloan's invitation to visit her at her family's 360-acre spread in Franklin, Tennessee.

No sooner did he return from Tennessee than William began pursuing yet another potential love interest—the stunning blond heiress with the tongue-twisting name, Isabella Anstruther-Gough-Calthorpe. William went so far as to spend time with Bellie Calthorpe at her family's impressive Chelsea manse, but she resisted his advances on the grounds that dating him would simply get in the way of her show business aspirations.

Kate, understandably, had had enough. Without saying as much, she and William decided that summer of 2004 to take a break from each other. Kate fled to Fergus Boyd's family vacation home in France with her old friends Ginny Fraser and Olivia Bleasdale. Late one evening Kate "got quite drunk on white wine and really let her guard down," a member of the group recalled. "She was debating whether or not she should text or call him. She said how sad she was and how much she was missing William, but she never mentioned it after that."

Feeling claustrophobic in the relationship but unwilling to end it, William scooped Kate up that August and took her for a romantic weekend at Balmoral. It marked the first time she met Camilla, whose friendly demeanor belied what Kate had already been told about the woman who broke up the marriage of Charles and Diana. If anything, Camilla was even more welcoming when Kate showed up with William at Highgrove to celebrate Prince Charles's fifty-sixth birthday—one of the most coveted events on the UK social calendar.

William and Harry wanted their father to be happy; after all, in the end even Diana acknowledged that the love Charles had for Camilla was something to be envied. But the brothers made it clear that they did not trust Camilla and, as Kate later told a friend, "It took everything I had not to let on."

In January 2005, the royals were hit by another headline-making scandal—and this time Kate played an unknown part in it. William and Harry had been invited to attend a costume party at the home of three-time Olympic-gold-medal-winning equestrian Richard Meade. The affair was to celebrate the twenty-second birthday of Meade's son Harry, and many of those attending were members of the Beaufort Hunt Club. When Harry balked about going, Kate called him up and urged him to reconsider.

Harry later explained in his memoir, *Spare*, that he thought the theme—"Natives and Colonials"—was a bit "cringy" for 2005, but Kate and William reminded him how much fun they always had together at what the British call "fancy dress" parties. Harry relented—but only if Kate agreed to help him pick out a costume.

Harry would have been forgiven for having second thoughts about their judgment when William tried on the lion costume Kate had selected for him, posing in a three-way mirror in his bedroom at Highgrove: "Some kind of feline outfit. Skintight leotard with . . . a springy, bouncy tail. He looked like a cross between Tigger and Baryshnikov." Kate and Harry "had a great time pointing our fingers" at William "and rolling on the floor."

Kate knew that Harry was one of the few people who could make her dissolve in laughter. "I liked making her laugh," he recalled in his book, "and I was quite good at it." He figured that his "transparently silly side" connected with her "heavily disguised silly side." Harry went alone to a costume shop in Nailsworth, a village not far from Highgrove, and narrowed the possibilities down to two costumes before calling Kate. Should he pick the RAF pilot's uniform, or a short-sleeved khaki uniform of Nazi tank commander Erwin Rommel's Afrika Korps, complete with the eagle badge of the Wehrmacht on the chest and a red-and-black swastika armband?

"Oh, the Nazi uniform!" replied Kate, who had opted for a safari outfit for herself. William agreed. Harry rented the costume—"plus a silly moustache"—then returned to Highgrove to try it on for Kate and William. "They both howled," said Harry, who then trimmed the fake moustache to resemble Hitler's.

No one seemed to enjoy the party more than Kate, who boasted to one guest, only half in jest, that she was responsible for picking out the brothers' "ridiculous" costumes. Most of the attention, in fact, was on William's leonine leotard. When she was told someone at the party had been taking photos, Kate worried that William's less-than-dignified skintight getup would wind up on the front page.

She was relieved—at least momentarily—when, two weeks later, it was Harry and his Nazi costume that were making world headlines. Reaction to the stories headed "Harry the Nazi" and "Heil, Harry" was swift and brutal. Harry was denounced by the Israeli foreign minister, Holocaust survivors, several Jewish and World War II veterans groups, and members of Parliament. There were even demands that Harry not be permitted to attend Sandhurst, the military academy that he had planned to enter in a matter of months.

Shocked and mortified that he had once again brought shame to the royal family, Harry placed his first call to William. Both the Heir and Kate told him how unfair it was for Harry to be pilloried over his choice of costume, but neither offered to share in the blame. Certainly Kate and William did not want to focus attention on themselves; she and William were still downplaying their relationship.

The second call Harry placed was to his father, who, much to the Spare's surprise, was sympathetic. There would, however, have to be some form of atonement if Harry was to be allowed to follow through on his plans to pursue an army career. Charles turned down an invitation for Harry to tour Auschwitz, the concentration camp where four million prisoners, mostly Jews, perished. But he did send the Spare to meet with the Chief Rabbi of Britain who, after scolding Harry for his stupidity, forgave him.

Kate watched helplessly as Harry was publicly flayed—the *Daily Telegraph* columnist Tom Utley described him as displaying "the stupidity of a rather backward child of twelve"—but at the same time Kate was thankful that no one had connected the dots about the role she and William had played in the Nazi uniform scandal. According to a friend of both brothers, Harry did not tell his father that William and Kate were complicit in picking out the offensive costume. The Palace was "happy to have Harry take the fall. He was expendable and William was untouchable." As genuinely fond as she was of Harry, "Kate knew pretty early on where her loyalties had to lie."

The ink on the "Harry the Nazi" tabloid headlines was scarcely dry when Kate was given a ringside seat to yet another royal drama that tested the bounds of family loyalty. Princess Diana had been dead less than a year when William first met Camilla during a hastily arranged summit at Clarence House. She soon claimed to be "shaking like a leaf" during the brief meeting and "in need of a gin and tonic" after it—details that both brothers told Kate had to have been leaked to the press by Camilla herself.

Harry's experience—at Highgrove over tea—was similar, although the meeting with Camilla itself was anything but tense. "I have a dim recollection of Camilla being just as calm (or bored) as me," Harry said. "I wasn't her biggest hurdle. . . . I wasn't the Heir."

By early 2005, Charles was speeding up plans for his marriage to Camilla. After those initial meetings years earlier, William and Harry had told their father that they wanted him to be happy—that they approved of his relationship with Camilla. There was one caveat, however. They did not want him to marry her. "We support you. We endorse Camilla. *Just please*," they pleaded, "*don't marry her. Just be together, Pa.*"

Now things were different. As soon as William and Harry made it clear that they did not want their father to marry Camilla, she set out to transform herself. New hair, new teeth, plastic surgery, new wardrobe—all designed to make her more salable to a public that still adored Diana. It would take seven years for Charles to convince the Queen to relent, but once he did, the boys fell into line. Again, with a caveat. Her Majesty granted permission for Charles to marry the undoubted love of his life—the woman she had once called "wicked"—only if Charles agreed she would never be queen. Charles made the same promise to his future subjects as well as to his own sons, who understandably felt their mother had been cruelly robbed of the title. Of course, under British custom and law, once Charles became king, his wife would automatically become the queen, regardless of what she was called. Still, Charles issued a statement promising that Camilla would never be queen, only "Princess Consort." The toned-down title did little to quell opposition to the marriage; polls at the time were showing that a resounding 93 percent of the population did not want Camilla as their queen.

Kate, like William and Harry, believed—naively, as it turned out—that Charles would keep his word. She had also grown genuinely fond of the Prince of Wales, and while she hadn't really gotten to know Camilla well, it

From top: Fearless from the start, toddler Kate clambers up a hillside during a family vacation in England's Lake District. When she was two, the Middleton family moved to Jordan, where her father, Michael, worked for British Airways. For the next three years Kate and little sister, Pippa, shown here with Daddy visiting the ancient ruins at Jeresh, learned Arabic phrases in nursery school by reciting passages from the Quran. Bottom, Kate, shown here in a school photo at age five, enjoyed dressing up like a princess during her childhood in the tiny hamlet of Bucklebury, Berkshire. Previous page: Kate at the November 22, 2022, Buckingham Palace State Banquet for South African President Cyril Ramaphosa—the first state visit during the reign of Charles III.

Left: Fourteen-year-old Kate hams it up at Marlborough College, the prep school she fled to after being mercilessly bullied at another private school, Down House. Like tens of millions of others, Kate tearfully watched William and Harry walk behind Princess Diana's coffin in 1997, unaware that eventually she would be called upon to help her prince cope with the PTSD caused by his mother's death and its aftermath.

Quiet and shy Kate caught William's eye in a serious way when she modeled a see-through outfit at a St. Andrews University fashion show. By the time they both graduated in 2005, Kate and William had been living together for three years.

Kate and her mother, Carole, a former flight attendant who made a fortune selling children's party supplies, watch William play polo near Highgrove. By 2007, the relentless paparazzi pursuit of "Waity Katie" infuriated William, but she never lost her cool.

Following the stunning announcement of their breakup in April 2007, Kate decided to steer a new course for her life—literally—by training to sail across the English Channel as a member of the all-female crew called The Sisterhood. The split lasted just six weeks.

The Wedding of the Century. Having deftly navigated the royal rapids for nearly a decade, Kate finally wed the future king on April 29, 2011, in a spectacular Westminster Abbey ceremony. Maid of Honor Pippa, who along with her sister was resplendent in Alexander McQueen, handled the bride's nine-foot train, causing something of a stir in her own right.

"The Kate Effect" was in full force when the Duchess of Cambridge made her official debut at a gala that raised $28 million for a children's charity on June 9, 2011. One month later, during their first overseas tour—a whirlwind nine-day tour of Canada and the US—Kate knelt down during a stop in Calgary to hug six-year-old cancer patient Diamond Marshall. The princess was heartbroken when Diamond succumbed to the disease three years later at age nine.

Kate and the queen share a laugh—as they often did—during a Diamond Jubilee visit to Nottingham in June 2012. Here, William has been mobbed by schoolchildren, and Her Majesty lets him know there isn't much she can do. In a rare public display of affection that August, the couple goes wild watching British cyclists compete during the London Olympics.

With cannons booming and church bells chiming, George Alexander Louis Mountbatten-Windsor—presumably the future King George VII—arrived on July 22, 2013. Less than two years later, he gives his newborn sister, Charlotte, a tender kiss on the forehead. Later, nanny Maria Borrallo looks on while the queen asks her great-grandson if he would like a peek inside the baby's pram.

As a master of soft diplomacy, Kate has always researched her wardrobe choices. For the state banquet at Buckingham Palace honoring Chinese President Xi Jinping in October 2015, she shrewdly wore red—which in China symbolizes luck, joy, and happiness.

Barack and Michelle Obama dropped in at Kensington Palace during their working visit to London in April 2016. Kate helped George show their guests how much he enjoyed the wooden rocking horse with the presidential seal on the saddle that the Obamas had given him for his first birthday.

On June 22, 2016, Kate and longtime friend and neighbor Rose Hanbury, the Marchioness of Cholmondeley, appear to be on the best of terms at a fundraiser for children's hospice care. Starting in 2019, however, baseless rumors would persist of an affair between the Marchioness and William.

was hard to deny that she and Charles were devoted to each other. Kate reassured the brothers that they were making the right decision by agreeing to the marriage. "Despite Willy and me urging him not to, Pa was going ahead," Harry later wrote. "We pumped his hand, wished him well. No hard feelings."

The day the Queen said yes, Camilla did too. At Highgrove, Charles got on bended knee and asked "Mrs. PB" (for Parker Bowles), as she was known around the Palace, for her hand in marriage. He then slipped an eight-carat emerald-cut diamond engagement ring that had belonged to the Queen Mother on Camilla's finger. "Well, Pa is finally going to be with the woman he loves," a resigned William told Kate. "Might as well make the best of it."

Incredibly, the furor over "Nazi Harry" was so all-consuming that Charles and Camilla's engagement remained secret for weeks. Then there were a series of delays, including a last-minute postponement so that Charles could represent the Queen at the funeral of Pope John Paul II in Rome. Throughout it all, there were also legal challenges to the marriage—Could the head of the Church of England even marry a divorcée?—and the persistent drumbeat of opposition from those who felt the planned marriage was an overt betrayal of Diana's memory. There was no way of quieting Diana loyalists, but there was a way around the legal challenges. Since they could not be married in the church, there would be a civil ceremony at Windsor Guildhall, followed by a service at St. George's Chapel on the grounds of Windsor Castle.

Kate and William watched with deepening concern as Charles grew increasingly bitter, claiming during a BBC interview that he had been "tortured" for his relationship with Camilla. By the time William and Harry took their father on a stag-week ski trip to Klosters, Charles made it clear that he was fed up. With press microphones just a few feet away as the trio posed for photos, the future Charles III looked at respected BBC royals correspondent Nicholas Witchell and blurted, "I can't bear that man. He's so awful. He really is. . . . Bloody people. I *hate* doing this." Trying to right the ship, William mumbled to his father, "Keep smiling, keep smiling."

William knew all too well what his father was going through. On the same trip, a reporter asked William if he was going to marry Kate. "Look,

I'm only twenty-two, for God's sake," he shot back. "I'm too young to marry. I don't want to get married until I'm at least twenty-eight or maybe thirty."

Kate, still officially being kept under wraps, was not invited to the civil ceremony at Windsor Guildhall—the Queen declined as well—nor to the subsequent religious service in St. George's Chapel, where Her Majesty sat glowering as Archbishop of Canterbury Rowan Williams made Charles and Camilla get down on their knees and confess their "manifold sins and wickedness."

From where she sat forty-five miles to the east in Bucklebury, watching the events unfold on television, Kate was impressed at how William and Harry both seemed to have put their bitterness over the wedding behind them. While Charles never actually kissed his new bride during the ceremony and the reception—and the Queen ignored her son's pleas to pose with the newlyweds on the chapel steps—both William and Harry bussed their new stepmother on the cheek. They spent much of the reception decorating the newlyweds' Bentley with Mylar balloons and using soap to scrawl "Prince + Duchess" across the windshield, then peppered the happy couple with handfuls of confetti as they headed for their waiting car.

William had shoved a potato in the Bentley's exhaust pipe, hoping to make the car backfire, and was disappointed when the gag didn't work. Still, as the newlyweds sped off to their two-week honeymoon at Balmoral, the brothers chased after it on foot, waving their arms and shouting, "Thank you for coming!" at the tops of their lungs. It was the line Charles and Camilla had repeated hundreds of times that day.

"The two boys were in fantastic form," Harry's godfather Gerald Ward said. "They were both very happy." But Kate knew better. The William she knew had done everything he could to stop his father from marrying the woman who had destroyed his parents' marriage—and left both the Heir and the Spare with deep-seated wounds even before the emotional trauma of their mother's death. At least, Kate reassured William when he returned to St. Andrews, "Camilla will never be queen."

As accustomed as she was to staying out of the limelight, Kate took center stage along with William when they graduated from St. Andrews on

June 23, 2005. The Queen was still battling a case of the flu, but showed up anyway. So did Prince Philip, who had never attended a family graduation before—not even Charles's graduation from Cambridge. Rounding out the front row center mezzanine seats in Younger Hall were Harry, Camilla, and the Prince of Wales.

Since the graduates were seated downstairs in alphabetical order, Kate Middleton was five rows ahead of her prince. She strode to the stage and knelt before university chancellor Sir Kenneth Dover, who, in keeping with tradition, tapped her softly on the head with a scarlet cap that allegedly contained a fragment of cloth from the pants of the great Protestant Reform leader John Knox. A red-lined black hood was then attached to the collar of her robe, and she was handed her master of art history degree. Kate returned to her seat, diploma in hand, looked over at William, and the two exchanged smiles.

As expected, the room exploded with thunderous applause, cheers, and flashing cameras when Dean of Arts Christopher Smith called the name "William Wales." Once he had gone through the ceremonial rigmarole and been handed his master of arts degree in geography, William looked up, smiling in the direction of the Queen, as he returned to his seat.

Launching into his commencement address, Vice-Chancellor Lang drew titters from the crowd when he told the new graduates, "You may have met your husband or wife. Our title as 'Top Matchmaking University in Britain' signifies so much that is good about St. Andrews, so we can rely on you to go forth and multiply."

Predictably, Lang's cringeworthy remarks elicited groans and eye rolls from everyone but the Queen, who beamed with delight. Afterward, Kate and William joined the rest of the families outside. The Heir dashed up to his father and the Queen, bending down to give each a kiss on the cheek.

Meanwhile, Kate, her long robe billowing in the wind to reveal a tight black miniskirt and high heels, went in search of the Middletons. She found her parents and siblings hanging back on the far side of the courtyard, wary of appearing too presumptuous. When William suddenly bounded up, impetuously grabbed Kate's hand, and offered to introduce Kate and her parents to the Queen, the Middletons wisely demurred. Kate, ever wary of appearing to overstep her bounds, pointed to all the proud parents armed with cameras and suggested that an introduction to Her Majesty in a more private setting was less likely to wind up on the front page of the *Sun*.

Meeting the monarch was just one of many hurdles that lay ahead. Now that William was out of college and heading for Sandhurst in January, the press was no longer obligated to leave them alone. He would be protected inside the walls of the military academy, but Kate would be fair game for the insatiable tabloid press. Moreover, this would be their first time living apart since they had moved in together three years earlier. Would their love survive this first extended period of separation? The overwhelming sentiment inside palace walls was that it wouldn't. "It's all very well to say that we're matchmakers," one St. Andrews faculty member commented. "The truth is that nearly all college romances fizzle out after people graduate and go their separate ways. When he has so many options, why would it be any different for Prince William?"

Perhaps, but this particular prince wanted to prove to Kate and all the doubters that William and Kate were still very much together. The first week in June, they had taken an important step by attending the wedding of William's friend Hugh van Cutsem to Rose Astor—incredibly, the very first time they had ever shown up as a couple at a public event. They followed up not long after to catch a match at the Beaufort Polo Club.

At the St. Andrews Graduation Ball, William and Kate "could not be pried apart," said another graduate. The celebration continued two days later at Boujis, where they danced until 1 a.m. before heading out separately to avoid the "paps" lurking outside.

Early the next morning, a seriously hungover William boarded a royal jet for the twenty-eight-hour flight to New Zealand. There he would make his solo debut as the Crown's official representative at ceremonies commemorating the sixtieth anniversary of the end of World War II.

Kate, meanwhile, was lying low at her family's Bucklebury mansion, trying to decide what kind of postgraduate life to make for herself. Even if William asked her to marry him—and there was no guarantee that he would—did she really want to give up her own identity for a life of walkabouts and plaque unveilings?

William's grandmother, for one, was rooting for Miss Middleton. For one thing, she had stood the test of time. The brief courtships of Charles and Diana and Andrew and Sarah Ferguson had led to disastrous marriages. Her Majesty now decreed that no senior royal should date for less than five years before exchanging vows.

Although Queen Elizabeth and Kate would not formally meet for another three years, the sovereign had been closely monitoring the young commoner and was favorably impressed. Not only had Kate convinced William to stick it out at St. Andrews for the full four years—an important gesture of solidarity with Scotland that would have backfired had he left—but she had effortlessly dealt with the daunting exigencies of royal life, from incursions on her privacy to elaborate security precautions. That Kate had neither bolted nor wilted in the white-hot glare of the media spotlight impressed Her Majesty even more. "The Queen," recalled her cousin Margaret Rhodes, "was beginning to think that this girl really loved her grandson. That was the most important thing, of course."

Kate was reassured when, on the spur of the moment, William whisked her off to Africa—until she realized it was to visit his old sweetheart Jecca Craig. This time, however, Kate did not give in to feelings of jealousy. No longer threatened by her boyfriend's past loves—and relieved that Jecca had fallen for British financier Hugh Crossley—Kate launched a charm offensive not only on Jecca but the entire Craig family. By the time William and Kate left a month later, she was proudly wearing a safari hat identical to the one Jecca had worn to the prince's Out of Africa twenty-first birthday party. "Kate won everyone over the minute she climbed out of Prince William's Land Rover," a Lewa staffer said. "She and Jecca hit it off right away, and that clearly made Prince William very happy."

So did Kate's enthusiastic embrace of the African experience. It was her first visit to William's favorite continent, and from the moment they hiked to their thatch-roofed banda at the exclusive Il Ngwesi Lodge with breathtaking views of mist-shrouded Mount Kenya, she was hooked.

Back in London, Kate again found herself shoring up her prince's self-confidence as he studied for Sandhurst's formidable entrance exams. Once he passed with flying colors, they returned to one of their old haunts—Purple—to celebrate in the VIP room. This time, he told the DJ to dedicate several tunes to the young woman he now openly referred to as "my girlfriend," and when they left the club they brazenly did so together.

Yet there remained occasions when Kate was required to step back into the shadows. When William was summoned to sit alongside his grandparents Prince Philip and the Queen at Scotland's Highland Games, Kate perused the shelves at Topshop, a clothing store on London's Kensington High Street.

Things were a bit murkier when William appeared without Kate at Falmouth Harbor to greet their friend Oliver "Olly" Hicks after Hicks had spent 124 days rowing solo from the United States to the United Kingdom. Tabloids seized on Kate's absence as a sign that the couple had split, but Kate was in fact there, only choosing to remain invisible.

No matter. When, the very next day, William and Kate were seated apart at the Institute of Cancer Research Gala at Whitehall, tongues were again set wagging. Talk of a breakup would continue that fall and winter of 2005 as the Heir undertook no fewer than three separate jobs before starting at Sandhurst. First, the prince donned an apron and a straw boater to serve customers from behind a counter in the farm store at Chatsworth in Derbyshire. Following that, he spent three weeks at the London headquarters of the financial titan HSBC that included visits to Lloyd's of London, the Bank of England, and the London Stock Exchange. Finally, William rappelled down the face of a two-hundred-foot cliff as part of a three-week stint with the RAF Mountain Rescue Team at Holyhead Mountain in North Wales. In between, he was brought up to speed on several of the causes he championed, most notably Centrepoint, a charity to end youth homelessness.

As frenetic as William's life undoubtedly was, Kate knew that these various tasks helped take his mind off Operation Paget, the ongoing investigation into his mother's death. The prince shared only a few details with Kate, but it was obvious to her that being grilled for hours by the head of Scotland Yard, Sir John Stevens (later Baron Stevens of Kirkwhelpington), had taken its toll.

Dredging up the gruesome details of Diana's car crash death only served to heighten William's growing concern that the same fate could befall Kate. As long as she was with the prince, his royal protection squad shielded her to some extent against intrusions by the newly emboldened press. But now that William only occasionally visited her at the Middletons' Chelsea flat, Kate was forced to fend for herself.

Whenever she stepped outside to meet friends or go shopping, she was tailed by six or seven photographers intent on chronicling her every move. They lunged from behind cars and crouched in the shrubbery, shooting her as she searched for her keys or angled her car into a parking space.

If this wholesale violation of her privacy bothered her, Kate was expert at not letting it show. Photos taken by the paparazzi invariably showed her going about her business, smiling, head held high. But when a German magazine published shots of William leaving Kate's apartment in the morning hours under the headline "The Love Nest"—with a red arrow pointing to the location on a street map—the prince flew into a rage. The royal law firm with the Dickensian-sounding name of Harbottle & Lewis fired a shot across the bow of Fleet Street, warning newspaper editors to leave Kate alone or face litigation.

The ploy failed. Newspapers were filled with stories about the charming young commoner who seemed destined to marry the future king. Suggesting that Kate was perhaps destined to outshine Diana, the *Independent* gushed that "the People's Princess may be replaced, in Kate, by a real princess of the people: a non-blueblood."

In all the years they had known each other, Kate and William had yet to spend a Christmas together. This year was no exception. The royal family always celebrated Christmas at Sandringham, and attendance by senior royals was mandatory. Although 2005 marked the first Christmas that Camilla was celebrating at Sandringham as an official member of the royal family, Kate had not yet made the grade; the Queen personally drew up the guest list, and no invitation to Miss Middleton was forthcoming.

No matter. There was always New Year's Eve. To throw the paparazzi off the couple's scent, Kensington Palace leaked information to the press indicating that William and Kate would ring in 2006 at one of their favorite spots—Verbier in Switzerland. While photographers scurried to Verbier, William and Kate were more than two hundred miles to the northeast, watching the snow fall outside the window of their small chalet in Klosters.

Eighteen years earlier, Prince Charles had nearly lost his life in an avalanche that killed his close friend Hugh Lindsay. Now Kate and William, apparently unaware of the danger, went off-trail at that same spot to ski atop Casanna in the Plessur Alps.

Fortunately, they managed to end their run partway down without incident—and without interference. They were a million miles from civilization and alone, or so they thought. The feeling was, Kate later said, "exhilarating." Pausing to take in the sweeping, uninterrupted view from an elevation of more than ten thousand feet, William wrapped Kate in his arms and pulled her close for a deep, lingering kiss. Incredibly, no one had ever photographed William and Kate kissing. This was an intimate moment that had never been captured for public consumption; it was a moment they had always somehow managed to keep all to themselves.

The next morning, the very first photograph of the prince kissing his girlfriend was on front pages everywhere. For most newspaper editors, the headline was foreordained: "Kiss Me, Kate."

Maybe she felt threatened by Kate, or perhaps more by William and Kate as a team.

—a St. James's Palace staffer, on Camilla

3

The Split of the Century

"The Star of the Show"

April 11, 2007

Kate could not believe what she was hearing. Clutching her cell phone close to her ear behind a closed door in a conference room at Jigsaw, the clothing firm where she worked as a children's accessories buyer, she listened to the man she had loved for five years tell her they were through. But why? Kate asked, knowing that her coworkers were straining to hear on the other side of the door. William stammered that he was unwilling to make a commitment, that he was "only twenty-five" and too young, and that the press would make her life "unbearable" as long as they were a couple. "Is that what you really want?" he reportedly asked. Did she really want to be "hounded like my mother," he demanded.

Even more important, he said, was that her life was in danger every minute they remained together. Now that he had graduated from Sandhurst and was about to embark on his army career, she would be more vulnerable than ever. She had never been entitled to royal protection when he wasn't around, and now their absences from each other would be more frequent and of longer duration than ever. While threats to the royal family were usually kept under wraps, there were plenty of them—from terrorists, would-be kidnappers, and the mentally ill.

William chose not to burden Kate with the knowledge that he sometimes woke up in a cold sweat after dreaming that she had met the same fate as Diana, chased down by the paparazzi and killed in a horrific car crash. The nightmares were becoming more and more frequent—and increasingly graphic.

Miss Middleton was not going quietly. She pleaded with William to reconsider. She would ask her parents to hire private bodyguards, if that's what he wanted. But it wasn't just that. Then what is it? she wanted to know. He was under so much pressure now that he was taking on the duties of a second lieutenant in the Blues and Royals Regiment of the Household Cavalry. Kate knew how he reacted at times like these, how his mood could turn dark in an instant—a sad remnant of his turbulent childhood and his mother's violent death. She urged him to take a deep breath and reconsider.

The call went on like this for over an hour, but William was adamant. "It isn't going to work" was his mantra. "It isn't fair to you." It wasn't until he finally told Kate that his father had suggested the breakup that Kate, who had come to view Prince Charles as a sort of surrogate father, became emotional. What initially seemed like another bump in the road now became a yawning chasm—the Prince of Wales had not only sanctioned this move but, for reasons Kate could not fathom, initiated it.

Down the hall, Kate's astonished coworkers could hear her voice rise and fall, careening from shock to frustration to panic, and, finally, tearful resignation. When she finally ended the call and emerged from the conference room, it was clear that she had been crying. "We knew who was on the other end of the line because she always asked to go into another room when the prince called," said one. "It was obviously a terrible quarrel. We were all shocked." But it never would have occurred to them that Kate and

William were splitting. "Over the phone? Really?" she added. "It didn't seem like Prince William at all."

Over her five months working four days a week at Jigsaw's headquarters in the leafy London borough of Kew, Kate had handled the ever-present media with considerable finesse—smiling, never allowing herself to be photographed looking rattled or annoyed. "She's been quite good," observed Kate's boss, Jigsaw founder and Middleton family friend Belle Robinson, "at neither courting the press nor sticking her finger in the air at them."

This afternoon, however, Kate could not face the photographers stationed, as they were every workday, outside Jigsaw's offices. After Robinson ushered her out the back door at 3 p.m., Kate drove straight home to Bucklebury. Meanwhile, the Queen was at Windsor preparing to visit the Earl of Carnarvon at Highclere Castle, where television's *Downton Abbey* was partially filmed, when she was told Prince William was on the phone. Even though they had not yet met, Her Majesty admired Kate and believed that an engagement was imminent. Instead, the Queen instructed the Palace to leak the breakup news now, rather than have speculation drag on for weeks.

As the next day's breathless headlines proved, this was the split of the century. "It's Over," the *Daily Mail* proclaimed the next day, while the *Sun* got right to the point with "Wills and Kate Split." Aware that the British electorate was as shocked as he was by the unexpected news, Prime Minister Tony Blair issued a press release asking the public to take a deep breath. "We've had the announcement," he said. "Fine. They should be left alone."

Kate had been gently pressing William for a commitment but was careful not to overplay her hand. Still, cracks had begun appearing in their romance. For the last four years they had managed to ring in every New Year together. This time, however, William decided at the last minute to turn down the Middletons' annual New Year's Eve invitation, choosing instead to remain at Sandringham—a move that left Kate in tears.

Similarly, since 2003, William had spent all or part of the Easter holiday in Bucklebury. When he didn't show for Easter either, Kate and her family were left to wonder if William's ardor was beginning to cool—and if so, why.

As far as their relationship was concerned, the last eighteen months had, on balance, been on an upward trajectory. When she was not invited to the prestigious Cheltenham Gold Cup, a highlight of the steeplechase racing season in Britain, in March 2006, Kate simply went on her own. Spotting her in the crowd, Prince Charles invited Kate to the royal box, where she charmed the Prince of Wales and Camilla for the next hour. This marked the first time Kate was seen in public flying solo with the royals, displaying an easy confidence and natural poise that made her appear right at home. "The star of the show," wrote the reporter for *Hello!*, "was not one of the Windsor clan—although many predict she soon will be."

She had won Charles over long ago, and now Kate left Cheltenham feeling particularly optimistic about Camilla. Kate's take on the Duchess of Cornwall was the same as virtually everyone else's upon first meeting the Prince of Wales's longtime inamorata: Camilla struck her as warm, self-effacing, and boisterously funny. These were qualities, William's girlfriend would soon discover, that served to disguise the private ambitions of one of history's most accomplished mistresses.

Kate's winning streak continued less than twenty-fours later, when William was allowed to interrupt his training at Sandhurst to compete as part of an "old boys" alumni team at Eton. For the first time, William and Kate seemed to be throwing caution to the wind—hugging, kissing, generally making a very public display of their love for each other as the paparazzi snapped away and hundreds of gape-mouthed Etonians and their families looked on.

That spring of 2006, William whisked Kate off to Mustique, a privately owned resort island in the Grenadines, where they stayed at villa Hibiscus, Belle and John Robinson's gated estate with jaw-dropping views of legendary Macaroni Beach. Even before Kate and William returned to London, images of the couple showering each other off on Richard Branson's yacht were everywhere. Not even the security measures taken by one of the world's wealthiest entrepreneurs were apparently enough to thwart a determined photographer armed with a telephoto lens.

Kate and William would soon both discover that nothing was off-limits as far as some tabloid editors were concerned. When details of their cell phone conversations and those of other royals wound up in the *News of the World*, at the time the most widely read English language newspaper on the planet, Scotland Yard launched an investigation that led to the jailing of the paper's royal editor Clive Goodman. (Ultimately, hacking complaints would bring down the 168-year-old publication altogether.)

Many of their phone conversations consisted of Kate lending a sympathetic ear while William complained about the ever-invasive press and the Palace operatives who were mapping out his life as a royal ribbon cutter even as he endured rigorous military training. William was particularly frustrated that, as heir to the throne, he was banned from any combat duty while Harry was perfectly free to fight. William didn't want to be "mollycoddled or wrapped up in cotton wool," he insisted, adding that he wanted "to go where my men went and do what they did." He didn't want to be held back for being "precious," he said, because that would be "the most humiliating thing."

There were times that summer when William was the one doing the comforting. In late July 2006, Carole's flamboyant, socially ambitious, chain-smoking mother, "Lady Dorothy," died of lung cancer at seventy-one. Two months later, Kate's World War II code-breaking granny, Valerie Middleton, passed away from lymphoma at the age of eighty-two.

By this time, Charles had been so won over by Kate that he dropped the appearances-driven pretense of assigning them separate bedrooms at Highgrove and gave them their own room furnished with a king-sized mahogany four-poster. Queen Elizabeth did not object when she heard the news, even though she had never even shared a bedroom with Prince Philip. But Her Majesty was beginning to wonder why Kate Middleton did not seem to have a job. The Queen did not demand that anyone in royal circles meet her high standards, said Lady Yolanda Joseph, the widow of Sir Keith Joseph (British statesman and a cabinet member under four prime ministers), "but she does expect them to work!"

Once she got wind of the Queen's concerns, Kate landed the job at Jigsaw. Leaving nothing to chance, the company's newest assistant buyer marched out the front door at workday's end and smiled at the small army of photographers waiting outside. The Queen was relieved to see the pictures of her grandson's girlfriend leaving her job, and perhaps even more delighted several days later when newspapers ran photos of Kate tromping through the grounds at Sandringham, swinging a clutch of bloody pheasants in both hands—and, in her stylish coat, fur hat, designer jeans, and suede boots, still managing to look as if she had stepped out of the pages of *Town & Country*. Kate, who had never fired a gun before meeting William, had already proven herself to be a crack shot.

Kate made her biggest splash to date at William's passing out (graduation) from Sandhurst on a blustery day in December 2006, when she wore a fire-engine red wool coat, black leather gloves, knee-high leather boots, and a broad-brimmed hat with a large bow designed by famed British milliner Philip Treacy. The Queen also wore red, but a protocol calamity was narrowly averted when courtiers decided that Miss Middleton's coat was scarlet, while Her Majesty's was claret.

It scarcely mattered that Kate wasn't invited to sit in the royal box—she and her parents were given front-row grandstand seats between two of William's three godfathers, Baron Brabourne and King Constantine of Greece. (The third godfather was Prince Charles's friend and mentor Sir Laurens van der Post, who died in 1996 at the age of ninety.)

The previous April, Harry had struggled to keep from laughing when the Queen paused before him while inspecting the troops. Now Kate laughed openly as she watched William try to contain himself as Granny stopped to give him a quizzical look. In fact, Kate seldom took her eyes off William throughout the half-hour-long ceremony. At one point, she leaned over to her mother and whispered, "I love the uniform. It's so, so sexy."

Notwithstanding the endearing exchange between Her Majesty and her favorite grandson, there was no doubt who had stolen the show that day.

"Kate Reigns at William's Parade" proclaimed the next day's *Daily Telegraph*. Headlines like that had the impact Kate was aiming for. After carrying odds of five to one against a royal proposal of marriage for months, British bookmakers dropped the odds to two to one before they stopped taking bets altogether—so certain was the prospect of an imminent engagement.

Unfortunately, not all the press coverage was flattering. Within days, newspapers were attacking Carole Middleton for chewing gum throughout the ceremony. They also carried reports that when she couldn't hear someone, Kate's bourgeois mom was in the habit of saying "Pardon?" instead of the aristocracy's more to the point "What?" Carole also committed the cardinal sin of boorishly asking for directions to the "toilet" rather than the presumably more acceptable "lavatory."

Behind closed doors, Kate did not disguise how upset she was about the attacks on her mother, who was being ridiculed for being an "insufferably middle-class," brash, gum-snapping social climber. Soon the line "doors to manual"—"Will flight attendants please secure the cabin doors" in the United States—would become a widely aped one-liner used to remind people of Carole Middleton's work history as a flight attendant.

William's grandmother, who devoured the racing forms and tabloids every morning, read the stories about Kate's allegedly ill-bred family and was not amused. "The Queen admires people who do honest work," Lady Margaret Rhodes said, "and she doesn't like it when people are made fun of." Her Majesty was particularly unhappy with the unflattering nickname her grandson's girlfriend was now saddled with: "Waity Katie."

The Queen decided to send a message about where Kate stood in the royal firmament. Miss Middleton had waited for years to be invited by the Queen to join the royal family for Christmas brunch at Sandringham. Now, in fairy-tale fashion, a footman arrived at the door of her Chelsea flat with the coveted gold-embossed invitation that began "The Master of the Household has received her Majesty's command to invite Catherine Middleton to Sandringham. . . ." It was the first time the Queen had invited any senior royal's girlfriend to Christmas at Sandringham.

No one was more surprised than William when Kate respectfully declined. Kate explained that as long as she was not even engaged to Prince William, she did not want to be the one responsible for breaking royal tradition. Besides, this would be the first Christmas without her grandmothers, Dorothy and Valerie, and Kate wanted to celebrate the holiday as she always did, with her own family—this time at Jordanstone House, an eighteenth-century estate the Middletons rented north of St. Andrews. The Queen understood, especially when she was told that Kate's family was spending the holidays in her beloved Scotland.

To a great extent, Kate's decision to begin pressuring William for a commitment was born of real concern for her own safety. Now that William was serving in the military, she was left on her own—and without the royal protection that came with being the Heir's fiancée—to deal with the increasingly bold paparazzi. One of William's former protection officers observed that there were "some genuinely scary moments" when photographers swerved in front of her car or chased her down the street on foot. "She was, to some extent, afraid."

Yet as far as William was concerned, Kate was simply fed up with the waiting game and was now resorting to ultimatums—no ring, no cozy Christmas at Sandringham. Humiliated, he spent much of Christmas week on the phone to his girlfriend, demanding to know why she felt the need to embarrass him by turning down the Queen's invitation. Even out shooting with Prince Philip and Prince Charles, William stopped frequently to have yet another spat with Kate over the phone. At the eleventh hour, William canceled his plans to join Kate's family in Scotland—a crushing disappointment for Kate, but nothing, her mother reassured her, that couldn't be overcome.

Unaware of the turmoil brewing behind the scenes, the press and public viewed an engagement announcement as a fait accompli. Diana's private secretary, Patrick Jephson, predicted in the *Spectator* that William would propose on January 9, Kate's twenty-fifth birthday. The *Times* concurred. Miss Middleton's "elegance, dignity, and beauty" made her "the People's Choice."

Not everyone was convinced, as it turned out. Back at Buckingham Palace and Clarence House, a small group of courtiers who had never been sold on Kate as future queen material watched with mounting interest as cracks began to appear in the relationship between Kate and the Heir. Increasingly, William was taking his breaks from tank training at an army base in Dorset to party hard in London with a number of nameless young women, leaving Kate to deal with the ever-present cadre of photographers camped on her doorstep.

Tensions bubbled to the surface in late March 2007, when Kate and William arrived together back at the Cheltenham Gold Cup, the scene of her triumphant appearance inside the royal enclosure just one year before. This time, a grim-faced Kate, hiding behind dark glasses, trailed after her downcast prince. "If there was ever a picture of two people who weren't getting along," Alan Hamilton said, "that was it." But the press and public would only see the brewing signs of trouble in retrospect; for now, Fleet Street was poised to break the news of a royal engagement.

The Prince of Wales was among those eager to learn that his son had finally popped the question. But when William came to him complaining that he felt "cornered" and "rushed," Prince Charles consulted his wife. Like everyone who had come in contact with Kate, Camilla liked and admired her. What the Duchess of Cornwall did object to were Kate's working-class roots.

As the granddaughter of a baron and a descendant of the Stuart bloodline—the Stuarts ruled England from 1603 to 1714—not to mention a descendant of one of the illegitimate sons of Charles II, Camilla was a distant relation of the future Charles III and a bona fide aristocrat. Moreover, her great-grandmother Alice Keppel was Edward VII's mistress, an intimate connection to the royal family that Camilla had always taken immense pride in. Throughout her life, Camilla moved in royal circles: "It was simply second nature to her," said a Parker Bowles family friend. Despite her hearty laugh and earthy demeanor—not to mention the fact that as the divorced mistress of a prince she herself hardly seemed qualified to marry a future monarch—Camilla was at heart "an awful snob."

Camilla had long lobbied on behalf of the highborn beauties with hyphenated names who swarmed around the Heir. It was she, after all, who along with another of Charles's mistresses, Baroness Tryon, handpicked Lady Diana Spencer to become Charles's bride. Barring a homegrown blueblood, then the member of a foreign royal household would, Camilla believed, also be preferable to a descendant of coal miners whose mother had grown up in public housing and once worked as a flight attendant. (Camilla was unaware at the time that Kate and William are, in fact, distant cousins.)

Then there was the matter of Carole Middleton, who was increasingly being portrayed in the press as a gauche opportunist. As much as she liked Kate, Camilla, who felt she knew a schemer when she saw one, feared her mother. "Camilla has a way of drawing you in and making you feel comfortable," another ex-mistress of Charles said. "But in the end it's really all about keep your friends close and your enemies closer. It's her way of keeping her eye on you."

There were other, more practical things for Charles to consider before offering advice to his son. If Charles was going to be an effective monarch, he needed to win over the hearts and minds of his future subjects—much the same as his mother, the Queen, had done. Charles and Camilla needed to be the stars of the royal show, but that was not going to happen as long as the public was consumed with the ongoing saga of the young prince and his romance with a dazzling commoner.

Internecine rivalry among the Windsors was nothing new. According to veteran journalist and Diana's friend Richard Kay, "Members of the royal family simply cannot stand being upstaged." Charles resented being overshadowed by Diana, and now he and Camilla were both being left in the dust while the press scrambled to cover Kate and William. National polls consistently showed that the overwhelming majority of Britons wanted William, not Charles, to succeed Elizabeth on the throne. If William and Kate were to continue at this rate vacuuming up all the attention, the inevitable result would be increased calls for Charles to step aside.

During a somber meeting on April 11, 2007, among the portraits and busts in Clarence House's cluttered drawing room, Charles offered his elder son an ultimatum: either propose to Kate now or break up with her. It wouldn't be fair to Kate, Prince Charles insisted, to keep dragging things out.

On Friday the 13—two days after William made the call that had shattered Kate's world—the prince and his tight band of Old Etonian pals drowned their sorrows in zombies and Dom Pérignon. "Everything is fine," he reassured his friends. "Let's drink the menu!" Before he picked up the $17,000 tab William asked the DJ to play the Rolling Stones classic "You Can't Always Get What You Want" and hit the dance floor. "I'm free!" the flush-faced prince proclaimed as friends rushed to steady him. "I'm *freeeee*!"

So, William quickly discovered, was Kate. In the immediate aftermath of the stunning, seemingly out-of-the-blue breakup, Carole secretly took her shell-shocked daughter to Dublin ostensibly to support Middleton family friend Gemma Billington at the opening of her art exhibition. But in truth, Carole and Kate needed time to regroup. Mother and daughter put their heads together and came up with a strategy for winning William back. Urging Kate not to mope, Carole suggested that instead she pick herself up and set out to make William appreciate what he would now be missing. To shore up her confidence, Michael reminded his daughter of the Middleton clan's ancient motto: *Fortis in Arduis* ("Brave in Difficulties").

At first, Kate struggled to appear unfazed. Hiding swollen eyes behind oversized sunglasses and with her brother, James, at the wheel, she went back to her Jigsaw office to pick up files that she could work on at home. Coworker Philip Higgs observed that Kate was "very emotional and on edge" as she stuffed papers into a cardboard box. Expressions of sympathy from concerned colleagues only made matters worse.

"It's because of his daddy!" Kate unexpectedly declared. Higgs recalled that "everyone raised their eyebrows" over this peek at "what she really thought, what was really going on behind the scenes." Kate had been "trying to keep it together," he added, but "momentarily lost her cool."

"It's really tough on her, but she handles it well," said Gemma Billington. "It's funny how you think people are different, but we are all just muddling our way through life. Whoever you happen to be going out with, you have to take the rough with the smooth."

William's ex-girlfriend wasn't about to crumble again, not for an instant. Looking far from heartbroken, Kate slipped into a series of microminiskirts and returned to London's club scene with Pippa riding shotgun.

Kate's bubbly younger sister had also had her share of romances with wealthy—and in some cases titled—young men, which led to them being labeled the "wisteria sisters" because of their "ferocious ability to climb."

Soon newspapers were brimming with stories about how much fun Kate seemed to be having with a succession of young men. She also signed on with the Sisterhood, an all-female rowing crew training for a twenty-one-mile race across the English Channel. As part of their training, the Sisterhood rowed up and down the Thames three times a week in a dragon boat, with Kate at the stern manning the tiller in her skintight racing suit.

Gone was the muted, classic, landed gentry look favored by the royals. Now that her diet and exercise regimen had taken her down a dress size, the Heir's ex-girlfriend tossed her sensible shoes and tweeds in favor of painted-on designer jeans and sky-high, slit-to-the hip miniskirts. "Far from appearing shattered," noted the *Daily Mail*, "Kate sans William is cutting a frankly far sexier figure."

Sir Henry Ropner agreed. An Eton schoolmate of William's and the dashing heir to a shipping fortune, Ropner had once dated William's old Africa flame Jecca Craig. When Ropner split from Craig, it was William who flew to Kenya to comfort her. Now the tables were turned, and it was Ropner who was doing the comforting. According to Jules Knight, when it was reported that Ropner and Kate were now in each other's arms on the dance floor, the Heir realized "he'd made a huge mistake." (Ropner's comparatively full head of tousled light brown hair was a particular sticking point for William; newspapers were already expressing concern about the twenty-five-year-old Heir's rapidly thinning pate. By 2007 William, who was also very sensitive about being photographed wearing the glasses he needed to correct his nearsightedness, often opted for wearing baseball caps whenever he and Kate went out in public.)

On May 26, precisely six weeks after their breakup, William and Kate were invited separately to a party at the seventeenth-century manor house home of their mutual friend, successful amateur jockey Sam Waley-Cohen. (A great-great-grandson of Shell Oil's founder and the grandson of a viscount, Waley-Cohen would go on to win numerous important races, including the Grand National.) Holed up together in a separate room, William pleaded with Kate to take him back.

Unbeknownst to Fleet Street, Kate and William were back in each other's arms by the time they showed up at the Household Cavalry's risqué "Freakin' Naughty" revels—a barracks costume party celebrating the end of troop leader training. Mingling with the other saucily dressed guests, William wore a London bobby's helmet and hot pants while Kate's naughty nurse getup included fishnet stockings and a starched white uniform with obligatory plunging neckline. Shortly after midnight, Kate's chastened prince took her by the hand and led her to his barracks quarters, where they spent the night.

Years later, Kate spoke of the rockiest period in their relationship. "I, at the time, wasn't very happy about it," she said of the abrupt breakup. "But actually, it made me a stronger person. You find things about yourself that maybe you hadn't realized." William was equally reflective. The split was "all about finding a bit of space and finding ourselves, about growing up—and it all worked out for the better."

On Saturday, June 30, Kate was behind the wheel of her black Audi when she was nearly run off the road in central London by four cars full of paparazzi. She pulled over, got out of the car, and, standing in a driving rain, begged her pursuers to stop. "There is going to be an accident," she told them. "Someone is going to get killed." Not surprisingly, they never paused to look up from their cameras.

The next day, the world would learn definitively that Kate and her prince were back together when Kate appeared in the royal box at the highly anticipated Concert for Diana. The charity event, held at the newly constructed Wembley Stadium on what would have been the Princess of Wales's forty-sixth birthday, was watched by a television audience of one billion people in 140 countries. For six hours Kate, seated two rows behind William, never made eye contact with him as they both clapped, swayed, and sang along with Elton John, Duran Duran, Rod Stewart, Tom Jones,

Kanye West, Pharrell Williams, and other superstars. When Britain's No. 1 group, Take That, sang their hit "Back for Good," all eyes were on the freshly reunited couple.

After the event's wild after-party, William and Kate nestled on a white leather couch in a dark corner and quietly discussed their future together. For the moment, no marriage plans were on the horizon—and Kate, who at twenty-five was only five months older than William, now was willing to accept that.

Yet the safety issues persisted. Kate remained ceaselessly in the crosshairs of tabloid photographers. After each potentially dangerous encounter with the paparazzi, William would instruct Harbottle & Lewis to fire another warning shot over Fleet Street's bows, threatening to cut off access to the coverage of royal events and possible legal action.

The Queen had grown increasingly fond of the resilient young woman who had so cleverly won back the heart of her grandson. But on the issue of providing her royal protection, she adhered to long-standing rules. Only members of the royal family or those who were about to become members—fiancées, in this case—were entitled to royal protection, she was reminded by the Men in Gray. It was left to Prince Charles to reach into his own deep pockets—as Duke of Cornwall his annual estimated income was in the neighborhood of $30 million—and pay for Kate's security detail. "It breaks my heart," he told his deputy secretary, "to see Kate chased down like an animal by those awful people."

Even as William fought to ensure his girlfriend's safety, he was still eager to put himself in harm's way on the battlefield. Kate and the Queen both understood that, as an army officer and the future titular head of all UK armed forces, William wanted to serve in combat just as Harry was doing in Afghanistan. Although both princes had a price on their heads, the future king was clearly the most sought-after prize for both the Taliban and Al-Qaeda—dead or alive.

It was terrifying enough for Kate to watch the love of her life take to the skies during the next phase of his military training at RAF Cranwell's Central Flying School. On April 11, 2008, she watched proudly as Prince

Charles, acting as air chief marshal, pinned his newly certified son with his provisional wings.

Unfortunately, by this time William—accompanied by a flight instructor and a three-person crew—had already gotten into the habit of buzzing Highgrove, Sandringham, and of course Oak Acre in Bucklebury at the controls of a $17 million twin-rotor Chinook troop carrier. The press finally got wind of William's joyrides—which wound up costing British taxpayers more than $65,000—after he picked up Harry at his barracks and flew off to a stag party on the Isle of Wight. When William actually landed a Chinook in the Middletons' backyard, aviation analyst and RAF-trained pilot Jon Lake slammed the maneuver as "ridiculous and inappropriate." William was subsequently denounced on the floor of Parliament for his "reckless" behavior, but that scarcely mattered. Once Clarence House had pressured the Heir's RAF superiors into taking the rap for the ill-advised sorties, the entire matter quickly blew over. "Even our editors thought the idea of Kate waving up at her aviator prince was rather charming," one reporter said. "He wouldn't be the first RAF pilot to buzz his girlfriend's house."

The Queen finally granted her grandson his fondest wish in late April 2008, when she reluctantly signed off on a plan that would allow him to see action with his unit in Afghanistan—albeit for just thirty hours. Undertaken in total secrecy, Prince William's mission was to fly a C-17 Globemaster troop transport to the front lines in Afghanistan and retrieve the body of a fallen British soldier.

Kate was one of the few who knew about the secret mission in Afghanistan, and she told a friend she "held her breath until it was over. I was so worried." That summer, she was blissfully unaware when William undertook another risky mission, this time while serving aboard the frigate HMS *Iron Duke* as part of his Royal Navy training. At the controls of a Lynx twin-engine battlefield helicopter, William chased down a cigarette boat northeast of Barbados and seized 1,900 pounds of cocaine worth an estimated $80 million. "He told me how exciting it was," Kate said. "I'm glad I didn't know until it was all over."

Kate had, in the interim, cleared a major hurdle of her own. For the first time, she served as a stand-in for William at the wedding of his cousin Peter Phillips (Princess Anne's son) and Autumn Kelly on May 17, 2008, at St. George's Chapel in Windsor Castle. Even more important, the occasion marked Kate's first in-person meeting with the Queen. Her Majesty "had wanted to meet Kate for a while," William later said, "so it was very nice of her to come over and say hello. There was a little chat, and they got on really well." Kate and Her Majesty would go on to form a strong bond, but in truth that first meeting struck William's girlfriend as anticlimactic. "It was in amongst a lot of other guests," she said, "and she was very friendly and welcoming—and no, it was fine."

Now that William's military training was coming to an end, his father and grandmother were eager to see him step up as a full-time royal in early 2009. The Palace had already whipped up a dizzying schedule of cornerstone layings, school visits, and whistle-stop tours, but the Heir was far from enthusiastic. "Kate pointed out rather rightly," a longtime friend of the Middletons said, "that if there was something else he wanted to do, now was the time to do it."

William's unilateral decision to sign up for five years in the RAF as a search-and-rescue helicopter pilot sent shock waves through the Palace. Stationed for additional flight training at RAF Shawbury, Flight Lieutenant Wales moved to Shropshire, a two-and-a-half-hour drive northwest of Bucklebury. Seeking to preserve a modicum of privacy, he opted out of living on the base with the other officers, choosing instead to move into a farmhouse on the grounds of a sprawling country estate. While the Defense Department insisted William was being treated like any other officer, his new residence was opulent compared to life at Shawbury's bachelor officers' quarters. There were tennis courts, a swimming pool, even stables. There was also a guest room for Harry, who had just broken up with longtime girlfriend Chelsy Davy and was also stationed at Shawbury for Army Air Corps training.

Harry remembered the place as "cozy, charming, just up a narrow country lane and behind some thickly canopied trees." The freezer was crammed with meals—"creamy chicken and rice, beef curry"—that had been prepared by Prince Charles's chefs at Highgrove. Unfortunately because of the proximity of the stables, Harry added, "there was a horse smell in every room."

Not that it mattered to Kate, who drove up to spend weekends in Shropshire when her Willy couldn't make the drive down to Bucklebury. On one of those occasions when the prince was spending time with the Middletons, two burglars tried to break into the farmhouse and were surprised when four bodyguards descended on them, guns drawn.

The Heir's decision to postpone his entry into the Firm was his own, but some of the blame inevitably fell on Kate. "She was always encouraging him to take control of his life and chart his own course," said an Eton chum of William's. "That's not exactly what a prince's job entails."

No longer with Jigsaw but still technically in the employ of Party Pieces, Kate labored under expectations of another sort. Was she, the Queen had inquired, involved in any philanthropic endeavors? Raising money for charity, after all, was one of the primary responsibilities of anyone seeking to be a member of the royal family. Prince Charles had raised more than a billion dollars over the years for a wide range of causes, Prince Harry was building an orphanage for African children whose parents had died of AIDS, and William was working to improve the lives of England's inner-city homeless. Palace operatives let it be known to Kate that, if she was going to join the Firm, lining up charities and causes of her own was an absolute must.

Kate, already smarting from the suggestion that she was either lazy or simply a shirker, moved quickly to silence her critics—and, more important, to appease Her Majesty. The previous September Kate had made a fairly spectacular debut as a charity fundraiser, donning pink leg warmers, yellow hot pants, a green sequined top, and lace-up roller skates for the Day-Glo Midnight Roller Disco. The event raised more than $200,000 for a new surgical ward at Oxford Children's Hospital, but that impressive achievement was overshadowed by the unladylike tumble Kate took and the awkward moments when she was splayed out legs akimbo on the floor—all documented in photos that appeared everywhere the next day.

Since then, Kate had embraced other causes, most notably actress Emma Samms's Starlight Children's Foundation that raised money to help seriously ill children and their families. Kate brought William along to the charity's swank Boodles Boxing Ball at London's Lancaster Hotel and later hosted a glittering charity auction—in the end using her undeniable star power to raise hundreds of thousands of dollars for the foundation.

Yet even though the entire Middleton family was pitching in to make Kate a success as lady bountiful, there was no stopping the ceaseless barrage of embarrassing stories targeting her family. Like Pippa, James Middleton at first enjoyed basking in his sister Kate's reflected glory. Yet in the end, he proved ill-equipped to handle it. Dyslexic and suffering from attention deficit disorder, James always felt like the failure in the family—struggling to get through school when his sisters were both star scholars and athletes. "It's forever frustrating to be compared," he later observed. "I did so badly in school, my poor mum was reduced to tears." Michael Middleton, in the meantime, complained that James's expensive education had been "a waste of money."

Although the prince quickly won Kate's brother over when he showed "genuine love" for James's beloved jet-black cocker spaniel, Ella, James's feelings of worthlessness intensified as Kate's popularity exploded. "I can't count the number of times I walked out the front door," James recalled, "to find a sea of photographers on the doorstep, bitterly disappointed that it is me, rather than William."

Somehow, James managed to get accepted by Edinburgh University—but dropped out after the first year to start his own cake-baking enterprise under the Party Pieces corporate umbrella in 2007. Kate's little brother was on no one's radar until late August, when several disturbing images of the then-twenty-one-year-old found their way onto the internet. A journalist printed them and showed them to Kate's mother and sister. In one shot taken at a booze-fueled party, James and other men are shown either in French maid costumes or naked; two of the men simulate an oral sex act. In a separate photo, James is wearing a French maid's outfit and full makeup; in yet another, he is stretched out for all intents and purposes nude in front of a fireplace; in another, he gives the middle finger gesture.

Carole and Pippa laughed it off. So did William, who had been caught doing more than his share of embarrassing things over the years. Kate was not so sanguine. She knew that Camilla and certain old-school courtiers were still opposed to a working-class commoner like Miss Middleton marrying a future king. Stirring up gossip was one thing, but did someone inside the Palace plant these mortifying snapshots in the press?

Matters only got worse when an additional handful of images appeared in the tabloids showing James and his chums employing a dead squirrel as a prop in several staged scenarios. In the United Kingdom, kinky sex was one thing, but anything even suggesting the improper treatment of animals—even dead ones—was quite another. Animal rights activists, who had already skewered Kate over her embrace of the royals' hunting culture, were aghast.

With matriarch Carole acting as family crisis manager, the Middletons simply ignored their critics—notwithstanding the occasional flash of temper. After James's twenty-second birthday at Boujis, Carole upbraided photographers as they took pictures of a bleary-eyed James and an equally sloshed Kate collapsing into the back seat of a cab.

Such incidents barely registered as a blip on the screen when it came to royal scandals; since the epic unraveling of her eldest child's marriage, Queen Elizabeth had learned to take it all in stride. But according to her deputy private secretary, even Her Majesty had to sit down when, on July 19, 2009, she was handed that morning's issue of *News of the World*.

"I Called Wills a Fucker: Kate Middleton Uncle Drug & Vice Shock," screamed the paper's front-page headline. The subhead: "Tycoon Who Boasts of Hosting Wills's Villa Holiday Supplies Cocaine and Fixes Hookers."

Kate was horrified. She had always been fond of her uncle Gary, whose antics were part and parcel of Middleton family lore. Like his sister, Carole, Gary had become a multimillionaire before the age of thirty. Founder of a firm that recruited staff for the computer industry, Carole Middleton's younger brother pocketed roughly $23 million when his company was sold for $425 million.

Back in the late summer of 2006, again at Carole's urging, Kate and William accepted Uncle Gary's invitation to spend few days unwinding at his home—vulgarly dubbed La Maison de Bang Bang—on the island of Ibiza off the coast of Spain. When William first arrived with Kate and his longtime pal Guy Pelly, the young men began tossing a tennis ball in the living room, accidentally smashing several glass pyramids Goldsmith had collected over the years. "Hey, you fucker!" Goldsmith shouted—the first words, he later boasted to *News of the World* reporters operating undercover, that he ever said to the prince.

In the piece that the Queen was now poring over in her Buckingham Palace study, Goldsmith blithely admitted to, among many other unsavory things, hiring prostitutes, frequenting live sex shows, and snorting cocaine in rolled-up one hundred euro notes. To make matters worse, Goldsmith bragged during the sting operation that he was very close to his Middleton nieces and nephew and a frequent presence in their lives. Over family dinners and game nights in Bucklebury, Goldsmith teased and joked with the Prince and Kate—"Winding people up is my favorite hobby"—without fear of stepping over the line. According to Goldsmith, no topic was off the table in the Middleton household—not even Kate's breasts. When she suddenly complained that hers were too small, William decreed that "more than a handful is a waste."

As for the distinct possibility that Kate and William would soon wed, Gary crowed to the stealth reporters that he planned on giving the bride away because he was "bloodline—*bloodline*. I'll be the Queen's uncle!"

The seismic furor ignited by Kate's outrageously behaved bad-boy uncle was more than just another bump in the road, and Uncle Gary knew it. Described by friends as being on the verge of committing suicide, Goldsmith was understandably horrified that he may have single-handedly destroyed the possibility of Kate ever becoming queen. He acknowledged that "the wheels came off a little" during that period in his life, and called the Middletons repeatedly to apologize. But Carole and Kate, both holed up in Bucklebury, refused to take his calls.

Uncle Gary would later change the name of Maison de Bang Bang to the more respectable-sounding Villa Tesoro de Oro (House of the Golden Treasure), but the damage was done. Once again Camilla, who had harbored doubts about Kate's origins from the beginning, teamed up with veteran courtiers to sound the alarm. In spite of Kate's own undeniably stellar qualities, could the monarchy really survive the antics of her nouveau riche, off-the-rails relatives?

Kate's detractors inside the Palace, who also complained that her brief stint working at Party Pieces after leaving Jigsaw hardly constituted real work, were not about to stop taking potshots at the Middletons. Camilla's friends leaked the false story that the family's royal connections had landed Party Pieces a multimillion-dollar deal to sell official England World Cup merchandise. Another bit of Palace-generated gossip had Kate's father researching possible coats of arms.

As she had done with her own misbehaving brood, the Queen sailed above the fray, confident that the newest headline-grabbing scandal involving Kate's family would soon blow over. Kate escaped with her family—sans Uncle Gary, of course—to Mustique, where they could sunbathe out of paparazzi camera range behind the high stucco walls of the Robinsons' bougainvillea-covered villa.

William literally rode out the storm in North Wales, practicing rescue flights over the Irish Sea. Less than a month after the bombshell revelations concerning Kate's notorious Uncle Gary rocked the Palace, Kate and William were together again in public—this time at the August 2009 London wedding of his old Eton chum Nick van Cutsem to event planner Alice Hadden-Paton. (Ironically, the bride's older brother, actor Harry Hadden-Paton, would go on to have key roles in both *Downton Abbey* and *The Crown*.) After William rushed up to congratulate the groom, Van Cutsem said, "You'll be next!"

If it was a fait accompli, Kate certainly did not feel it. Now that she qualified for royal protection and was followed everywhere she went by bodyguards, the Heir's girlfriend was beginning to chafe at the idea of driving for hours to spend stolen moments in a farmhouse that smelled of horses—an experience made all the worse by the equine allergy Kate had suffered from since childhood. There were also William's increasingly frequent training trips to Wales, where he would eventually be stationed. With her prince away for days at a time, she felt more isolated and alone than ever. "Yes, it's fine what William is doing," the Queen commented to a guest at a Buckingham Palace garden party honoring seniors. "But I hope Kate won't feel too lonely when they're up in North Wales. It can get," she added with a feigned shiver and a faint smile, "so awfully cold."

By way of making it clear that Kate still had her backing, Queen Elizabeth had already given the couple the keys to their own love nest at Balmoral: Brochdu, a totally refurbished, nineteenth-century three-bedroom, granite-walled farmhouse overlooking the River Muick that was not far from Charles's pad at Birkhall. But before William and Kate could snuggle up at Balmoral, Kate kept the home fires burning in Wales while William was dispatched on his first official overseas assignment substituting for the Queen—alone.

Not surprisingly, "When are you and Kate getting married?" was the question repeated with cloying frequency at every one of the stops on William's breakneck five-day tour of New Zealand and Australia. His default reply: "Wait and see."

How she'd have loved Kate, and how she'd have loved seeing this love you have found together.

—Harry, in his wedding toast to Kate and William

4

"Our Lives Will Never Be the Same"

"Something I Wanted to Do For Myself"

"The Happiest Job in the World"

Kate had waited nearly a decade for this moment, and yet when it came it took her by complete surprise. On October 20, 2010, William and Kate went fishing on Lake Rutundu, a haven for large equatorial rainbow trout nestled at 12,500 feet above sea level on the northeastern slopes of Mount Kenya. When they were done, he went to his backpack, pulled out the blue velvet ring box he had been carrying with him for days, and got down on one knee to propose. Even after all this time, "Waity Katie" was taken aback. "It was," she later said, "a *total* shock."

William admitted that he had been dragging his feet before making the decision to propose. "As every guy out there will know," he later said, "it takes a certain amount of motivation to get yourself going." Some of the motivation came from higher up the royal food chain. The Queen's Diamond Jubilee celebrating Elizabeth II's sixty years on the throne was scheduled to take place the first week in June 2012. Less than two months later, London was scheduled to host the Olympic Games. Cramming another major event like a royal wedding—*the* royal wedding—into such an already packed calendar was deemed not an option. That meant asking Kate and the world to wait until 2013—again, not an option.

With a 2011 wedding date a fait accompli, William turned his attention to the circumstances of the proposal itself. There was never any question in his mind about the venue. "The African continent holds a very special place in my heart," William later explained. "It is the place my father took my brother and me shortly after our mother died. And when deciding where best to propose to Catherine, I could think of no more fitting place than Kenya to get down on one knee."

It would be a month before news of the engagement was announced via the Queen's Facebook page and Twitter. "It's brilliant news," cooed Her Majesty, while Charles sounded more relieved than anything else. "I'm thrilled," he said. "They have been practicing long enough!" The Duchess of Cornwall was snagged by reporters coming out of a West End matinee performance of the hit musical *Wicked*. "It's the most brilliant news," Camilla said. "I am just so happy and so are they. It's wicked." Harry was "delighted" with the news. "It means I get a sister," he said, "which I've always wanted."

Then–Prime Minister David Cameron went so far as to predict a royal wedding would unite the country, but Patrick Jephson was more concerned about what would happen to Kate. "There will be a tidal wave of sentimental slush," said Diana's ex–private secretary. "But if Kate were my sister, I'd tell her to get a good prenup." (Like all Windsor brides before her, Kate did not.)

Jephson went on to publicly urge Kate to consider what kind of life she wanted inside the royal family—and eventually as the Queen of England. "If they want her to be a wife, a pretty face, to keep quiet and stay in the background, get that straight now," he cautioned. "If they want her to be more active and carry on Diana-style, let's get that straight, too. If you get it right, it's the best job in the world. It can be fantastic. It doesn't have to be a drain, the way Prince Charles sometimes sees it. William should set off with making it the happiest job in the world."

Even before their engagement was announced to rapturous applause,

Kate and William had begun crafting a quiet life for themselves far away from the spotlight on a remote island off the rugged, windswept coast of North Wales. As soon as he completed training in September 2010, William signed up for three years with 22 Squadron, C Flight, as a search-and-rescue pilot and was given orders to report to RAF Valley air base on Anglesey Island.

There was never any doubt in William's mind that once they were wed, Kate, who had chalked up tensions in their relationship to their extended periods apart after leaving St. Andrews, would follow him to Wales. "I am not interested," she bluntly declared, "in a long-distance relationship. They never work."

Finally—and firmly—headed toward the altar, Kate began supervising the move into their new $1,000-a-month, four-bedroom, two-bathroom, slate-roofed, whitewashed stone farmhouse, just twenty-five miles south of the air base. The young couple's comfortable rental—on the Bodorgan Estate owned by Lord and Lady Meryick—had direct private beach access, four fireplaces, and large bay windows with sweeping views of the Newborough Forest and the Irish Sea. Yet the property was also isolated and therefore vulnerable in the eyes of Scotland Yard—so much so that the couple's security detail was beefed up by an additional fifteen officers. Total annual cost to the British taxpayers: $2 million.

Like fellow officers' significant others, Kate was left to her own devices while William did several twenty-four-hour shifts per week. She continued to work remotely for Party Pieces, taking and organizing the photographs to be used in displays, in catalogues, and on the company website. She also drove into town to go grocery shopping at the local Waitrose supermarket in Menai Bridge, browse the stalls at the Beaumaris Artisan Market, shop for linens at James Pringle Weavers, or pick up barbecue at the Bryn Celyn Farm Shop—all without fear of being run off the road by paparazzi. When William was around, they often dropped into their favorite pub, the White Eagle overlooking Rhoscolyn Bay, for fish and chips. Their domestic life together now was, he said, "incredibly easy, because we took the time."

Unlike the general public, she was painfully aware of the danger her fiancé faced every day as a search-and-rescue helicopter pilot. "I jump," she told one of the few women she befriended on the island, "every time the phone rings. But after a while, you have to stop that or you'll go crazy."

Much of the time, Kate found herself listening to William tell harrowing life-and-death stories—heartbreaking accounts of the carnage and death he routinely witnessed—and struggling to contain her own tears as she consoled him.

Even before he officially started his tour of duty, William was on a training mission when a taxi driver went on a shooting rampage in northwestern Cumbria county, killing twelve people before taking his own life. Because so many helicopters were needed to transport the victims to area hospitals, William's Sea King helicopter was rerouted to save a mountain climber who had fallen off a cliff. Sadly, the young man succumbed to his injuries before William's crew could get him to a hospital.

Not all William's early rescue attempts ended in tragedy. Not long after the young climber's death, the prince piloted his chopper through a storm to pluck a heart attack victim off an oil rig in the Irish Sea and airlift him to an emergency room. The man, who like many of those William would rescue was stunned to see the future king at the controls, survived.

Anglesey was more than just the couple's first totally out-in-the-open home together, it was the place Kate made her official debut as a working royal, or at least a soon-to-be one. On February 24, 2011, Kate, wearing the same chic beige Shetland herringbone overcoat she had worn to impress Prince Charles at the Cheltenham Gold Cup five years earlier—only now cut off at the knees by designer Katherine Hooker to show off Kate's toned legs—accompanied William to the Trearddur Bay Lifeboat Station to christen her first ship. Since the *Hereford Endeavour* was inflatable, she could only pop open a bottle of champagne and, smiling, pour it over the hull.

Then the princess-to-be embarked on her first walkabout in the blustery cold, shaking hands with well-wishers, effortlessly making small talk, and graciously kneeling to accept flowers from eager young children who would remember this moment for the rest of their lives.

As with any good performance, no one saw the sweat that went into it.

Every detail from the fascinator she wore—pheasant feathers adorned with the insignia of Royal Welch Fusiliers—to her much-rehearsed and flawlessly delivered rendition of the tongue-twisting Welsh national anthem "Hen Wlad Fy Nhadau" ("Land of My Fathers") was calculated to win over the locals.

The *Sun* had said there would be "tremendous pressure on Kate today," and at least one royal expert predicted that she would be "incredibly nervous." In the end, all would agree that Kate Middleton seemed better suited to the role than anyone born into the royal family. Comparisons to Diana were inevitable. Like the late Princess of Wales, Kate had the human touch: she connected with the average person, she was warm and gracious, unaffected. She was undeniably glamorous, already a fashion icon, and yet there was nothing stiff or formal about her.

William basked in the success of his future wife's official debut, beaming as she worked her special brand of magic on the crowd. Both troupers, neither gave the slightest inkling that just four days earlier he had been again turning to her for solace. The prince had tried to rescue another climber—this time a young woman—who had tumbled from a cliff. From his position as copilot, William guided efforts to winch paramedics down to treat her, and then winch the victim back up for transport to the hospital. Sadly, she was pronounced dead on the way. Even for an experienced pilot like William, journalist Duncan Larcombe said, the incident had been "pretty harrowing." One of his fellow search-and-rescue officers conceded that "it does get to you sometimes. You have a job to do, but we're human, after all. We can go to pretty dark places mentally, and I think she obviously pulls him out of it. . . ."

April 29, 2011

Westminster Abbey, London

"It almost looks," a normally blasé US anchorman among the seven thousand reporters covering this moment said, "as if God is having a hand in this." The newly minted Duchess of Cambridge—the Queen bestowed the titles of Duke and Duchess of Cambridge that same day—certainly thought so as she stepped out of the classic 1977 black Rolls-Royce Phantom VI limousine in front of Westminster Abbey. Kate glanced up briefly to see London's ubiquitous gunmetal-gray storm clouds part, then turned to wave to the cheering throng as abbey bells pealed. Meanwhile, Pippa gathered up the nine-foot train of her sister's wedding dress of ivory silk overlaid with Chantilly lace by Alexander McQueen's star designer Sarah Burton.

Kate took her father's arm and glided serenely up the red carpet leading toward the abbey's Great West Door, at nearly one thousand years the oldest door in Britain. Golden sunlight pierced the clouds and fell on Kate's \$1.7 million Cartier Halo tiara, glistening with 739 brilliant-cut diamonds weighing 57 carats. (Kate had wanted to depart from tradition by wearing a simple crown of fresh flowers, but changed her mind when she realized the Queen, who had been given the tiara as an eighteenth-birthday present, wanted to loan it to her for the occasion.) Paired with the tiara were pear-shaped diamond pendant earrings—a gift from Kate's parents. The earrings' oak leaf and acorn motif reflected the oak leaves and acorns in the Middletons' new coat of arms, which Kate had a major hand in designing. The Middleton coat of arms, which would be "impaled"—merged—with William's the moment they were married, was made up of three acorns and oak sprigs, representing Kate and her siblings, and a gold chevron through the center to represent both Carole's maiden name—Goldsmith—her central place in the family, and the family name: Middleton.

Ironically, it was Kate's given name, not her surname, that set off alarm bells at Clarence House. Charles and Camilla each had a royal monogram that consisted of interlocking *C*'s beneath a crown, and they expressed concern that a third royal cypher with a *C* was overkill. Would Kate mind if she changed the spelling of her full name from "Catherine" to "Katherine"? Camilla pointed out that such a change also made sense on the grounds that, to most of the world, she was known simply as Kate. Offended by yet another command from on high essentially aimed at placating Camilla, a fuming William replied on his wife's behalf. The request was nothing less than "insulting," he told his father, not only to Kate but to her entire family. The bizarre suggestion that "Catherine" become "Katherine" simply to make Charles and Camilla happy was summarily dropped.

Unlike Diana, who at twenty years of age had little control of her own wedding ceremony beyond picking the designers of her dress, Kate took charge, insisting on approving even the most minor detail. "She has been made to wait a terribly long time," Countess Mountbatten said. "You can't blame her for wanting everything to be perfectly the way she wants it."

Even the Rolls-Royce that carried the bride and her father to the abbey had been the subject of debate. This was the very vehicle that, just five months before, Charles and Camilla had been riding in when a crowd of anti-monarchists shouting "Off with their heads!" attacked the car with bottles and rocks. Kate was offered another Rolls, but insisted on making a statement: the monarchy was here to stay.

The bouquet Kate clasped as she walked up the aisle, like nearly everything else in the ceremony, was steeped in symbolism. It included sweet william, lily of the valley (Queen Elizabeth's favorite flower), and myrtle from a shrub planted by Queen Victoria using a sprig from *her* wedding bouquet. Kate carried the theme inside the abbey itself, transforming the aisle into an avenue of trees, with six field maples and two hornbeams—all to reflect the newlyweds' love of the English countryside.

Yet nothing was more evocative of the moment's historic importance than Diana's twelve-carat Ceylon sapphire surrounded by fourteen diamonds. Arguably history's most famous engagement ring, it occupied what royals call "pride of place" on the ring finger of Kate's left hand.

Standing ramrod straight at the altar were William, wearing the ceremonial red tunic with blue sash and shamrock-embroidered collar as a colonel in the Irish Guards, and best man (or so the public thought) Harry in his braid-bedecked Blues and Royals uniform. The brothers' calm demeanor masked William's frustration over not having any say in the wedding—not even when it came to what he would wear. William had gone directly to the Queen asking if he could wear his dark blue Household Cavalry frock coat uniform, but since she had appointed him colonel of the Irish Guards only weeks earlier, Her Majesty insisted he wear the regiment's red tunic. "I was given a categorical 'No! You'll wear this!'" William later recalled. "So you don't always get what you want. . . . So you just do as you're told!"

William, who had sported a beard for the first time in public during the Christmas holidays in 2008 and wanted to be bearded during his nuptials, was also forbidden from being anything but clean-shaven. In fairness, the Heir was in uniform, and the century-old ban on beards in the British military was still very much in force. (It would be lifted in 2024.) For her part, Kate was actually a fan of the hirsute look and wanted to exchange vows with a bearded prince. "I think it gives a man's face character," she said when he showed up sporting facial hair at his graduation from the Royal Air Force College Cranwell. "I find it very sexy."

According to Harry, William also was denied the ultimate say when it came to choosing a best man. The Spare wasn't really William's best man—or even his second pick. That honor, though never officially disclosed, went jointly to William's closest pals, James Meade and Thomas van Straubenzee. Kate agreed with William that, as much as she loved Harry, he was too much of a loose cannon to give an official best man's speech before an audience at the reception that was going to include his grandmother the Queen. But once again, William and Kate had little say in the matter. The public had long assumed that each prince would be the other's best man, and the Palace did not want to convey any sense of a rift within the royal family. "The public expected me to be the best man," Harry said, "and thus the Palace saw no choice but to say that I was." (One tidbit, if that is the right word, had not been shared with the public: during a charity expedition to the Arctic, Harry's penis had been stricken with frostbite, and during the wedding weeks later his "todger," as he referred to it, remained a source of considerable pain.)

The guest list had also been something of a sensitive issue. When Kate and William were handed a list that contained the names of 777 people they didn't know, they went straight to the top and asked the Queen what they could do about it. "Get rid of it and start with your friends," she said. "We'll add those we need to in due course. It's your day." Now that Kate was looking out over the crowd of 1,900—of which more than one hundred were directly in line for the throne—she understood what the Queen meant. The newlyweds were free to add the names of the people they actually knew, but the original 777 strangers—all handpicked by the Men in Gray—remained.

Accordingly, with the exception of her new in-laws, Kate still only recognized a relatively small minority of the faces staring back at her in the abbey. There were the famous ones, of course: Elton John, David and Victoria Beckham, Guy Ritchie, Prime Minister David Cameron, who thirty years earlier had slept on the street in hopes of getting a glimpse of newlyweds Charles and Diana. Notably, Kate and William agreed to invite all their old pals from St. Andrews and more than a few old flames. Kate's former boyfriends Willem Marx, Harry Blakelock, and Rupert Finch were there, as were the groom's former love interests Isabella Anstruther-Gough-Calthorpe, Arabella Musgrave, Rose Farquhar, and Jecca Craig.

At the bride's insistence, the Middletons made sure to include some of their favorite Berkshire townsfolk on the guest list. Among those who had been part of Kate's life growing up in Bucklebury were the hamlet's convenience store clerks, the postman, the local grocer, and the local butcher. The bride smiled broadly when she spotted John Haley, owner of her favorite local pub, the Old Boot Inn, seated wearing a cutaway, his top hat in his lap. (Kate dropped into his establishment frequently for a pint. "It's not like cold frothy beer like you have in America," Haley boasted to a guest from the United States. "It's proper beer. Real beer. It's warm beer, but it's wonderful.")

William had also wanted to connect with the common folk. After a small dinner hosted by Prince Charles at Clarence House on the eve of his son's wedding, the groom nervously knocked back a half-dozen Cuba libres (rum and Cokes) as an increasingly alarmed Harry looked on. Gazing out the tall windows, the brothers could see thousands of people camped outside, hoping for a glimpse of the wedding procession the next day.

Suddenly William announced he wanted to mingle with the spectators—"It's the right thing to do!"—and pulled Harry outside. Soon people were rushing up to them, telling William how much they loved Kate, how happy they were for them both. Yet William would later confess to Kate that he was haunted by the memory of Diana's funeral—that the tearful words of praise from total strangers reminded them of the day when they walked through the "tunnel of grief" behind Diana's coffin.

That night, William did not sleep. When he and Harry climbed into the back seat of the custom-made burgundy stretch Bentley that would take them to the abbey, there was no ignoring the fact that William—"His face gaunt, his eyes red," Harry said—was still drunk. "You reek," the Spare blurted to his big brother, and handed him a mint.

Once inside, William, still smelling of rum and visibly shaky on his feet, "looked absolutely terrified," said reporter Duncan Larcombe, who was sitting just a few feet away. While they waited for Kate to arrive, Harry abruptly pulled his brother into the Crypt, a side room off the Poets' Corner where such giants of literature as Geoffrey Chaucer, Rudyard Kipling, and Charles Dickens are buried—not to mention Charles Darwin and Isaac Newton in the "Scientists' Corner" nearby. Harry was trying to get his brother, in Larcombe's words, "to compose himself," but that was easier said than done.

Surrounded by death—among the more than three thousand corpses entombed at the Abbey are Queen "Bloody Mary" Tudor, Queen Elizabeth I, and the beheaded Mary Queen of Scots—both William and Harry were suddenly flooded with memories of their mother's funeral. Both men began pacing, waving their arms in the air to relax themselves—all symptoms, they would eventually discover, of the post-traumatic stress disorder that still plagued them. Larcombe watched as the brothers emerged from the Crypt minutes later "and gave a deep breath. William was ashen." It was clear to others present that this wasn't a simple case of nerves.

William later admitted that he was "sort of paralyzed" by his "deep sadness" over the sudden realization that his mother wasn't there to witness this important moment. "It's the one time since she's died, where I've thought to myself it would be fantastic if she was here," he later explained, "and just how sad really for her, more than anything, not being able to see it." It took some extra moments in the Crypt for William to "sort of prepare myself beforehand," he said, "so that I was sort of mentally prepared. . . . I didn't want any wobbly lips or anything going on."

Kate, who had done her own makeup after taking private lessons with makeup artist Arabella Preston—such was the bride's insistence on controlling even the smallest detail—smiled broadly as she arrived at the altar. "You look beautiful," William told her before whispering to the father of the bride, "I thought this was supposed to be a small family affair." Kate, who had stayed the night before at London's historic Goring Hotel in Belgravia—every prime minister and reigning monarch since 1910 has been welcome there—had spent the night worrying about William's state of mind. He still suffered from night terrors, dreaming of the chase through Paris streets that had ended in his mother's violent death, and of the funeral that had made the world stand still. Would being inside these Gothic walls trigger an anxiety attack, cause him to hyperventilate, or even pass out just as they were about to exchange vows?

To be sure, the groom was anything but laid-back. While Kate walked toward him, clutching her father's arm, William was "constantly clasping his hands together—a sign of apprehension and nerves," observed body language expert Darren Stanton. The groom was also frequently biting his lower lip—"a common self-soothing gesture." But once she was standing before him, William "instantly relaxed, you could see his shoulders drop, his smile widen. Kate calmed him down, she was William's rock."

The bride, who had lost ten pounds so she could slip into her wedding dress, had asked that her wedding ring be resized so that it wouldn't slide off her finger. The job fell to the prestigious London firm of Wartski, which fashioned the band from a sliver of Welsh gold sliced off the same nugget used to make Queen Elizabeth's wedding ring as well as Princess Diana's. Kate neglected to try it on before the ceremony, however, so now William struggled before a global TV audience of three billion people in 180 countries to slip the uncooperative ring on her finger. The resizing explanation aside, others present felt the ring snafu had just as much to do with the groom's drinking, his sleeplessness the night before, and the

PTSD that would plague him for years to come. (William's wedding ring presented no problems—he declined to have one made and, like his grandfather Prince Philip, has never worn one.)

Like Diana, Kate omitted the word "obey" from her wedding vows. When they were finished and pronounced man and wife, an earsplitting roar of approval went up from the crowd listening to the ceremonies being broadcast on speakers outside. By now, Kate was pleased that William seemed to have to overcome whatever anxiety he had been experiencing that most commentators chalked up to "wedding jitters." As they walked outside and climbed into the open horse-drawn 1902 State Landau that would take them past one million cheering, Union Jack–waving well-wishers on the way to Buckingham Palace, William and Kate looked every inch the fairy-tale prince and princess—poised, dignified, confident, and, well, regal. At this moment as they pulled away from Westminster Abbey, Kate looked at William and said, simply, "I'm so happy."

So, too, were those who worked tirelessly to keep the monarchy afloat. The wedding "was an image of vitality and strength mixed with pure joy," rhapsodized Palace veteran Paddy Harverson, communications secretary to the Prince of Wales. "They were the perfect couple enjoying a perfect moment and it gave a lift to the whole country."

From the time they fell in love at St. Andrews to her new life on a windswept island and everything in between—all of it was prelude to this moment on a sunny Friday in late April. Just two months after making her royal debut with the launch of an inflatable rescue boat, Kate stood on the balcony at Buckingham Palace facing a crowd of more than a half-million Britons. The happy couple kissed, but, sensing how disappointed the crowd was with a glancing peck, did it again—this time lingering just long enough to ramp up the decibel level.

Later, following the tradition started in 1863 when wedding photos had been taken of the future Edward VII and Princess Alexandra of Denmark, Kate posed in the Throne Room for portraits of her new blended family. Determined to make a memorable exit, they shot out of the front gates with William behind the wheel of his father's blue Aston Martin Volante convertible with license plates that read JUST WED. Trailing streamers and Mylar balloons with the initials *C* and *W*, they made the three-minute drive to Clarence House to rest—not noticing that the tires were beginning to smoke. William had forgotten to take off the parking brake.

By comparison, the banquet thrown that night for three hundred guests in the "Buckhouse" ballroom—largest of the palace's 775 rooms—went flawlessly. The Prince of Wales, who hosted the evening, lavished praise on his new daughter-in-law: "A wonderful girl; we are so lucky to have her in the family." Harry, who had been told by William he was basically there to introduce Tom van Straubenzee and James Meade as the legitimate best men, instead did fifteen minutes of partly improvised stand-up. The most eye-opening story involved an American fan who promised to make a special wedding gift for Kate—an ermine thong, which Harry proudly held aloft to a collective gasp from the guests. Then a moment of awkward silence—until Kate's laughter gave everyone else permission to do the same.

Aside from repeatedly referring to the newlyweds as "the Dude and Duchess" and mock-apologizing to Kate for "having to marry a bald man," Harry did manage to capture the emotion of the moment. In addition to saying he loved Kate like a sister, the Spare tugged at hearts with his closing remarks. "Mummy: how she'd have loved to have been here," he said, not daring to make eye contact with his father or his brother or Kate for fear of crying. "How she'd have loved Kate, and how she'd have loved seeing this love you've found together." Then, as promised, he introduced the two friends William had selected over him to share the best man honor.

Kate, the real star of the evening—with the possible exception of Her Majesty Queen Elizabeth II—dazzled in a long white satin strapless Sarah Burton gown worn with a white angora bolero. Once the speeches were over, guests moved to the Throne Room, which had been transformed into a nightclub where the newlyweds danced to "You're the One That I Want" from the musical *Grease*. At one point toward the end of the Beatles classic "All You Need Is Love," friends gathered around the happy couple on the dance floor and began chanting, "She loves you, yeah, yeah, yeah," a "very special moment," recalled one guest, "that gave everyone goose bumps."

At 3 a.m., a fireworks display over the Buckingham Palace Garden brought the wedding celebration to an end. The Cambridges were about to head off to their suite of rooms to spend their wedding night, but not before a bleary-eyed and quite pixilated Harry grabbed them both. "I love you, I love you," he said as he began to weep. "Mummy would have been so proud of you."

It was impossible to imagine that anything would surpass the Wedding of the Twenty-First Century. Much of the credit went to the bride, and deservedly so. Not only had she proven over nearly a decade that she truly loved her prince, but she had navigated the treacherous waters of the monarchy with grace, wit, savvy, and style. She was resilient, capable, intelligent, funny, loyal, and kind—soft, understanding, and supportive when those qualities were called for, but Kate was certainly no pushover.

Now that she was officially inside the lion's den, Kate would need to marshal all those qualities and more if she was to survive. A new generation of Men in Gray—the courtiers, advisors, and bureaucrats who Diana accused of undermining her efforts to make the monarchy more relevant—were now intent on exerting control of the newest princess. And she *was*, by order of the Queen, to be addressed as Princess Catherine—a change in Palace protocol, since her formal title was Catherine, Princess William of Cambridge, Duchess of Cambridge, Countess of Strathearn, and Baroness Carrickfergus. Elizabeth II had not made similar allowances for Camilla, who, though by rights now the Princess of Wales, was still to be addressed as Duchess of Cornwall.

The Queen's decision to loosen up the rules for Kate was notable because she invariably followed the strict guidelines set down by the monarchy's entrenched gatekeepers; incredibly, even the sovereign did not wish to run afoul of these shadowy figures. "Be careful, Paul," she had once told

Diana's longtime butler and confidante Paul Burrell. "There are powers at work in this country about which we have no knowledge."

For now, Kate and William were content to resume their more sequestered life in Wales. Prior to the wedding, William's grandmother had agreed that the Cambridges could postpone their full-time royal duties for two and a half years—until his tour of duty with the RAF was up.

Not that the couple wouldn't be dragooned into making the periodic public appearance. With postwedding polls showing that William and Kate were now the most beloved members of the royal family—a Reuters poll actually showed that two-thirds of Britons felt the same affection for Kate that they had had for the late Princess Diana—the Palace would be hard-pressed not to exploit their popularity.

In the long run, there would be no escaping their destiny. Yet there was still the matter of their honeymoon. Kate, who had been so focused on the wedding ceremony itself, gladly turned responsibility for planning their honeymoon over to William. On May 10, 2011, William, who somehow had managed to pull off a surprise proposal in Kenya, whisked Kate away on a private jet bound for one of their favorite spots: the Seychelles. This time they stayed on the North Island in Villa 11, the eight-thousand-square-foot, $5,000-per-night thatched-roof, open-air villa with its own pool and private beach access. After ten days spent snorkeling, scuba diving, surfing, kayaking, and simply lolling on the white sand beach, the couple headed back to London to undertake their first official assignment as a royal couple.

On May 24, the Queen welcomed US President Barack Obama and First Lady Michelle to Buckingham Palace. After being shown to their quarters, the palace's Belgian Suite—last used by William and Kate on their wedding night—the Obamas met the Cambridges in what is arguably the most important room at Buckingham Palace: the opulent, rose-walled 1844 Room. Named after the year Queen Victoria received Russian Czar Nicholas I there, the 1844 Room glittered with blue-and-gold silk-upholstered furniture, crystal chandeliers, and gilt woodwork. It is here where the monarch receives world leaders, accepts diplomats' credentials, and bestows damehoods and knighthoods.

For twenty minutes, Kate, dressed in a $290 off-the-rack beige Reiss bandage-style Shola dress and clutching a small black evening bag, chatted amiably with Michelle Obama about the royal wedding while President Obama quizzed William on his "day job" as an RAF rescue pilot. They also briefly discussed a rapidly developing story back in the United States: the series of tornados that at that moment were tearing through the American Midwest.

Kate had reason to believe that the Obamas would be easy to connect with; two years earlier, during their first official visit to Great Britain, Michelle Obama had been denounced by Fleet Street for having the temerity to place her hand on the Queen's shoulder. Although laying hands on the sovereign constituted an obvious breach of protocol, Her Majesty was touched by the spontaneous gesture of affection. After the Obamas returned home, the Queen and the First Lady forged a bond of friendship, sharing their thoughts on everything from organic gardening and child-rearing via emails, written correspondence, and the occasional phone call.

The next day's headline in the *Daily Mail* failed to mention either the visiting US president or the heir to the British throne: "Michelle Obama Hails Kate, Britain's First Lady of Style . . . and Her £175 Dress That Is Selling Out Across the Country." Within minutes of the Buckingham Palace meeting, the dress had sold out online before overwhelming demand crashed the retailer's website.

Kate and William returned to Anglesey, but the prince managed only a handful of missions before being called back just two weeks later to attend the Queen's private party at Windsor Castle celebrating Prince Philip's ninetieth birthday. Then, in rapid succession: an appearance with the Queen and the rest of the Windsors at the Epsom Derby (Kate wore an off-white jacket over a diaphanous white dress with a "cappuccino-colored" hat); a Kensington Palace fundraising gala for a children's charity (Kate made headlines yet again in a show-stopping pink sequined Jenny Packham gown dripping with Swarovski crystals); and, finally, William's debut riding in the annual Trooping the Colour parade. One of the most important dates on the royal calendar, Trooping the Colour (also known as the Sovereign's Birthday Parade) marks the monarch's official birthday—not his or her *actual* birthday—and is usually held on the second Saturday in June. Why? Edward VII's birthday was in November, and he determined that the weather for reviewing his troops would probably be better in June. While Kate once again garnered praise for her outfit—white Alexander McQueen coat paired with a black basketweave hat—it was William, sporting the traditional bearskin hat, who stole the spotlight.

Just a few weeks later, the Cambridges had been launched on their first official overseas trip, a whirlwind nine-day tour of Canada and the United States—the first time Kate had set foot in North America. From the moment they stepped off the plane in Ottawa, Kate continued her winning streak—at first intimidated by Canadians who showed up in the thousands to scream her name, but growing in confidence with every little girl who rushed up to shyly present the princess with a bouquet.

It quickly became clear to William's stalwart private secretary Jamie Lowther-Pinkerton, who hovered on the sidelines, that Kate was "exceedingly talented" at working the crowd—perhaps with one small exception. "Everybody teases me in the family that I spend far too long chatting," she said with a laugh, adding that she still had "to learn a little bit more" to master the art of the walkabout.

Kate also had to learn to at least appear to be enjoying elaborately staged spectacles with her as the centerpiece. A crowd of a half-million people—nearly two-thirds of Ottawa's population—waved maple leaf flags and cheered wildly as the Cambridges arrived to Canada Day celebrations on Parliament Hill in an open nineteenth-century landau escorted by dozens of Mounties on horseback and 150 bearskin-hatted Canadian Grenadier Guards. With the sun beating down on the couple and temperatures soaring into the nineties, Kate nevertheless stood up to wave at crowds lining the streets. "I'm just so hot," she told Laureen Harper, Canada's First Lady, smiling broadly even as her makeup began to run and the red faux maple leaves adorning her hat began to wilt. "So, so hot! It's incredible."

That evening, an estimated three hundred thousand people showed up for the open-air Canada Day pop concert on Parliament Hill and when the royal couple returned, Kate once again seemed overwhelmed by the crowd's euphoric reaction. No wonder. Already keenly aware of the symbolic importance of her wardrobe, Kate had spent much of the day in red and white—Canada's national colors—and proudly sported on every outfit the diamond Maple Leaf brooch given to the late Queen Mother in 1939.

Now, for the concert, Kate wore an eye-catching purple Issa jersey dress that, said one journalist, "made it impossible to miss her from a mile away." Despite the fact that Kate insisted she didn't want to be seen as "just a clothes horse," wrote the *Daily Mail*'s Rebecca English, "Kate does not disappoint." During her first twenty-four hours on Canadian soil, Kate wore five different outfits with three different hairstyles.

Parallels with her adored late mother-in-law were inescapable, and never more so than when she visited the playroom at a pediatric cancer ward at Sainte-Justine University Hospital in Montreal. Kate, like Diana before her, exuded warmth and empathy as she focused her attention on each child, asking them about their favorite games, their artwork, their friends, their pets. Whenever one of the older children wanted to talk about their cancer and the treatment they were undergoing, Kate listened patiently, asked questions, offered encouragement. "Princess Catherine was just amazing, and so was Prince William," one nurse observed. "It reminded us all so much of the video we used to see of Diana, the way she bent down to the child's level and made eye contact. You knew she cared, and you know Kate cares."

After sailing up the St. Lawrence River aboard the Canadian frigate *Montreal*, Kate looked on from the shore as her husband expertly landed a Royal Canadian Air Force CH-124 Sea King helicopter on Prince Edward Island's Dalvay Lake as part of a search-and-rescue demonstration. Then Kate got in on the action, racing against Prince William in opposing dragon boats. William was one of the twenty rowers on his crew, but all eyes were, not surprisingly, on his bride. Kate was given the tiller—a nod to her widely photographed stint as the "sweep," or steerer, aboard the Sisterhood's dragon boat during the couple's brief breakup in 2007. Going head-to-head for the first time, neither was about to give in without a fight.

But in the end, William's boat pulled in ahead of Kate's by inches—and no one seemed more excited than the prince. "It's not that often," he said as he climbed out onto the pier, "that I beat her at anything!"

After a quick trip to Yellowknife, capital of Canada's Northwest Territories, the couple took a seaplane ride to remote Blachford Lake where they sifted through pelts, examined a wigwam, and ended up being taken to an uninhabited island where they dined on reindeer steaks and Arctic char.

Next stop: the province of Alberta, where they donned white Stetsons—a Calgary tradition—western shirts, jeans, and cowboy boots to press a giant button that officially started the iconic Calgary Stampede Parade. Kate clapped wildly and cheered along with the crowd during the bull-riding and bronco-busting competitions, but the most memorable moment of the trip was when she knelt to hug Diamond Marshall, a six-year-old girl who had lost her hair to chemotherapy.

Diamond, whose mother had died of cancer just four years earlier at age thirty-two, wrote a touching letter to the Palace saying that she had watched the royal wedding from her hospital bed and that Kate "looked pretty. . . . My Mommy's in heaven with Princess Diana. . . . I like playing princess dress-up. My favorite princess is Aurora," she wrote, referring to the title character in Disney's *Sleeping Beauty*. "Who is yours? I would really like to meet you. Do you want to meet me, too?"

Diamond was selected to present the bouquet to Kate, but when Kate reached down to accept it, the little girl rushed up to hug her. Kate, wide-eyed with surprise, gave her a lingering hug back. The real-life princess complimented Diamond on her dress, and the two chatted for a few moments before Kate was pulled away. Diamond's stepmother, Danielle Marshall, praised Kate for being "so lovely and so gracious. For a little girl who has dreamed of meeting a princess it was a dream come true." As for Diamond's reaction: "She told me she liked the flowers a lot. She was as fancy as she looks on the TV." (Sadly, after battling her cancer on and off for years, Diamond died in 2014 at the age of nine.)

Moments like these would be captured on video and go viral—cementing the image of Kate as Diana 2.0. Yet, just as they had with William's beloved late mother, such encounters with the suffering would inevitably take a heavy emotional toll. Once they were out of camera range, Kate, like Diana, would suddenly and without warning find herself fighting back tears. "It's just so very sad what some people have to go through—heartbreaking," she later confided to a Kensington Palace staffer. "It's hard, sometimes, to listen to these stories and not cry."

Ever since meeting William, Kate had been reticent to speak of his late mother. She knew that he still suffered deep psychological wounds stemming from Princess Diana's death, and Kate did not wish to inadvertently dredge up any memories that might cause him pain. Eventually, she would convince him to get the therapy that both he and Harry should have gotten in the immediate aftermath of the fatal Paris car crash that had rocked the world.

There were rare moments—during their BBC engagement interview in November 2010, for example—when she was forced to discuss her own feelings about Diana. "Well, obviously I would have loved to have met her," Kate replied. "She's obviously . . . she's an inspirational woman to look up to." And what about living up to Diana's legacy? "There's no pressure though," William chimed in. "There's no pressure, because . . . it is about carving your own future. No one is going to try to fill my mother's shoes, what she did was fantastic. It's about making your own future and your own destiny and Kate will do a very good job of that."

The Duchess of Cambridge was certainly off to a good start. "While many were keen to see the prince," proclaimed the *Daily Mail* as the Cambridges departed Canada, "there is little doubt that it is Kate who is winning their hearts in what is widely considered to be a dress rehearsal for the rest of her public life."

Back in London, the Queen was ecstatic—"thrilled and touched" were the words she used—that Canada had embraced its future king and queen. Elizabeth II was also pleased that, in one of his speeches, William referred to her as "the Queen of Canada"—which, as head of state, she was. The line drew cheers from the crowd at every stop, signaling to Her Majesty that the anti-monarchist movements in Canada's English-speaking provinces and Quebec's chronically cantankerous separatists were beginning to fade.

In fact, a poll taken around the time of the Cambridges' visit showed that opposition to the monarchy in Canada had suffered a sharp decline; 60 percent of the population now strongly supported keeping England's monarch as their own. When asked to describe their feelings about William and Kate, most respondents used words like "pride," "enthusiasm," and "joy."

Tellingly, a separate poll revealed that no fewer than 80 percent of Canadians would view the monarchy even more favorably if William were to become king. "It's unbelievable," a senior Clarence House official said. "I don't think any of us expected anything like this."

Next stop: Southern California, where they went straight to a technology summit in Beverly Hills aimed at promoting US investment in British tech firms. Then, it was on to a charity polo match at the Santa Barbara Polo & Racquet Club, where fans rushed the field to catch a glimpse of the royal couple before being pushed back by security. William, who scored four goals as his team went on to win the match, stepped up later to accept the large silver trophy from Kate. When the crowd yelled "Kiss!," Kate drew her husband close and gamely complied with a peck on both cheeks.

The main event: a BAFTA "Brits to Watch" gala at LA's historic Belasco Theater. As dozens of Hollywood stars waited anxiously to meet the guests of honor, BAFTA official Duncan Kenworthy asked them to "please don't all rush over, be cool in this coolest of towns. Trust me, they will try and chat to all of you. You can call them whatever you want: sir, madam, Will and Kate. . . . They are very relaxed. . . ."

The Duke and Duchess would eventually get around to chatting with the likes of Tom Hanks, Jennifer Lopez, Nicole Kidman, and Prince Charles's old pal Barbra Streisand. But it was clear who they most wanted to meet. As soon as they entered the room, William and Kate rushed past Hanks and Kidman and excitedly introduced themselves to *Sopranos* star James Gandolfini, who, quipped British commentator Stephen Bates, "greeted them with a sly Mafia grin." The next morning's *Guardian* headline summed up the evening perfectly: "William and Kate Leave Stars Starstruck."

"I can only say," William concluded as the couple headed home, "that the experience has exceeded all our expectations." So had Kate, whose potential as a global superstar and avatar for the United Kingdom seemed limitless. Yet Kate was also the first to realize that such breathtaking success came at a heavy price. "Our lives will never be the same after this, you know," William warned her as they made the 5,440-mile flight back to London aboard a British Airways commercial flight. (The couple's environmentally conscious decision not to fly aboard royal aircraft or private jets earned them even more points with an already adoring public.) The Palace, William rightly predicted, "will want us out there all the time now. There will be no stopping them."

There was an added complication: William did not want to overshadow his father, who had never stirred passions the way the Cambridges were doing. Every time a survey showed that the public overwhelmingly wanted William to succeed the Queen, "it hurts him deeply. He is an amazing man," the Heir often said of his father. "He has done so many amazing things. I only wish people would see that more. He's been given quite a hard time. . . . I wish that people would give him a break."

Besides, William loved his job as a search-and-rescue pilot, and was eager to get back to it. Kate was eager for a return to some semblance of normalcy, as well. Over the next two years, the couple divided their time between their stone farmhouse in Wales and Kensington Palace. "KP" was added to the royal family's collection of lavish palaces shortly after William and Mary assumed the throne as joint monarchs in 1689. King William was a severe asthmatic, and the main palace of the time, fog-shrouded Whitehall, was far too close to the dank, flood-prone Thames.

Enter the legendary eighteenth-century architect Sir Christopher Wren, who transformed the original Jacobean mansion sitting far from the river at the western end of Hyde Park into a redbrick Baroque masterpiece. The second royal occupant, Queen Anne, added extensive formal gardens and the Orangery, a colossal greenhouse with two dozen towering Corinthian columns initially designed to protect her cherished orange trees in winter.

Queen Victoria had a miserable childhood at Kensington Palace, where she was brought up under the rigid and unyieldingly strict Kensington System invented by her mother, the Duchess of Kent. It was there that, upon the death of Victoria's uncle King William IV in 1837, the eighteen-year-old was awakened in the middle of the night and told she was now queen. Victoria held her first privy council in Kensington Palace's Red Saloon, then promptly moved to Buckingham Palace to start her new life there as queen away from her bitter childhood memories.

Conversely, William's memories of his childhood years spent at KP were largely happy ones, despite his parents' chaos-filled marriage. While rumors of a royal pregnancy had already begun to circulate, the Queen intervened to allow the Cambridges to move into her late sister's Kensington Palace residence, Apartment 1A. Anything but a ground floor flat, Apartment 1A was actually a four-story, twenty-one-room brick manor house that took up half the Clock Tower wing designed by Wren for King William and Queen Mary. It boasted five reception rooms, three main bedrooms with fireplaces, two nurseries, three kitchens, a gym, and his-and-hers dressing rooms. In addition to its own private walled garden—a strong selling point for Kate, an avid grower of white lilies, hyacinths (her favorite flower), and roses—Apartment 1A also featured its own tennis courts. There were nine additional bedrooms on the top floor for staff, all easily summoned with the push of a button.

The space had been vacant since William's once-flamboyant, hell-raising Great Aunt Margaret died in 2002, so it would wind up taking two years and a jaw-dropping $7.6 million to bring Apartment 1A up to code with asbestos removal, new wiring, plumbing, and of course redecorating. Most of the rooms, much to Kate's amazement, were still painted in Margaret's favorite colors—turquoise, shocking pink, and electric blue.

For the time being, when they were in London the newly married couple would be bunking in Nottingham Cottage (Nott Cott), a two-bedroom, 1,324-square-foot house with a gym in the basement and ceilings so low that six-foot, three-inch William and six-foot, one-inch Harry had to stoop to avoid hitting their heads. At five foot nine, Kate only had to duck going through doorways.

Kensington Palace Apartment 1A was, by definition, a grace-and-favor residence; the Crown owned the property, and the Cambridges were permitted by the sovereign to live in it rent free. The Queen did not actually own Kensington Palace, but she did own Sandringham, and on its sweeping grounds was Anmer Hall.

Thirty-one years earlier, the Queen had given stunning pieces from the royal jewelry collection to Diana as a wedding gift, including Queen Mary's famous $1.4 million Lover's Knot tiara and Queen Mary's emerald choker, worth an astonishing $20 million. This time, however, Her Majesty chose real estate as her gift to the newlyweds—specifically Anmer Hall, a ten-bedroom, eighteenth-century Georgian brick-and-stone estate. Once occupied by the first Baron Rugby, who served as governor-general of the Sudan and England's first official representative to the Republic of Ireland, Anmer was rented from 1991 to 2001 to Charles's friend, Van Cutsem family patriarch Hugh van Cutsem. Beyond the Van Cutsem connection—and the fact that William had spent every Christmas at Sandringham—Diana Spencer had been born at Park House, a stately home that was also part of the Sandringham estate. She grew up there, leaving in 1975 at age fourteen when the family moved to Althorp, the Spencers' thirteen-thousand-acre spread in Northamptonshire.

Eventually, the Queen would spend $3 million out of her own pocket to pay for a new roof, new wiring, a conservatory, and a modernized family kitchen. The kitchen, intended as the social center of the house, would mirror the expansive open kitchen Kate had as a child growing up in Bucklebury. (On her first visit to the remodeled Anmer Hall, the Queen "couldn't wrap her head around the kitchen as a place for socializing," an aide observed. "In her mind, that is where all the kitchen staff work.") It would take two years, but eventually Anmer Hall would become the Cambridges' principal base of operations.

In the meantime, Kate's parents decided to step it up as well, reportedly paying more than $7 million for Bucklebury Manor, a Georgian manor with five reception rooms, seven bedrooms, a pool, tennis courts, walled gardens, and a steel-framed conservatory. The ostensible reason for upsizing: now that their daughter was married to the future king, they needed the added space for security reasons.

There were other reasons for upsizing, as well. Months before the wedding, William had casually told an interviewer that he and Kate were "looking forward to having a family"—an offhand remark that predictably started the royal pregnancy clock ticking.

Both the Queen and Diana had delivered their first child within a year of getting married, but William and Kate had their reasons for holding off. In the wake of their epic nuptials, the Cambridges didn't want to seem as if they were competing for attention with the Queen's Jubilee and the London Olympics. Nevertheless, rumors of an impending pregnancy ramped up in the fall of 2011, fueled by the passage on October 28 of the Perth Agreement to end the centuries-old practice of primogeniture—giving preference to the firstborn male in the line of succession. The new law went into effect once the leaders of the sixteen Commonwealth governments, who recognized the British monarch as their own, signed off on the change.

UK Prime Minister David Cameron formally announced the end of primogeniture in Parliament. "Put simply," Cameron said, "if the Duke and Duchess of Cambridge were to have a little girl, that girl would one day be our queen."

One week later, the Cambridges flew to Denmark to help pack food and medical supplies at a UNICEF relief center. At one point, William dug into a bag of peanut paste with his fingers and then offered some to Kate, who turned it down. Within minutes of the video airing, rumors spread on the internet that Kate was pregnant—that she, like many other expectant mothers, had been advised by her doctors not eat peanuts to prevent allergies during the early development of the baby. Despite repeated Palace denials, tabloids continued to run photographs zeroing in on Kate's midsection in search of evidence that she was sporting a "baby bump."

With "Peanutgate" behind her, Kate now looked forward to spending her first Christmas at Sandringham as a full-fledged member of the Firm.

Not surprisingly, Kate was stumped about what would be a suitable present for William's granny. Members of the royal family had long ago solved that ticklish problem by tacitly agreeing to give each other gag gifts. One year, Prince Charles was given a toilet seat upholstered in white leather (which he in fact took with him on trips abroad); another Christmas, Harry gave his grandmother a Big Mouth Billy Bass electronic singing fish plaque that the Queen liked so much she hung it in a place of honor at Balmoral. (An earlier gift to the monarch from Harry—a shower cap emblazoned with the words "Ain't Life a Bitch?"—apparently didn't go over as well, but not for reasons of taste. According to a royal butler, Queen Elizabeth was, unsurprisingly, very old-school and only took baths.)

As a newcomer, Kate wanted to make her gift more personal. "I thought, 'I'll make her something,'" Kate later recalled, "which could have gone horribly wrong." Using her own grandmother's recipe—featuring onions, apples, and marrows (British for summer squash)—Kate presented the Queen with a jar of homemade chutney. "I was slightly worried about it," Kate remembered. But the next morning, Kate's jar of chutney was on the table for all to share. "Such a simple gesture went such a long way for me," she said. "It just shows her thoughtfulness, really, and her care in looking after everybody."

Kate's thirtieth birthday—her first as a royal—was a low-key affair that came on the heels of their not-so-low-key appearance at the London premiere of the Steven Spielberg film *War Horse*—the Duchess's first royal premiere. The usual red-carpet mayhem ensued when the Cambridges arrived at the Odeon Leicester Square Theater in a downpour and made their way through the black-tie crowd to their seats. At one point, the film reduced Kate to tears. "Right in front of my face, my wife passed a Kleenex to the Duchess of Cambridge," said Spielberg, who was sitting with Kate to his left and his wife, actress Kate Capshaw, on his right. "But I didn't want to ruin her experience of watching *War Horse* so I never glanced over."

In its story on the excitement created by Kate and William's mere presence at the premiere, CBS News reported "that sometimes the people going to the movie can be bigger stars than the people in it."

On February 1, 2012, RAF pilot William Wales was to depart for a six-week tour of duty in the Falkland Islands. Before he left, James Middleton summoned his sister and brother-in-law to his house in Berkshire. James knew that William was still mourning the loss of Widgeon, the Labrador that he and Harry had grown up with, just eighteen months earlier. He also "reasoned that a puppy would be company for Catherine," James added, "on the nights he was away on duty."

Kate's brother had managed to get his cocker spaniel, Ella, to breed with another cocker named Spartan. Nine weeks later, Ella gave birth to five male pups. Now James was offering one of the dogs as a "belated wedding present. All you have to do is choose your favorite."

Kate and William bent down to stroke the glossy black pups nestled in a cardboard box. They chose one, and named him Lupo—Italian for "wolf." Why Lupo? she was asked. "No reason," she replied with a shrug. "We just like the way it sounds." They waited until Lupo was eight weeks old before bringing him to Kensington Palace, where Kate was soon spotted walking Lupo the two blocks to the Starbucks on Kensington Church Street with two royal protection officers shadowing her at a distance. On the way back, neither bodyguard interfered as she held on to a grande decaf soy latte in one hand while picking up after Lupo with the other. "We try not to get in the way," a guard explained, "of them having a normal life."

Even Kate had to admit that, dog poop or no, she would never again have a truly normal life. With William away, she quickly came in for criticism for not doing enough. Averaging three hundred or more royal engagements per year, Camilla in particular was feeling overworked—and, in part, she blamed the newcomer. The Duchess of Cornwall told friends that Kate wasn't pulling her weight, having racked up a paltry thirty-four official appearances during her first full year as a royal—a figure Camilla's allies were eager to leak to Fleet Street. For fear of rankling her husband, Camilla refrained from mentioning that William had managed only ninety royal outings in 2011—which seemed like plenty given his ten-hour shifts as a search-and-rescue pilot, not to mention a stint in the Falklands.

Of course, only Charles and the indominable Princess Anne would surpass the monarch's record of engagements, which would top out in 2012 at 425. That same year, Charles blew the competition out of the water with a staggering 592 official appearances—more than ten every single week.

An unrepentant workaholic, Elizabeth II nonetheless appreciated the fact that Kate was still learning the ropes. At the same time, the Queen believed a military wife should keep busy while her husband was away serving his country. She also knew that, in the crowd-pleasing Kate, the monarchy now had a valuable asset that it could not afford to let go to waste. Likening Kate to one of her racehorses, the Queen told an equerry that "with William away, there is no reason to keep her in the paddock."

Feeling the pressure to do more, Kate sifted through hundreds of charities before picking a handful to support. In January, she announced that she would be zeroing in on the Art Room, which provides art therapy to children from five to sixteen; Action on Addiction; the Scout Association (Britain's equivalent of the Boy and Girl Scouts); and the East Anglia's Children's Hospices.

Kate made her first solo public appearance on February 8, 2012, attending an exhibition at London's National Portrait Gallery, another one of the institutions she signed up to support. Wearing a gray tweed A-line coat dress, the princess moved through the exhibition of Lucien Freud portraits, including a famously unflattering one of the Queen making her look pasty and lumpen faced. Elizabeth II, who sat for Freud many times over a nineteen-month period, actually liked it.

With the Heir still on maneuvers abroad, Kate made her second solo tour—her first outside London—this time a Valentine's Day trip to Liverpool, where she began by visiting the Brink, an alcohol-free bar that provides assistance to those suffering from alcoholism or other substance abuse. In her honor, Brink bartenders created an alcohol-free smoothie named, appropriately, the Duchess. After being serenaded by the Raucous Caucus Recovery Chorus, the Brink's choir made up of alcoholics and former drug addicts, Kate visited a children's hospital and the local Ronald McDonald House. There, she again proved herself to be the new People's

Princess, spending time with every child who had waited to present her with flowers, cards, and cupcakes.

No one was more touched than Jacquie Johnston-Lynch, who founded the Brink after her brother Garry was killed by a drunk driver. Kate put her arm around Johnston-Lynch. "She had her arm around me and I could feel myself starting to cry," Johnston-Lynch recalled. "I told her 'I just want to thank you for putting recovery on the map. You've got no idea what you've done for us.' "

The Duchess rubbed Johnston-Lynch's shoulder. "Don't cry," Kate pleaded, "because then I will, too, and that wouldn't be a good idea on my first solo engagement!"

Kate's next solo stop was Oxford, where she spent hours taking part in art therapy classes for disadvantaged and special needs children. Following a little girl's instructions on how to draw a cat's earlobe, Kate laughed when she got red paint on the sleeve of her Orla Kiely jacquard shirt dress, then rushed to save several children's paintings when another pupil accidentally spilled water on the table. Ever the fashionista, she advised one young artist on how to dress the owl she was drawing—"Is it going to be brown trousers and a belt?"—and when the child reached for some glitter, Kate nodded. "Ah, there's the bling."

Juli Beatie, who founded the Art Room in 2002, echoed the sentiments of all who came in contact with Kate this early in her royal life. The Duchess's patronage—a much sought-after honor that signified her official endorsement and support as a member of the royal family—was "overwhelming. We are one of the smallest charities in the country," Beatie said, "and the difference she has made already is incalculable." Kate, she went on, "is a young, independent, intelligent woman who really wants to make a difference."

As the nation approached the first of 2012's epic celebrations—the Queen's Diamond Jubilee celebrating her sixty years on the throne—Kate was enlisted to appear with Her Majesty on several outings. The first included Camilla and was just a short ride from Buckingham Palace: London's renowned Fortnum & Mason gourmet shop, which had been catering to Britain's aristocracy since 1707. The generation-spanning trio shared a spot of tea, and then shopped for goodies—giving the world a glimpse of one current queen and two queens-to-be gazing with wonder into personalized wicker gift baskets.

If anyone harbored doubts at this point that Kate had become a personal favorite of Her Majesty, they vanished when she joined the Queen and Prince Philip on a two-hour train trip to the city of Leicester (pronounced "Lester") in the East Midlands. Kate, wearing a teal peplum jacket in contrast to the Queen's fuchsia wool coat dress, had confessed to her grandparents-in-law that, in William's absence, she still felt a tad "jittery" when suddenly confronted with large crowds.

The Queen and the Duke of Edinburgh spent much of their time on the train reassuring Kate, but once they arrived at their destination, Kate looked perfectly at ease as she worked the rope lines. Shaking hands and chatting amiably with a broad cross-section of the population that included young women and men, schoolchildren, the disabled, and seniors, William's wife looked very much in her element.

In this, Kate was quite unlike most Windsors. At one point or another, every member of the royal family had been rightly accused of appearing uninterested, condescending, patronizing, imperious, dismissive, churlish, stiff, awkward—or at various times all of the above. Even the Queen, who was not the worst offender in the family, maintained a studied air of detachment throughout her long reign. The very idea of Queen Elizabeth II hugging a cancer patient or cradling an infant suffering from AIDS would have seemed preposterous.

Only three other senior royals—Diana and her two sons—had the magic touch, and now the Queen was seeing firsthand just what a powerhouse the monarchy had in Kate. The highlight of the Leicester tour was an alumni fashion show at De Montfort University, where Her Majesty and the Duchess of Cambridge kibitzed and laughed for thirty minutes. According to Leicester MP Liz Kendall, who was seated nearby, Kate "looked amazing, and they were smiling and talking. They obviously have great affection for each other." "They seemed very relaxed together," said Dr. Julie

King, head of the Department of Fashion and Textiles. "The Queen has been doing this for so long . . . and just seems to set everyone at ease. And Kate's got that manner as well." Kate Bostock of the British department store chain Marks & Spencer was struck by the easy rapport between the Queen and Kate, and described the experience of being in their presence with one word: "tingly."

To mark another first for the Duchess of Cambridge—her first solo military engagement—Kate pinned the late Queen Mother's golden shamrock brooch on her forest green Emelia Wickstead coat dress to attend the 1st Battalion Irish Guards St. Patrick's Day Parade at Aldershot barracks in Hampshire. There Kate, whose $300 Lock & Co. "Betty Boop" hat sold out online within one hour of her wearing it, carried out a tradition started by the immensely popular Queen Alexandra in 1901—personally handing out springs of shamrocks to bearskin-hatted Irish soldiers. She also affixed shamrocks to the collar of Conmael, the battalion's massive Irish wolfhound mascot.

There was added significance to this appearance. Even though he was still serving overseas, William had been promoted to colonel of the Irish Guards the year before. Once again, Kate did not merely show up, shake hands with a few generals, and exit. Before having lunch with battalion officers, she visited enlisted men in the mess hall, where they toasted her with glasses of Harveys Bristol Cream sherry and Irish lager. Over the course of several hours, she chatted and laughed with the rank-and-file soldiers, stopping to ask as many as she could about themselves, their service, their families. She also inquired several times about one of the soldiers who, during the parade, had passed out under the weight of the bearskin hat and his heavy scarlet uniform. Kate was reassured that the young soldier was perfectly fine. "Princess Catherine really cares about us, and we don't always see that. She is so warm and engaging," a lance corporal said. "Even Conmael loved her. She reached down to pet him, and you could see his giant tail wagging."

For all her people skills, Kate had yet to make a speech on her own and was terrified at the prospect: "I find doing speeches nerve-racking," she confessed. When the princess stepped up to give her maiden speech to staff, volunteers, and families at the East Anglia Children's Hospices Treehouse, her deer-in-the-headlights demeanor took many by surprise. The first few moments were halting and awkward; Kate looked down repeatedly to read from her script, then looked up, trembling, to deliver the lines. She soon found her footing, however, and in the end her clearly heartfelt message shone through. Confessing that she had a preconceived notion of what to expect, Kate pointed out that "far from being a clinical, depressing place for sick children, it was a home. Most importantly, it was a family home, a happy place of stability, support, and care. It was a place of *fun*. The Treehouse is all about family and fun—a home away from home enabling families to live as normally as possible."

The weeks leading up to Her Majesty's four-day Diamond Jubilee celebration in June were a maelstrom of receptions, banquets, garden parties, teas, and concerts—not to mention one of the equine-loving Elizabeth's favorite annual events, the Royal Windsor Horse Show.

Kicking off the jubilee in earnest, Prince Charles cued up the Windsor home movies for a special hour-long BBC tribute to his mother. Kate was touched by the number of times her father-in-law seemed to grow emotional as he narrated the amateur family films, usually taken by Prince Philip. In one, eight-year-old Charles and six-year-old Anne are buried up to their necks in sand at the beach while one of the Queen's corgis looks on; in another Winston Churchill is among guests unwinding at a Windsor family picnic. William also stepped up to pay tribute to the Queen, admitting that where once he found her "very daunting," they were now "very close."

On Sunday, June 3, an estimated 1.2 million people lined the banks of the Thames to see a flotilla of more than one thousand vessels drawn from the far corners of the Queen's beloved Commonwealth—cruisers, tall ships, steamers, fireboats, cutters, tugboats, pleasure craft, fishing boats, trawlers, skiffs, the vessel that carried Winston Churchill's coffin during his state funeral, gondolas, a pirate ship, a Māori war canoe, a motorboat steered by the last survivor of Dunkirk, Viking longships—sail past in a thunderstorm. Reviewing this eclectic jubilee fleet was Elizabeth II aboard the *Spirit of Chartwell*, a 210-foot sightseeing boat that had been convincingly dressed up with flowers, flags, and ornate carvings of red, gold, and purple to resemble royal barges of centuries past.

Joining the Queen on board were the Duke of Edinburgh, Charles (who had actually conceived of the floating pageant as a tribute to his mother), Camilla, William, Kate, and Harry; lesser royals like Charles's siblings and their families were relegated to separate, considerably less majestic water craft. The message was clear: this was the vessel carrying three queens and two kings—the future of the British monarchy.

What also seemed evident—from a considerable distance, in fact—was Kate's unexpected desire to stand out, even in this far-from-drab group. While Prince Charles and his father wore their gold-braided and medal-bedecked ceremonial admirals' uniforms, William looked every inch the aviator in his slate blue RAF uniform, and Harry wore both his Blues and Royals uniform and the powder blue beret of the Army Air Corps.

The sovereign's longtime personal designer, stylist, and confidante, Angela Kelly, spent over a year creating her boss's outfit: a white coat studded with Swarovski crystals and a large white Tudor-style hat. Trying to blend in, Camilla wore off-white with a similarly large, sixteenth-century-inspired hat. If she got the memo about wearing white—and the first question out of every female royal is "What will Her Majesty be wearing?"—Kate decided to ignore it. With the help of her trendsetting stylist and pal, Natasha Archer, Kate was piped on board the royal barge wearing a scarlet dress by Alexander McQueen with a striking cardinal red hat to match.

Kate's dress "just screamed, 'Look at me!'" wrote the *Daily Mail*'s Amanda Platell, joining a chorus of journalists who took the Duchess of Cambridge to task for trying to upstage the Queen. "Oh, Kate, what were you thinking?" Not everyone agreed—not even other writers for the *Daily Mail*: Kate was "resplendent in red," proclaimed Deborah Arthurs, "cutting a swath through the gloomy weather." The *Hollywood Reporter*'s headline writers couldn't resist the opportunity for a fashion pun: "Kate Middleton is RED HAUTE in Alexander McQueen!"

Still, Kate might have wondered if she had pushed things too far had it not been for Harry. "Oh, Kate!" he chided her after the headlines appeared. "You wore a red dress. How *dare* you?" Not always able to count on the sometimes-brooding William to lift her spirits with a joke, Kate relied more and more on Harry for a healthy dose of playful ribbing. "Harry teases me all the time," she told a longtime family friend. "He keeps me sane, if you want to know the truth."

Lost in the shuffle was nearly ninety-one-year-old Prince Philip, who, after standing in the cold and damp for four hours, was hospitalized with a severe bladder infection. Assured that her husband was going to be fine, the Queen went ahead with the scheduled pop concert in front of Buckingham Palace—a star-packed show featuring performances by Stevie Wonder, Ed Sheeran, Kylie Minogue, Dame Shirley Bassey, and sirs Tom Jones, Elton John, and Paul McCartney.

At one point, Prince Charles asked the crowd of a half-million people in front of the palace to yell so that his father, who was in the hospital, might hear them. When thunderous shouts of "Philip" went up from the throng, everyone was moved—especially the Queen, Camilla, and Kate. The next day's *Daily Mail* and *Daily Telegraph* shared the same headline: "The Show Must Go On!"

Once again, no one appeared to be having a better time than Kate. This time wearing a body-hugging blue patterned wrap dress by another of her favorite labels, Whistles, Kate waved the Union Jack and sang along with "Our House," being sung by the British group Madness from the roof of the palace.

Later, the Cambridges rode in an open horse-drawn carriage for the first time since their wedding, following the Queen, Charles, and Camilla as they made their way from a Thanksgiving service at St. Paul's Cathedral to a Queen's Jubilee Luncheon with seven hundred volunteers at Westminster Hall. One million people jammed the streets to wave flags and cheer their queen, but the cheers for top-hatted William and his elegantly attired bride were equally, if not more, enthusiastic.

The scene was amplified that afternoon when, as Her Majesty stepped out onto the Buckingham Palace balcony, a sea of humanity stretching to the distant horizon roared its approval. As Prince Charles, Camilla, William, Kate, and Harry came into view, the frenzy went into overdrive. "A bit wild," William said to the Queen, who also appeared overwhelmed. "Amazing," she said, waving to her subjects. "Oh, my goodness, how extraordinary." In the meantime, Kate once again stole the show in an Alexander McQueen creation—this time a champagne-colored dress covered in eggshell white lace. Standing slightly apart from her husband, Kate leaned in to Harry and the two began chuckling about the pandemonium. "Have you ever seen anything like this?" she asked her brother-in-law, who nodded in agreement.

William was more focused on Granny. "Those cheers are for you," he told her before aircraft from the Battle of Britain—including Spitfires and a Hurricane—flew overhead, followed by the RAF's Red Arrows aerobatic team trailing white, red, and blue smoke over Buckingham Palace.

If there was ever any doubt before, the Duke and Duchess of Cambridge were, with a little help from Harry, giving the monarchy a much-needed shot in the arm. In the process, Kate in particular had stepped forward as the new ideal of grace, style, charm, and youthful energy. She was, in a word, fun.

Kate and William kept up the pace when the Summer Olympics came to London. Not that they had any hope of topping the Queen's entrance during the opening ceremonies. Picked up by 007 star Daniel Craig at Buckingham Palace and then "parachuted" into the new Wembley Stadium, Her Majesty reduced the rest of the royal family—none of whom had been clued in on the stunt—to open-mouthed hysterics. "She did such a good performance," William later cracked, "that she's been asked to star in the next Bond film. I'm thrilled for her."

Throughout the remainder of the games, however, it fell to the Cambridges to keep morale high. William and Kate were anointed Official Ambassadors of Great Britain's athletes ("Team GB"), a role they took seriously. Athletes became accustomed to seeing Kate and William on the jumbotron screens, leaping to their feet and cheering wildly. The Cambridges even offered fans a rare public display of affection when they leapt into each other's arms after watching Team GB cyclists whiz home to gold. "Do they give out gold medals for most enthusiastic spectators?" asked *E*'s Gina Serpe. "Because if they did, the spectacular cheer squad of Prince William and Kate Middleton would be a shoo-in."

There were times when Kate flew solo—at the gymnastics and handball competitions, for example—proving that she didn't need her husband at her side to excite the crowd. Waving a Union Jack and cheering each contestant who took to the floor, Kate, observed the *Hollywood Reporter*, "added her star power to every event."

With William summoned back to duty with the RAF's Search and Rescue Force in North Wales, the Queen asked Harry to represent the royal family during Olympic closing ceremonies—all part of a concerted plan to use the games to sell a new generation to the British public. Throughout the ceremonies, Kate sat alongside Harry, schmoozing and laughing and, said the *Daily Mail*, "clearly enjoying herself."

Kate and Harry felt closer than ever, bonded by the simple realization that their main purpose in life was to love and support the Crown. She worried about her brother-in-law now that he had completed his training as an Apache attack helicopter pilot and was being deployed to Afghanistan for a second time.

Harry gave Kate and everyone in the royal family something else to worry about in late August when, while vacationing in Las Vegas before his deployment, someone took cell phone shots of the Spare frolicking in the altogether with an equally nude young woman in his $8,000-a-night hotel suite.

Sadly for Harry, what happened in Vegas didn't stay there. Two of the photos showed the naked Spare coyly trying to conceal his private parts—by now having recovered from his bout with Arctic frostbite—with cupped hands. The racy images, taken during a game of strip pool, were soon splashed across front pages everywhere. The Spare, who had turned to drugs and alcohol to escape the dark, unresolved feelings that had haunted him since his mother's death, was once again a national embarrassment. Once more Harry was denounced on the floor of Parliament—"A new low, even for the royal family," said Labour MP Stephen Pound—and skewered in the press. "It was only a matter of time," reported CBS News, "before Harry was caught with his pants down. . . . Is the party prince back?"

Harry rushed to Birkhall in Scotland to apologize to his father, and was surprised that this time Prince Charles was "gentle, even bemused"—perhaps because in 1994 a German magazine had published naked photos of him as well, taken through the window as he toweled off in his room at the French chateaux where he was staying.

Kate also reached out to reassure Harry. Yet even she couldn't convince him that he hadn't once again "screwed up badly. . . . At the end of the day, I let myself down. I let my family down." Not that Harry felt it was entirely his fault. "There is no such thing as privacy now," he complained. "Everyone's got a camera on their cell phone. You can't move an inch without someone judging you."

The Duchess soon found that out for herself. The Cambridges were in the Malaysian capital of Kuala Lumpur—halfway through a nine-day Jubilee Tour of Southeast Asia and the Pacific—when topless photos of Kate appeared on the covers of the French magazine *Closer* and Italy's *Chi*. "Oh My God" were the only English words scrawled on the cover of *Closer*, alongside color snapshots of Kate taking off the top of her swimsuit and the couple slathering their naked torsos with sunscreen. "The future Queen of England, such as you have never seen her . . . and such as you will never see her again." *Chi*'s red-letter cover headline was less wordy, and a little premature: "La Regina E Nuda!" ("The queen is nude!")

Kate was visibly shaken when she was shown the images, taken a few weeks earlier while the couple was sunbathing during a vacation at a secluded French château owned by the Queen's nephew (and William's first cousin, once removed) Viscount Linley. Visitors had to make their way down a narrow private drive that wound through 650 acres of woods and fields to find the viscount's villa, but that didn't stop an enterprising female photographer from taking the photos from a public road 1,500 feet away using a telephoto lens.

As humiliated and violated as she justifiably felt, Kate managed to quickly compose herself. After all, at different stops throughout the Southeast Asian tour they chatted unselfconsciously with bare-breasted islanders "and," Kate told a royal handler, "it's all perfectly natural. They seem very happy and free." In any event, she added, "We are not going to let it [the publication of topless photos] ruin this trip!"

It certainly helped that the photos were flattering, for the most part. Within a short time, Kate was back to being "the picture of cool, calm, and utterly unruffled elegance," recalled journalist Rebecca English, who was in Malaysia with the royal couple when they were shown the images. "We were all marveling how she was able to smile, shake hands, and make small talk, without the slightest quiver or indication that anything was amiss."

The Heir, however, saw red. "I'd never seen William as furious as when those cruel pictures of Kate were leaked," English said. "He was so angry, jaw clenched, he could barely contain his fury." The incident dredged up memories of his mother sobbing in her room after being chased by the paparazzi. It also reminded the prince that, despite his promise to Kate's parents that he would protect her, he had failed miserably—a gnawing sense of guilt that, despite the Middletons' protestations to the contrary, William wore like a hair shirt.

Like his father, William had enlisted the help of royal lawyers from time to time to threaten publications with legal action—a negotiating tactic that often succeeded in getting the press to pull back, if only slightly and for a short time. This time, however, he wanted blood: an injunction and damages exceeding $2 million. The decision to move against the French publication stemmed from that country's strict criminal privacy laws, which can carry a prison sentence of up to one year.

"Diana would be absolutely devastated and utterly distraught by what William and Kate are having to deal with," said handbag designer Lana Marks, one of the late princess's close friends. "But she would be proud of how William is handling things. . . . She would want him to take a stand against this." William, Marks continued, "knows more than anyone what his mother had to endure. He would not want his wife to be hounded in the same way."

Not everyone was so sympathetic. "Who wouldn't take Kate's picture and make lots of money," tweeted Donald Trump, "if she does the nude sunbathing thing? Come on, Kate!" The Duchess shrugged it off, but William was reportedly apoplectic. The Heir was already aware that, just months after Diana's death, Trump had told radio host Howard Stern that he could have "nailed" William's mother. "I think I could have," said Trump, who also joked with Stern about having Diana get "a little checkup" for HIV before having sex.

It would take five years for the case to finally reach a verdict, and then only after William wrote a letter to the court saying that the naked photos were "particularly shocking because it reminded us of the harassment that led to the death of my mother, Diana, Princess of Wales." While everyone managed to avoid jail time, the French court ordered the defendants to pay $250,000 in damages and fines.

Even as William fumed behind the scenes, Kate was determined not to appear the suffering victim. They marveled at orangutans in the dense, steaming jungles of Borneo and gamely agreed to strap on harnesses and be yanked on a pulley system more than thirteen stories high to the top of a lush, domed *Parashorea tomentella* tree. At her suggestion, the couple even took time off in the middle of the tour to take what they billed as a "second honeymoon" at the Tavanipupu Island Resort in the Solomon Islands.

A high point of the tour was Kate's first official speech abroad, at a children's hospice in Malaysia. In one particularly heart-melting moment, Kate gave a birthday card to a terminally ill fifteen-year-old named Zakwan Anuar, who had postponed a blood transfusion so he could meet the princess. Anuar had been asleep in his wheelchair but sprang to life when Kate walked into the room and held his hand. "You are very, very brave," she told the young leukemia patient, "and very handsome." Anuar's mother was in tears. "Zakwan had almost given up hope, but today, my God, it was as if the leukemia had gone," she said. "God bless Princess Catherine. I cannot repay that kindness."

Earlier, when the royal couple had met the Solomon Islands' governor general, Sir Frank Kabui, at a reception in London, William admitted that he and Kate were "extremely excited. Both of us have never been anywhere near there." Her husband, Kate added, "has been practicing his dance moves." Now as they arrived in the island nation of Tuvalu, draped in garlands of gardenias and frangipani and carried above the crowd in sedan chairs, the Cambridges had the opportunity to try out those moves. Kate and William both donned colorful straw skirts and, towering over their diminutive hosts, waved their hands and shimmied their hips as part of the *fatele*, Tuvalu's traditional welcome dance. Oddly, the ritual requires guests to spray the dancers with cologne to show their appreciation; the Cambridges happily spritzed their hosts with Paul Smith Eau de Toilette, William's preferred scent.

As perfectly choreographed and executed as the South Pacific tour undoubtedly was, even the most minuscule mistake generated raging headlines. There was an international uproar, for example, when the royal couple showed up wearing clothing not by local Solomon Island designers but by a designer from the Cook Islands seventeen hundred miles away. Of course, Kate took the heat—despite the fact that William was also wearing the wrong getup. "A Right Royal Wardrobe Gaffe! Kate's Solomon Islands Error!" trumpeted the *Daily Mail*'s front page. "Oops!" the *Hollywood Reporter* chimed in, "Kate Middleton Commits Fashion Faux-Pas in South Pacific!" In the end, it was discovered that an aide had inadvertently placed the Cook Islander attire on the Cambridges' bed, and an open suitcase obscured the correct, locally manufactured Solomon Island outfits.

No matter. When they returned to the United Kingdom, Princess Catherine was again hailed as one of Britain's greatest assets—especially when it came to fashion. "Kate is a style icon," designer Karen Millen gushed, "and a great ambassador for British fashion and fashion everywhere." What the press had already dubbed "the Kate Effect" was now more in force than ever. For the second year in a row, she was named one of *Time* magazine's "100 Most Influential People in the World," and a *Sunday Times* poll showed that 73 percent of the British population believed Kate was breathing new life into the royal family.

Once again, Kate was on her own back in the United Kingdom, this time substituting for her husband while the Heir attended the funeral of his former nanny Olga Powell. In the northern city of Newcastle, Kate met hundreds of locals who had volunteered to make the London Olympics a success, including fourteen-year-old triple-amputee William Hardy, who carried the Olympic torch through part of the city. Later, she met with schoolchildren, planted seeds in a community garden, and spent time with members of her charity Action on Addiction, which helps families where one of the parents is battling drug abuse. Northumbria University student Megan Bartle, who was among the two thousand people in Newcastle who showed up hoping for a glimpse of Kate, summed up the Princess's populist appeal: "She is such a brilliant role model and an inspiration. She carries herself beautifully, but at the same time she is modest and at ease with the public. It's almost as if she's saying, 'I'm not better than you.'"

In the coming weeks, there would be more engagements: the couple were guests of honor at a scholarship fundraiser for their alma mater, St. Andrews, marking the university's six hundredth anniversary; Kate wore three poppy pins in memory of her three great-uncles, who died in World War I, at Remembrance Day ceremonies in London, and the Cambridges made their first official visit to their namesake city. Looking happy and fit, Kate and William barnstormed through Cambridge like seasoned politicians, visiting homeless shelters and schools, waving to thousands of cheering fans from the balcony of Cambridge's guildhall, tirelessly working the rope lines, and opening a new hospital in nearby Peterborough.

At another St. Andrews—the prep school for ages three to thirteen she had attended as a girl in Berkshire—Kate showed up alone to unveil a plaque and meet the field hockey team that she had once been a part of. Wearing an Alexander McQueen navy and green plaid coat and high-heeled black boots, she still managed to pick up a stick and show off her skills in a spirited game on the school's new Astroturf field. It was left to the school's athletic director to point out that, seventeen years after she had left at age thirteen, Kate still held the school record in the high jump.

For all her athletic prowess and seemingly radiant good health, Kate was, in fact, sick—desperately so. She was also ten weeks pregnant. In the past three weeks since confirming her pregnancy with a home test, Kate had been able to battle back feelings of nausea that surged during her public appearances. But once she and William had decamped to Bucklebury Manor, the Middletons' extravagant new estate in Berkshire, Kate began vomiting uncontrollably.

At first, the family reassured Kate that she was experiencing the unfortunate symptoms of run-of-the-mill morning sickness. After a twenty-four-hour period of nonstop nausea and violent heaving—nothing stayed down, not even water—there were clear signs that Kate was becoming seriously dehydrated. Dr. Marcus Setchell, who for twenty years had been the Queen's gynecologist, made the command decision to have Kate hospitalized immediately.

Setchell brought impressive credentials to the job. In addition to serving as one of the Queen's most trusted physicians, Setchell had performed Camilla's hysterectomy in 2007 and an emergency cesarean on Prince Edward's wife, Sophie, the Countess of Wessex, in 2003. At sixty-nine, Setchell had agreed to delay his long-planned retirement until after the Cambridges' first child arrived.

William and Kate had wanted to wait a few weeks longer before making the happy announcement, but now he was working the phones, calling his grandmother—royal protocol dictates that the sovereign is always notified first—and Prince Charles with the happy news. Harry, who was still serving with the British Army in Afghanistan, got the news via email. That Monday morning, December 3, with one of their ever-present royal bodyguards in the driver's seat, William and Kate sped the eighty minutes to King Edward VII's Hospital.

It did not take long for Dr. Setchell to diagnose his famous patient with hyperemesis gravidarum, a severe form of morning sickness experienced by less than 2 percent of pregnant women. If left untreated, the condition could lead to a number of complications, including low birthweight for the baby and malnutrition for the mother—and, in the most dire cases, death for either the mother or the child, or both.

After years of speculation about a "baby bump," Kate and William had managed to catch everyone—including family members—by complete surprise. A statement from St. James's Palace read: "The Queen, the Duke of Edinburgh, the Prince of Wales, the Duchess of Cornwall and Prince Harry and members of both families are delighted with the news."

So, too, was everybody else. Prime Minister David Cameron tweeted that he was "delighted by the news. . . . They will make wonderful parents." Not to be outdone, opposition party leader Ed Miliband tweeted, "Fantastic news for Kate, William, and the country. A royal baby is something the whole nation will celebrate." Barack and Michelle Obama sent their congratulations from the White House, the Archbishop of Canterbury invited the "whole nation to join in celebrating this wonderful news," and William's uncle Earl Spencer declared himself to be nothing less than "thrilled for them both. This wonderful news tops off what's been quite a year for Britain."

Following Queen Elizabeth's Diamond Jubilee and the London Olympics—back-to-back spectacles that commanded the world's undivided attention—the announcement of a royal pregnancy in the closing days of 2012 did seem to provide the perfect capstone for one of Britain's most memorable years. But during the same twelve-month period, the country also chalked up some unforgettable scandals—most notably Prince Harry's naked Las Vegas photos and the legal firestorm ignited by Kate's topless (and some bottomless) snapshots.

Sadly, a bizarre tragedy would strike even as the world celebrated news of the royal pregnancy. A nurse at King Edward VII's Hospital, forty-six-year-old mother of two Jacintha Saldanha, received a call the morning after Kate was admitted from two people inquiring about her condition. Claiming to be the Queen and Prince Charles, they were put straight through to the Duchess's nurse.

Unfortunately, the callers were two Australian radio shock jock hosts, Mike Christian and Mel Greig, using what they later called "ridiculous comedy accents" to impersonate the royals. "When is a good time to come and visit her," Greig asked in "an absurd, plummy" voice, "because I'm the Queen and I need a lift down there." After asking about "how my granddaughter's little tummy-bug is going," and squabbling with "Prince Charles" over whether or not he would give her a ride to the hospital, Greig asks Christian, "And when are you going to walk those bloody corgis?" Christian replies, "Mummy, I'll go and take the dogs outside." Christian then impersonates the Queen's yapping dogs in the background.

All obvious silliness aside, the hoax sparked a Fleet Street furor. The Australian radio station apologized, as did the hospital for not protecting Kate's patient confidentiality rights. No one was blaming either of the two hospital nurses; but William, who visited Kate in the hospital every day, was angry that once again his wife's privacy had been violated. Kate, focused on her own recovery from hyperemesis gravidarum after three days on an IV drip, took the whole radio prank call controversy in stride. When she left the hospital at 10:30 on a Thursday morning, Kate was smiling broadly and clutching a bouquet of yellow roses as reporters peppered her with the same question: "How are you feeling, Kate?" The answer was always the same: "Much better, thanks."

The next day, Jacintha Saldanha, still distraught over her role in the prank call scandal, hanged herself in her nurse's quarters at the hospital. Saldanha had tried to kill herself twice before, was on antidepressants, and one of the three suicide notes she left behind was a litany of long-brewing complaints against the hospital. None of this assuaged Kate's feelings of guilt over the nurse's tragic death. "How terrible!" Kate said when she heard the news. "None of it would have happened if I hadn't been there."

Kate wanted to reach out to the nurse's family directly, but that idea was nixed by St. James's Palace. Instead, the Palace issued a statement. "The Duke and Duchess of Cambridge are deeply saddened to learn of the death of Jacintha Saldanha. Their Royal Highnesses were looked after so wonderfully well at all times by everybody at King Edward VII Hospital, and their thoughts and prayers are with Jacintha Saldanha's family, friends and colleagues at this very sad time."

For the remaining thirty weeks of her pregnancy, Kate spent most of her time at Bucklebury Manor with her mother by her side, locked in a battle with HG—a struggle that left her feeling "utterly rotten! I was really sick. I am not the happiest of pregnant people."

At a time when most expectant parents are tossing around baby names and decorating nurseries, the Cambridges, informed that HG increases the risk of miscarriage, concentrated almost entirely on bringing Kate's pregnancy to term. During ultrasounds and other tests, the royal couple asked not to be told the sex of the child—they wanted it to be a surprise—but they allowed that she wanted a boy and he wanted a girl. "All that matters," she said, "is that the baby is healthy."

Toward that end, Kate gave up artificial sweeteners, alcohol, caffeine—and her favorite artificial tanning spray. None of that seemed to matter. Still unable to keep food down, she struggled to gain the weight she needed to sustain her pregnancy. "I was unable to consume the nourishing foods I should have been, and yet, miraculously, my body continued to extract the essential nutrients required to nurture new life. I find that absolutely fascinating."

Kate later conceded that coping with HG was "definitely a challenge. Not just for me but also for your loved ones around you—and I think that's the thing—it impacts everybody in the family." William felt "helpless." The Heir "didn't feel he could do much," she said, "and it's hard for everyone to see you suffering without actually being able to do anything about it."

To help combat her morning sickness, Kate called in an expert on "hypnobirthing"—a method that combines self-hypnosis, visualization, music, positive thinking, and prompts from partners to relax the body before and during labor. The technique was also effective in tamping down some of hyperemesis gravidarum's most unpleasant symptoms. "It was through hyperemesis that I really realized the power of the mind over the body," she said, "because I really had to try everything . . . to help me through it."

William's good intentions aside, Kate did not have the patience to enlist him in the hypnobirthing process. "I'm not going to say that William was standing there sort of chanting sweet nothings at me," Kate said. "He definitely wasn't! I didn't even ask him about it, because it was just something I wanted to do for myself. I witnessed the potency of these techniques. It dawned on me that this was something I could harness, a source of empowerment."

That Christmas, only Kate's second since becoming a member of the royal family, the Cambridges had to pass on festivities at Sandringham. Instead, they spent the holidays with the Middletons—and with a bathroom always close at hand.

Kate managed an outing with family and friends on January 11, 2013, to celebrate her thirty-first birthday, catching the Cirque du Soleil show *Koozå* at Royal Albert Hall. She also showed up the next morning at the National Portrait Gallery for the vernissage of her first official portrait. While she had only kind words for the artist, Paul Emsley, critical reaction to the oddly washed-out portrait was brutal. Michael Glover of the *Independent* described it as "catastrophic," and Waldemar Januszczak of the *Sunday Times* called the portrait "disappointing." The *Guardian*'s Charlotte Higgins bemoaned the "dead eyes: a vampiric, malevolent glare beneath heavy lids. Then there's the mouth: a tightly pursed, mean little lip-clench." The *Scotsman* arts editor Andrew Eaton-Lewis asked why any artist would want to make "a pretty young girl look less pretty and less young."

Incredibly, between hours at a time spent retching at either Bucklebury Manor or Kensington Palace, Kate managed to pull it together enough to make several major appearances. One wintry day in March, she wore jeans, a Barbour coat, and boots to teach Cub Scouts in northwestern Cumbria wilderness skills, like how to build a fire and pitch a tent. In early April, she and William toured Scotland, where she played a fast-paced game of Ping Pong and shot some baskets with him at Glasgow Sports Center. Two weeks later, she made her customary fashion splash wearing a black-and-white polka-dot dress to visit the *Harry Potter* movie set in London.

To be sure, throughout her pregnancy Kate was the epitome of maternity-wear chic. Although every senior member of the royal family was on hand to mingle with the eight thousand guests at Her Majesty's annual Buckingham Palace garden party, all eyes were on the now quite visibly pregnant Duchess of Cambridge. Navigating the lawn in four-inch stilettos—heels were the one thing she refused to give up—Kate stood out in a lemon-yellow coatdress by British designer Emilia Wickstead and a cream-colored Jane Corbett hat decorated with wide ribbons.

Started in 1868 by Queen Victoria as a way for the monarch to connect with her subjects, the party gave a chance for everyday Britons to quiz royal family members—and no one was peppered with more questions about the baby than Kate. "No," she insisted repeatedly, "we don't know if it's a boy or a girl, and, no, we haven't picked out names. But thank you so much for asking. . . ."

Still wearing skyscraper heels, Kate gamely trooped up and down treacherous gangways to christen the newest Princess Cruises ship, the *Royal Princess* (fittingly, since Diana had christened the first *Royal Princess* in 1984). Her striking dalmatian-print coat by High Street retailer Hobbs sent thousands of Kate-watchers scurrying to the store's website. Struggling to keep gusty winds from blowing up her coat and the skirt beneath, Princess Kate launched the new 3,560-passenger vessel with a $2,000 bottle of Moët & Chandon champagne and then took a tour of the bridge. Pressing the ship's horn, she threw up her hands in delight at the deep, bellowing sound. "Brilliant," she said. "I was expecting something high-pitched."

Kate had one last gig before going into labor—the Trooping the Colour ceremony marking the monarch's official birthday. (Queen Elizabeth's actual birthday was April 21.) Riding in an open carriage with Camilla and Harry, the pregnant duchess wore a pale pink Alexander McQueen coat, a matching hat by Jane Corbett, and Annoushka baroque pearl drop earrings. Not surprisingly, Kate's choice of pink—which again made her a standout among the other Windsor women on the Buckingham Palace balcony—was widely interpreted as a signal that the Cambridges were expecting a girl.

Did it really matter? "This child," royal historian Kate Williams reminded anyone who cared to listen, "will come to the throne as the king—or queen."

Princess Catherine has an almost old-fashioned,
Queen Mother attitude to drama—she just doesn't do it.

—Jamie Lowther-Pinkerton, former private secretary to Kate and William

5

"She Is Straight from a Fairy Tale"

"A Precious, Unforgettable Moment"

"Cunning? Me?"

Waity Katie, as she had been known for over a decade, was at it again. Anticipation had been building for months, and now, with England in the grip of searing summer heat, she was a full week overdue. "We've all been waiting," Camilla fretted as tension mounted, "at the end of a telephone."

Amazingly, air-conditioning had not yet been installed in their spacious new quarters at Kensington Palace, so Kate opted to remain in the cool confines of Bucklebury Manor. But at 3 p.m. on Friday, July 19, Kate and William departed for Kensington Palace in a motorcade with a half-dozen members of their royal protection detail and a police escort. Moving into a portion of KP where air-conditioning had been hastily installed, the couple remained sequestered until the early morning hours of July 22 when Kate went into labor.

More like an anxious suburban dad-to-be than a prince of the realm, William—the first heir apparent to be born in a hospital instead of a palace—swung into action. Vetoing a flashy motorcade that would attract attention, the prince bundled his wife into a town car and ordered protection officers to follow in an unmarked sedan. Five minutes later, they pulled up to the back entrance of the Lindo Wing of Paddington's St. Mary's Hospital—the same hospital where William and Harry were born—and, with television cameras, still photographers, and reporters all staked out at the front entrance, miraculously managed to sneak in undetected.

Dr. Marcus Setchell also managed to sneak past the reporters who had been camped out in front of the hospital for weeks. With William at Kate's side throughout the fourteen-hour labor, Kate gave birth to an eight-pound, six-ounce boy at 4:24 on the afternoon of July 22, 2013. "It was a precious, unforgettable moment when I held the future King of England," Dr. Setchell recalled. "Wonderful baby. Beautiful baby. But I had to remind myself that Prince George was just another baby. You just keep reminding yourself that although it's very important, it's just another healthy young couple giving birth to a hopefully very healthy baby."

As positive as the outcome was for both mother and child, the birth process itself was not without difficulty. Dr. Setchell praised the team of midwives that had assisted in the baby's delivery, but made it clear he needed to be in the room. "What happened in labor is an entirely private matter," he said. "But I do think there are certain situations . . . that it's important not just to have a specialist sort of available at the end of a telephone but actually in the same room to deal with anything that's immediately going to be wrong."

It was customary to proclaim a royal birth to the waiting world without delay. But Kate insisted, with her husband's backing, that the Palace wait four hours so that they could savor the moment in private "as any young family would." Nor would they be divulging the infant's name quite yet. It had taken one month before Charles's name was revealed in 1948—a long-standing royal tradition up until then—and William was a week old before his name was known. Although the new parents had already settled on a name for their son, William in particular was in no rush to let the world at large in on it. "Baby Wales," as their son was being called for the moment, would become "public property" soon enough.

In the meantime, Kate spent the night in the hospital with her newborn son. Summer thunderstorms crashed over London all night, keeping Kate awake, but she was grateful that George "did sleep, which was really great." The new mom was "keen to get home" because being in the hospital triggered memories of her grueling bout with acute morning sickness. "It wasn't a place I wanted to hang around in," she said. "So I was really desperate to get home."

Later, Dr. Setchell and three members of his medical team who witnessed the birth signed a single typewritten page—a relic from days when the prime minister or some other high official had to sign off on the authenticity of a royal birth. The letter was then taken by a royal driver directly to the Queen at Buckingham Palace. Once she approved it, the announcement was carried by two Palace staffers to the forecourt of the palace. There it was then carefully placed on the same ornately gilded wooden easel that had announced William's birth in 1982:

Her Royal Highness The Duchess of Cambridge was safely delivered of a son at 4:24 p.m. today.

Her Royal Highness and her child are both doing well.

The King's Troop, Royal Horse Artillery in Green Park next to Buckingham Palace fired forty-one rounds, while a sixty-two-round salute boomed from cannons at the Tower of London. Public fountains were bathed in blue light, church bells pealed, London cabbies honked their horns, and everywhere throughout the Commonwealth people were toasting the birth of the future king. The Queen and Prince Philip were "delighted" at the news, while Prince Charles was not only "thrilled" and "overjoyed" for the new parents, he was "enormously proud and happy" to find himself a first-time grandfather at sixty-four.

He wasn't the only grandparent, of course, and suddenly Charles and Camilla found themselves racing to be the first ones to see the baby. Michael and Carole Middleton were staying at their London flat, so they had the advantage; the Prince of Wales and his wife were two hours away touring the North Yorkshire village of Bugthorpe where, after Camilla commented that Charles was "brilliant with children," a six-month-old in the crowd burst into tears upon meeting him.

The Middletons pulled up to the hospital in a cab, waving at reporters before they dashed inside. Kate handed her infant son to Carole, who sat with him for fifteen minutes before giving Michael an opportunity to hold their first grandchild. Then Carole gave new dad William some tips as she watched him attempt to change his first nappy (diaper).

Kate had spent much of her difficult pregnancy at Bucklebury Manor, where William was a frequent guest. The Middletons had been pillars of support for their daughter and son-in-law, and Carole in particular was destined to be a major presence in the life of the new prince. More than an hour went by before they reappeared on the Lindo Wing's front steps. The new parents were doing "fabulously," Carole told reporters. And what was the first "cuddle" like? "Amazing! It's all coming back."

Charles and Camilla, having hastily summoned a helicopter to return to London, finally arrived in a royal car. "You've had a long wait," the Prince of Wales joked with reporters before ducking inside with the Duchess of Cornwall. Ten minutes later, they emerged to tell the startled reporters that the newest Windsor was "marvelous," then zoomed back to Clarence House.

Nearly twenty-seven hours after Kate gave birth, mother, father, and infant stepped outside and were met with a barrage of questions from waiting reporters. Kate was engulfed in a swirl of "mixed emotions. Both William and I were really conscious that this was something that everyone was excited about . . . and you know we wanted to share that joy with the public." At the same time, those feelings were "coupled with a newborn baby, and inexperienced parents, and the uncertainty of what that held."

There was also the issue of Kate's appearance—and how people would react to what remained of her baby bump, clearly visible beneath her empire-waist blue-and-white polka-dot dress. The moment she stepped before cameras while William held the baby was "slightly terrifying, slightly terrifying, I'm not going to lie," said Kate, whose conscious decision not to conceal her post-birth belly made headlines and sparked an online discussion about how self-conscious women often feel after giving birth. The founder of Netmums, a popular online UK parenting site, praised Kate for being a healthy role model for mothers everywhere and dispelling the myth that all women should be "perfect postpartum. In a couple of minutes on the steps of the Lindo Wing," Siobhan Freegard wrote, "Kate has done more for new mums' self-esteem than any other role model." Agreed journalist Heather Marcoux: "The iconic images of her in that polka-dot dress taught a generation of women that the female body isn't an elastic band and that recovering from birth takes time."

"He's got a good pair of lungs, that's for sure," William informed the press. "He's a big boy, quite heavy. He's got her looks, thankfully." The equally self-deprecating Kate was quick to correct her husband. "No, no," she said. "I'm not sure about that." The baby's hair color? Not certain, "but," said William, "he's got way more than me. Thank God!" William also apologized for keeping the press waiting. "I'll remind him of his tardiness," William said, "when he's a bit older."

Later, Kate got in the back of their Range Rover while William—who had been rehearsing this moment for days—expertly clicked their $160 Britax infant car seat into place. Wiping his forehead to make the familiar "phew" gesture, the new dad climbed into the driver's seat and headed off to Kensington Palace.

Harry was waiting for them outside Nottingham Cottage, the Cambridges' two-bedroom refuge at Kensington Palace until renovations of Apartment 1A were finally completed. Allowing that it was "fantastic to have an addition to the family," Harry cracked that "I only hope my brother knows how expensive my babysitting charges are."

For the first time since Queen Victoria had held her great-grandson Edward VIII in 1894, a monarch was about to meet her third-generation heir. Soon the Queen pulled up to Kensington Palace in a dark green Bentley and stepped into Nottingham Cottage where Kate, William, Harry, and the baby were all waiting to greet her.

It would be another day before the baby's name was announced to the world; not even Prince Charles and Camilla were in on the secret. Kate and William wanted the Queen, who made a practice of never interfering with suggestions of her own, to be the first to know. Not that they didn't feel pressured anyway. Kate later admitted that she and William had at one point wanted their "little grape"—their nickname for the baby in utero—to be named Alexander. That would have been a popular choice as far as Scotland was concerned, since Scots revere Alexander III as one of their greatest kings.

As it turned out, there was another name they liked just as much, and it paid tribute to the Queen's adored father. The newest prince of the realm was to be called George Alexander Louis—His Royal Highness Prince George of Cambridge. Alexander still figured in the equation, as did Louis, which honored Charles's great-uncle and mentor, Lord Mountbatten. Her Majesty was touched, in part because of the obvious nod to her father, George VI, but also because of the historic significance: George had been the name of six British kings, the first four of whom lent their name to the Georgian era.

Two hours later, the Queen was back at Buckingham Palace and the Cambridges departed for Bucklebury Manor, where the Middletons had already set up a nursery. During her first few weeks as a mother, Kate learned the ropes from Carole while Will, committed to being a hands-on dad, commuted from Berkshire to his search-and-rescue job in Wales.

The Cambridges returned to Anglesey in mid-August, and with William doing search-and-rescue night shifts, Kate suddenly felt "so isolated, so cut off." The constant presence of royal protection officers nearby made little difference. "George was a tiny, tiny little baby," she said. "I didn't have family around. . . ."

A month later, as William's tour of duty wound down, the Cambridges departed for their newly refurbished digs at Kensington Palace—and a new life as full-time royals. It quickly became clear to Kate that, even with a light schedule of official duties, she was going to need a little help. While his wife interviewed candidates for the job, William asked his former nanny, seventy-one-year-old Jessie Webb, if she would come out of retirement to fill in. Webb, who had witnessed the turmoil surrounding William and Harry's childhood firsthand and once said the boys were going to "need a lot of help if they're not going to end up as barking mad as their mum and dad," agreed.

Predictably, the world was besotted with Baby George. When Kate and William showed up for Christmas at Sandringham without him, even the Queen registered her disappointment. Kate explained that George was having a "wonderful Christmas" with the Middletons in Bucklebury, and like most infants "loves bright colors" and was "more interested in the wrapping paper than the gifts inside."

Determined to keep George away from the spotlight for just a little while longer, Kate took George along with her on the Middletons' annual January vacation in Mustique—the little prince's first trip outside the country—while William wrapped up his military obligations. Then, in April 2014, all three Cambridges embarked on a three-week tour of New Zealand and Australia—Prince George's first *official* trip abroad. It also marked the debut of George's new full-time nanny, Maria Teresa Borrallo. Easy to spot in her distinctive brown Norland Nanny uniform and bowler hat, Borrallo was always on hand throughout the trip to care for George—a "godsend," Kate said of George's new caretaker. "I have absolutely no idea what I would do without her."

Kate and William made their usual good-natured, fun-loving impression, coaching primary grade children in a rugby match in the New Zealand city of Dunedin (William's team beat Kate's), racing yachts in Auckland (Kate led her crew to victory over William's), posing in front of Uluru—formerly known as Ayers Rock—in the Australian Outback. Thousands turned out to greet Kate and William, but the biggest cheers were reserved for George on the two occasions when he appeared—during a children's play group in Government House, the governor-general's official residence in Wellington, and then coming face-to-face with a rabbit-like bilby named—what else?—George at Sydney's Taronga Zoo.

For fans of the royal family, George provided a much-needed reprise of the time thirty years earlier when William, nicknamed "Wombat" by his mother, had won over the hearts and minds of the Queen's subjects Down Under. "On each occasion," wrote veteran royal correspondent Nicholas Witchell, "the appeal of a nine-month-old future king has upstaged even the glamour of a future queen consort and her husband." Moreover, polls were showing that William, Kate, and George had injected new life into the royal family; support for ditching the monarchy in favor of a republic was suddenly at its lowest point in decades. Even more encouraging, much of the support came from young adults. They could identify with the exuberant, sporty, down-to-earth Cambridges who, like most new parents, spent an inordinate amount of time trying to hold on to their squirming bundle of joy while wiping dribble from his chin.

In a speech before Parliament welcoming the Cambridges, Liberal Prime Minister Tony Abbott fired a shot over the bow of his country's anti-monarchist movement. "Many decades hence," Abbott told Kate and William, "when a currently unknowable Australian prime minister welcomes your son, King George VII, to this building, that will be a sign of the stability and the continuity in the life of our nation."

In the midst of all the accolades, the Cambridges were stunned to learn that Camilla's only brother, noted wildlife conservationist and legendary bon vivant Mark Shand, had died in a fall while exiting a Manhattan hotel after a night of partying. Camilla and the sixty-two-year-old Shand were extremely close, and, understandably, she was devastated. While Kate knew that Camilla had tried to undermine her chances of marrying William, the two women now maintained a grudging respect for each other. On hearing the news, Kate found herself becoming emotional over Camilla's sudden and tragic loss. They sent their "deepest condolences" from Australia, but there was nothing else they could do. "The show," William was overheard saying to his wife as they wound down the tour, "must go on."

Their squealing son was, in fact, proving to be something more than just a reboot of Wombat; he was turning out to be something entirely new for the United Kingdom. Because his mother was not merely a commoner but from a decidedly working-class background, George embodied "almost American-style upward mobility with a British twist," wrote *Time* magazine's Andrew Ferguson. "If you work hard and play by the rules, regardless of race, color, or creed, you, too, can marry your daughter off to become the mother of a King . . . the future King of England and Defender of the Faith has emerged from a mother who is without a drop of peerage blood. My guess is the boy, quite apart from his personal qualities, will prove an inconvenience to anti-royalist and monarchists alike."

On the heels of their first overseas triumph, Kate and William journeyed to Normandy with the Queen to mark the seventieth anniversary of D-Day. At one point during a gathering described by the Palace as a "tea party" for World War II veterans, eighty-eight-year-old Arthur Jones asked Kate if it was "okay to kiss a princess."

"Of course it is," she replied, at which point Jones planted a kiss on her cheek. Later on, William jokingly accused Jones of flirting with Kate. "Were you chatting up my wife?" he demanded.

"I only gave her a kiss!" Jones replied. "William laughed," the veteran later said, "but I bet I'll be picked up now and taken to the Tower of London." Reflecting on the moment with Kate, Jones said, "It was a lovely kiss. I lost my wife ten years ago, and I'm on my own now, so I don't get many opportunities for kisses anymore."

Two months later, the Cambridges were back in Europe, this time to attend ceremonies in Belgium commemorating the hundredth anniversary of the start of World War I. No sooner did they return than Kate suddenly fell ill with the all-too-familiar symptoms of hyperemesis gravidarum. The Duchess of Cambridge, Kensington Palace announced via Twitter, was pregnant with her second child.

"Not entirely surprising," the BBC's Nicholas Witchell said of the announcement. "They want to get on with it." Prince Charles, who called the news "splendid," wasted no time stating his preferences. "It's wonderful to become a grandfather again," he said. "I'm looking forward to it, but I hope it will be a girl this time."

Prince Charles would get his wish, but first Kate would spend the next eight months trying to balance her literally gut-wrenching battle with HG with royal duties. She would pull out of events and overseas trips—to Malta, for instance—leaving William to go solo. But when she did manage to venture outside Kensington Palace or their Anmer Hall home on the grounds of Sandringham, Kate was the event's undisputed star.

One of the events Kate most regretted missing was the opening ceremony for the very first Invictus Games. Kate was uniquely aware from William's own night terrors that both brothers still suffered from their mother's sudden death and the earthshaking events that followed. She also understood that, despite her own obvious affection for her brother-in-law, Harry had felt untethered and to some degree abandoned during the two years since William and Kate had wed.

While Harry was delighted to be an uncle, every new addition to the family spelled more than just being pushed another rung down the ladder of succession. George and the baby who was coming further distanced William from his brother, and Harry felt cast adrift. With the Cambridges ensconced in Apartment 1A and Harry just across the courtyard in Nottingham Cottage, the Spare expected to see them all the time. "I assumed they'd have me over any minute now. But day after day it didn't happen," he recalled. "I get it, I thought. They're busy! Building a family! Or maybe . . . they don't want a third wheel?"

Harry's girlfriend at the time, actress and model Cressida Bonas, was a particular favorite of Kate's. It was a tenderly posed question from "Cress" about Princess Diana while they were on a ski holiday in Switzerland that actually made Harry weep—the first time he had cried about his mother since her burial at Althorp. But despite receiving both Kate's and William's stamp of approval, Cressida could not handle the pressures of royal life, and she and Harry broke up.

Kate often heard Harry talk about finding his own soulmate, just as William had, and joining the Cambridges as a foursome. The Heir was not always so encouraging, reminding Harry that not everyone was lucky enough to find a perfect love match and that he might have to reconcile himself to spending the rest of his life alone. Kate did her best to undo the damage when she could, pointing to her own decade-long trek to the altar. "You'll find someone," she told Harry. "It just takes time. . . ."

Until now, Harry had somehow managed to tamp down his anxiety, to convince himself and others that things would improve if he just soldiered on. But it all came apart as he, Kate, and William drove together in the Cambridges' Range Rover from Anmer Hall to a charity polo match in Gloucestershire. It was during the three-hour-and-forty-minute trip that Harry suffered his first-ever, full-fledged panic attack. William was behind the wheel, and looked in his rearview mirror to see his brother sweating and crimson faced in the back seat. He asked "Harold," as he often called Harry, if he was okay. In truth, every few miles Harry wanted to ask his brother if he would pull to the side of the road so, as he recalled, "I could jump out and try to catch my breath."

Kate, sitting in the front passenger seat, reached back to take Harry's hand and asked what she and William could do to help. Did he want to skip the polo match and talk it out? Consumed by feelings of dread and recurrent nightmares, the Spare admitted that he was "on the edge of a complete breakdown . . . when all sorts of grief and sorts of lies and misconceptions are coming to you from every angle." Harry was "always on the verge of punching someone. . . . I didn't know what was wrong with me."

At Kate's urging, William had sought counseling for the first time. Now they pleaded with Harry to get the therapy he so obviously needed. "Look, this is not right, this is not normal," William told his brother. "You need to talk about this stuff. It's okay." Harry credited William with getting him the help he needed to cope with his unresolved feelings of grief and abandonment—help that was never forthcoming from the royal family. "My brother, you know, bless him," Harry said. "He was a huge support to me. I owe him so much."

Yet therapy wasn't enough—at least not therapy alone. Knowing that he would soon be leaving the British Army, Harry wanted to do something significant for his fellow combat veterans. For two years, Harry had worked on establishing the Invictus (Latin for "undefeated") Games—an international competition among hundreds of injured, sick, or wounded war veterans—and now it was becoming a reality. Charles, Camilla, and William were all there—along with a videotaped message from US First Lady Michelle Obama—but Kate, whose HG symptoms were most serious during the early weeks of her pregnancies, was simply too sick to leave Kensington Palace.

Kate had hoped to be well enough to attend at least one day of the games, but she was out of commission the entire week. When the Invictus Games ended after five days with a concert staring James Blunt, the Foo Fighters, and Bryan Adams, Harry was exhausted but thrilled at what he had achieved. Moreover, the games had helped him overcome those recurring panic attacks that had left him "pouring with sweat, like, heart beating boom, boom, boom, boom." The games were, he later said, "a cure for myself."

Kate had watched Invictus unfold on television and called Harry twice to say how proud she was of him. Ironically, even as the once-disparaged Spare was now being universally praised for his philanthropic efforts, William was starting to be chastised for not working hard enough on behalf of the Crown. The press began referring to the Duke of Cambridge as "Workshy Wills," but there was a catch-22: Charles and Camilla did not want Kate and William overshadowing them, diverting attention away from the next in line for the throne. The Prince of Wales had flown into crimson-faced rages when Diana had upstaged him, and now he angrily chastised his son whenever he felt the Cambridges were getting too much attention. Kate, in particular, was in the crosshairs of "Pa's team," as William and Harry referred to Prince Charles's Clarence House advisors. For example, Kate was instructed not to hold a tennis racket when she visited a tennis club because such a charming image would knock the Duke and Duchess of Cornwall off the front page. On another occasion when Charles and Camilla were touring a factory in northern England, Kate's team was told to postpone a planned visit to a London animal shelter. "Can you imagine?" asked a courtier. "Pictures of Kate—with puppies? Too adorable. Those were the kinds of things that terrified Prince Charles."

Kate was still struggling with HG symptoms in the fall of 2014, but her health had improved by October when she made one of her customary fashion statements wearing a gray plaid Alexander McQueen dress coat to welcome Singapore President Tony Tan to the United Kingdom. When Tan's wife, Mary, asked how she was doing, Kate shot back, "Well, I've been looking forward to getting out of the house, that's for sure!"

That same day, Kate changed into a sky blue Jenny Packham wrap dress to attend the Wildlife Photographer of the Year awards at London's Natural History Museum. Two days later, she was beaming at the Autumn Gala for one of her favorite charities, Action on Addiction. The "Fashionista Duchess," as she was now labeled in the press, wore a daring black Temperley London "Emblem Flare" dress, which featured slashed panels over a nude slip to mimic stained glass ironwork. The bold $953 dress sold out within minutes.

Determined not to be driven into seclusion by HG, Kate managed a half-dozen other appearances in and around London, including a visit to an oil refinery in Wales and the Royal Variety Performance at the London Palladium starring, among others, Ed Sheeran and the group One Direction.

By design, George had been nowhere to be seen since returning from Australia. When nanny Maria Borrallo told Kate that she and George were being stalked by two photographers in nearby Hyde Park, William ordered his lawyers to tell them to back off or face charges of harassment. A Palace spokesman explained that it was "more the fundamental weirdness of two grown men following a fourteen-month-old baby around London that we're concerned about."

Kate's morning sickness subsided to the point where she could travel overseas in December—this time on a whirlwind three-day trip to New York. Hundreds of fans greeted the royal motorcade as it pulled up to the Carlyle Hotel on East 76th Street—once John F. Kennedy's "New York White House" and Diana's favorite hotel in the city (photos of Jackie Kennedy Onassis and the late princess entering the Carlyle hang in the lobby).

In a country where Diana was venerated even more than in her own, comparisons between the Duchess of Cambridge and the late Princess of Wales were preordained. But Kate undeniably brought a magic all her own. It helped that, as one American journalist put it, Kate was "regally dressed, flawlessly groomed, and bejeweled for every occasion."

The royal couple's packed schedule included a visit to the Northside Center for Child Development in Harlem, where Kate helped wrap Christmas gifts with volunteers. At one point, one of the women volunteers snapped loudly at the Duchess, telling her to "keep wrapping!" Kate glared at the woman and rolled her eyes—a seldom-seen view of the future queen that instantly went viral. Later that afternoon, the Cambridges met Bill, Hillary, and Chelsea Clinton at the British consul general's residence. Then it was on to Brooklyn's Barclays Center for a Nets game, where they chatted with fellow courtsiders Beyoncé and Jay-Z, and seemed genuinely thrilled when LeBron James gave them a Cleveland Cavaliers jersey for Prince George.

There would also be a visit to the twin reflecting pools of the 9/11 Memorial, a reception at NeueHouse in Manhattan's trendy Flatiron District (where Kate was especially thrilled to meet *Star Trek: The Next Generation* actor Sir Patrick Stewart for the first time), and finally a splashy fundraising dinner celebrating the six hundredth anniversary of the Cambridges' alma mater, St. Andrews University. The event was held at the Metropolitan Museum of Art's gallery that holds Ancient Egypt's spectacular Temple of Dendur.

At each and every stop, the number one topic of conversation was Kate—specifically her maternity wardrobe now that she was a quite visible four months along. "Kate Middleton may not be able to see her toes," wrote the *New York Post*'s Alev Aktar, "but she's still flaunting her fabulous legs in short skirts and high heels—unless, of course, she's wearing a floaty evening gown." Kate "dazzled New Yorkers on her first official trip to Manhattan in seven sassy and sophisticated outfits," Aktar continued, and in the process "made the crown seem cool." Fashion journalist Eva Chen praised Kate for doing "a really good job of being tasteful, refined, and still modern. She looks pretty much exactly how you would want a young pregnant princess to look."

As always, there was ample proof that Kate was the world's most influential style setter. From the $1,063 black wool and ivory crepe "Washington" coat by the London womenswear label Goat to the $595 Tory Burch "Bettina" gray bouclé coat shot with metallic thread to the $99 turtleneck "Vanessa" dress from Seraphine (adorned with an $80,000 Cartier Trinity necklace in rose, yellow, and white gold), everything the Duchess wore was suddenly placed on back order.

Kate returned home to London, in the words of one of the seven Palace staffers who accompanied the royal couple to New York, "completely spent. She just collapsed. The strain can be just overwhelming, but Princess Catherine would never let you see it."

The Cambridges had finally moved into the newly upgraded Anmer Hall, just five minutes away from Sandringham House via the aptly named King's Avenue. Now that she was a mother, Kate was determined to host her first family Christmas there—even though the place was haunted. During the renovations, the Cambridges learned that sixteenth-century Jesuit martyr Henry Walpole was born on the grounds of Anmer and captured there by agents of Elizabeth I for being a Catholic priest. Walpole was brought back from York to the Tower of London, where he was tortured on the rack and then hanged, drawn, and quartered.

As far as William and Kate were concerned, the fact that the ghost of Walpole was said to roam the halls of Anmer Hall merely added to the character of the place. "No old home," Kate said, "would be complete without a ghost now, would it?"

At Anmer Hall, Kate was set on re-creating the kind of family Christmases she'd known as a child—days spent wrapping gifts, decorating the tree, playing board games, and singing carols by the fire with Michael Middleton dressed up either as Father Christmas, an elf, or a reindeer. (One Christmas, Kate's fun-loving dad wore an inflatable sumo wrestler costume because he was "getting bored.")

But first, William had to seek permission from his grandmother for the

Cambridges to host the Middletons on Christmas Day, with the proviso that Kate and William attend the royal family's annual black-tie Christmas Eve dinner and Christmas morning services at St. Mary Magdalene Church on the Sandringham estate. Along with everyone else, the Queen was disappointed that George had stayed home at Anmer Hall with his nanny. William told well-wishers gathered outside St. Mary Magdalene that George had been kept under wraps because "it's a little cold" and added that he and Kate were "really looking forward to going back to see what destruction he's caused." Kate admitted that George was a bit "rambunctious" to be attending a religious service with the Queen. "Believe me," she said, "you would have heard him in the church. He's just too noisy!" When one of the locals handed Kate a bouquet and told her she looked "beautiful," the five-months-pregnant princess replied with a sigh, "I feel . . . big."

By way of providing their daughter with a much-needed distraction—not to mention an opportunity to escape Britain's dreary January weather—the Middletons headed off on an island holiday with the Cambridges in tow. "Kate's Mum Never Does Things by Halves" read the *Daily Mail*'s front-page headline describing the "tireless social climber's" sixtieth birthday bash on Mustique. Joining William, Kate, George, and the Middletons were twenty-seven other guests flown in to toast the future king's grandmother with signature cocktails—a pink champagne and grenadine concoction for the birthday girl and, for Kate, a mocktail blend of maple spice, passion fruit syrup, pineapple, and ice.

No sooner did she return home than Kate was dispatched to spend time with the UK's America's Cup yacht team. Even with the new baby's due date rapidly approaching, there would be more engagements for the Cambridges. But to everyone's surprise, Harry was emerging as something of a royal workhorse. Buoyed by the success of the Invictus Games, the Spare was making several appearances a day, shaking hands and giving speeches sans the heart-pounding anxiety attacks.

Harry was nearing the end of ten years in the military—halfway to the twenty years he once said he would serve to qualify for a pension. Instead, in March 2015 he announced he would soon be leaving the armed forces.

Kate was delighted, and for reasons that were not entirely unselfish. A month earlier, William had signed a two-year contract to fly helicopters with the East Anglian Air Ambulance service in Cambridgeshire, just an hour's drive from Anmer Hall. With a second child on the way, Kate could not count on her husband to be on hand as they raised their young family in the Norfolk countryside—and out of royal duty reach. Conveniently, Harry, who remained behind at Kensington Palace, would now be available to take up the slack.

Charles and Camilla were of two minds when it came to the Cambridges' decision to at least temporarily jump off the nonstop carousel of tree plantings, ribbon cuttings, and walkabouts. On the one hand, there would be fewer opportunities for Kate—and to a lesser extent William—to hog the spotlight the senior royals so desperately craved. On the other hand, even after his departure from the army, Harry wasn't exactly filling the void left by his brother and much-adored sister-in-law. In 2015, William, Harry, and Kate would manage a combined total of two hundred appearances. By contrast, Queen Elizabeth and Prince Philip racked up four hundred while Charles, Camilla, and Princess Anne scored nearly five hundred official engagements *each*.

In the early morning hours of March 2, 2015, Kate checked back into the Lindo Wing of St. Mary's Hospital and at 8:34 a.m. gave birth to an eight-pound, three-ounce daughter. Again, while both parents hoped for a daughter, they wanted the baby's sex to be a surprise. As before, church bells pealed and cannons boomed—but this time pink light illuminated landmarks like the London Eye, Tower Bridge, and the fountains in Trafalgar Square.

The new princess's arrival differed in other ways, as well. Most important, the Cambridges' daughter made history: she was the first daughter of a future monarch born since the abolition of royal primogeniture, which meant she was now fourth in line for the crown behind her big brother George. Kate and William were also less reluctant to introduce their daughter to the world than they had been with George. When she was not quite ten hours old, their infant daughter was taken out to meet the press and whisked off to

Kensington Palace, where Carole, Michael, and Pippa Middleton were the first to arrive and hold the baby. Later that day, her name was announced: Charlotte Elizabeth Diana—Her Royal Highness Princess Charlotte of Cambridge. Since Charlotte is the feminine form of Charles, the name paid tribute to three of the most significant people in William's life.

The Queen was next to arrive, once again in her jade green Bentley. "She was really thrilled," Kate said of the monarch, "that we'd had a little girl." Charles, delighted that he now had the granddaughter he had always wanted, followed the Queen and even came back the next day for an extra peek at the baby. Once he left, the Cambridges headed off to their new full-time life at Anmer Hall. The Prince of Wales was not alone in his enthusiasm for adding a little girl to the royal family. "It's very special," Kate said. "I feel very, very lucky that George has got a little sister."

Presumably because they would one day be king and queen, the Cambridges continued to shoulder most of the blame for not lightening the onerous load borne by their royal elders. But then there were the sort of magical moments that only their young family could provide. During Trooping the Colour ceremonies that June, twenty-two-month-old George made his debut on the Buckingham Palace balcony wearing the same powder blue romper that William had worn thirty-one years earlier. Charlotte remained home with her nanny, but the thousands of onlookers cheered as William, wearing the scarlet uniform of a colonel in the Irish Guards, held George with Kate at his side.

"Prince George Steals the Show" ran the headline in several newspapers on both sides of the Atlantic. The point was also made that Kate, who wore a blue floral silk dress by Catherine Walker—one of Diana's favorites—"looked nothing less than radiant" just six weeks after giving birth.

One person on the balcony who decidedly did not look radiant was Harry, who seemed to sulk even as the throng went wild over his nephew. In the span of two years, he had been pushed from number three to number five in the line of succession, but that's not what was bothering him. Harry had often spoken of his desire to someday have a family like his brother. But now that Cressida Bonas, like Chelsy Davy before her, had essentially been chased away by the press and the pressures of royal life, he wondered if it was in the cards for him.

Kate, more than anyone, appreciated that both brothers were still living on the edge of a deep well of depression. With the success of the Invictus Games and a little extra help from therapy, Harry had only recently begun to confront his demons head-on and put his life back together. But despite brief hookups with one or two models and actresses, Harry's love life had fallen apart, and those old feelings of anger, isolation, and self-loathing that had pushed Harry to the brink were making a comeback.

Harry needed a pep talk, and Kate arranged for the brothers to meet at Kensington Palace. The right woman was going to come along, William reassured the Spare. It was only a matter of time, as their mother said, that he would also "find that someone who is everything to you."

In the meantime, Kate pushed Harry to focus on the more than one hundred charitable organizations he and William supported. After a brief summer holiday with the Queen and the rest of her royal in-laws at Balmoral, Kate was once again sucked into the royal spin cycle. Soon she was back to making a minimum of three appearances a week. To quell the nagging and unfair criticism that she and William were somehow loafing on the job, Her Majesty made a show of presenting Kate with the Royal Family Order of Queen Elizabeth II, the highest honor that she could bestow on a female member of the royal family.

Kate's value as a representative of the Crown was on display once again in late October, when she attended her first state banquet at Buckingham Palace, thrown in honor of Chinese President Xi Jinping. Kate, as always, had done her homework, researching which colors spoke to the honored guests—in this case red, which both honored the flag of the People's Republic and also represented joy and good luck in Chinese culture. When she walked into the massive ballroom wearing a cinnabar-red, floor-length, cap-sleeved Jenny Packham gown and the diamond-and-pearl-encrusted Lotus Flower Tiara—on loan from Her Majesty—the normally unflappable President Xi appeared dumbstruck.

"Kate Dazzles" were the first two words in dozens of headlines, and in

China, praise for the Duchess of Cambridge was equally effusive. "Kate Is Wearing Chinese Red to Greet the President" trumpeted a headline in the state-owned *China Daily* newspaper. "Kate is everything you want in a princess," wrote a Hong Kong commentator. "She is straight from a fairy tale."

Yet Kate knew all too well that she provided a necessary distraction from the weighty issues facing both countries. "Behind her glittering debut at a Buckingham Palace state dinner," wrote Cecilia Rodriguez in *Forbes* magazine, "unseen but important political and economic interests were hard at work." Rodriguez went on to write that Kate's dress was "universally approved as impeccable elegance but also symbolic of a crucial economic agenda." Prime Minister David Cameron wanted stronger ties with China, and the Queen agreed. Trouble was, Prince Charles was a friend of the Dalai Lama and an outspoken critic of China's harsh policies toward Tibet. Since Kate's father-in-law chose not to attend the banquet—widely interpreted as a deliberate snub—the Cambridges were put in the awkward position of choosing between Prince Charles and the Queen. They chose to side with the woman Diana used to call "the Boss."

The next day, Kate and William met with the Chinese president and his fashion-conscious wife a second time. Once again, the princess left nothing to chance, wearing a high-collared Dolce & Gabbana lace dress in a color called Chinese violet. William wore a purple tie to match. Action star Jackie Chan was introduced to the Chinese leader, as was the cast of the television series *Poldark*, and someone dressed up as Kung Fu Panda. They also gave Xi a peek at the Aston Martin DB10 driven by Daniel Craig as James Bond in the film *Spectre*. Despite it all, it was Kate who took center stage online and in the press.

Kate understood the public perception of her—poised, stylish, smart, kind, charming, athletic, compassionate, devoted wife, dutiful member of the royal family, hands-on mom. She also knew that, even though she had waited for a decade to land her prince, she was not viewed as ambitious—not even after a hit West End play called *King Charles III* landed on Broadway in November 2015.

Members of the royal family traditionally took dramatized depictions of their lives in stride. The Queen was so fond of Dame Helen Mirren's Oscar-winning portrayal of her in *The Queen* that she invited the actress to tea. Mirren played Her Majesty yet again in 2015, this time winning a Tony for her performance in the Broadway production of a Peter Morgan play called *The Audience*. Morgan, who had also written *The Queen*, would go on the following year to create a Netflix series called *The Crown*. (Like other members of the royal family, Kate enjoyed early seasons of *The Crown*, but that interest tapered off over the years as storylines hit closer to home.)

King Charles III differed wildly from these other efforts, however. Written by Mike Bartlett in blank verse, the play is set in a future England where Kate's father-in-law is now an embattled monarch. The Duchess of Cambridge emerges as the villain of the piece, scheming to undermine the King. Ultimately, Charles abdicates, William is crowned as William V, and Kate becomes the new queen. *King Charles III* was later adapted for television and aired on both the BBC and PBS's *Masterpiece* in the United States. No royal admitted to seeing either the play, which in the US was nominated for five Tony Awards, or the TV production. But Kate was reportedly nonplussed at the cunning and manipulative qualities embodied in her fictionalized character. "Cunning? Me?" she quipped to an advisor who had seen the production at London's Almeida Theatre. "I'll have to give that a thought."

Once again, the grown-up Cambridges made it to Christmas Day church services at Sandringham, with Prince William gallantly holding an umbrella over his wife's head as the rain pelted down. Cloudburst or no, Kate once again made fashion news wearing a green felt cloche with a matching forest green belted wool Sportmax coat over a "Cezanne" pleated dress by the British brand Great Plains. *Glamour* proclaimed it "one of her most iconic looks ever."

Things were a little more informal back at Bucklebury Manor, where the rest of the Middleton clan kept up their family tradition of weekly game nights. In the beginning of his relationship with Kate, William unhesitatingly joined in. After all, competition ran in the royal blood. No one enjoyed a spirited contest more than Queen Elizabeth II, whether cheering on her horse at Ascot or watching a tug-of-war at the Highland Games. Prince Philip was a world champion four-in-hand carriage driver, Princess Anne competed in equestrian events at the Olympics, and Prince Charles was so passionate about polo that he suffered countless injuries on the field. And William and Kate did not hesitate to compete against each other for the cameras—be it a rowing contest or a footrace.

Kate's family was a different matter altogether. Carole and Michael Middleton taught their children that winning was everything, and their heated board games often devolved into shouting matches that ended when one of the players angrily flipped the board over and stormed off. The Middleton family games—their favorite was a rapid-fire multiplayer version of solitaire called Racing Demon (Pounce or Nerts in the US)—were so heated and all-consuming that William now made excuses to avoid getting sucked in. Usually, he'd jump up from the kitchen table and offer to take James's dog, Ella, for a walk.

"William would flinch at our ruthless determination to win at all costs," Kate's brother said. "He'd be delighted to be the first out, and when no longer compelled to take part, he'd slink off to cuddle Ella. Better still, he'd absent himself from the game entirely. 'James, does Ella need a walk?' he'd ask before we'd even started dealing the cards. My sisters and I would exchange a knowing glance."

That January a quick ski trip to the French Alps—their first holiday as a family of four and the first time either George or Charlotte had seen snow—showcased the blurred line between reality and royal staging for public consumption. Royal photographer John Stillwell was supposed to snap some shots of Kate and William skiing, but the weather was too hazy. At one point, Stillwell tapped her on her shoulder, took her aside, and whispered, "Kate, make a snowball and have a snowball fight . . . but push it in his face."

"Pardon?" she replied.

"Just whack him in the face with a snowball." Later, the photographer admitted he "didn't think she'd do it, but she did. William saw the funny side of it." Later, Stillwell took the first shots of the family in the snow—

George wearing a navy snowsuit and red bobble hat, baby Charlotte in a white padded snowsuit, pink boots, and matching pink-striped hat.

Once they were ensconced back at Anmer Hall, William picked up where he had left off with the East Anglian Air Ambulance service, working ten-hour overnight shifts while nanny Maria Borrallo and Kate looked after the children. Granny Carole Middleton frequently made the three-hour drive up from Bucklebury to help out, a degree of involvement in the Cambridges' lives that was alien to upper-class Britons who were raised by nurses and nannies from birth.

Kate and William took another major step away from the way things had always been done by enrolling two-year-old George at Westacre Montessori School in Norfolk. Diana broke the royal mold when William became the first royal family member to attend preschool. But William's $20,000-per-year nursery school was located near Kensington Palace and catered almost exclusively to London's privileged class. By contrast, Westacre Montessori charged a reasonably modest $50 a day per child, and still provided financial assistance to 85 percent of its pupils.

In April, George and Charlotte stayed behind while their parents embarked on a punishing seven-day tour of India and the Himalayan kingdom of Bhutan, where the country's fifth *Druk Gyalpo* (Dragon King), Jigme Khesar Namgyel Wangchuck, and Queen Jetsun Pema welcomed them as "William and Kate of the Orient" during a spectacular ceremony featuring scores of sari-clad dancers and saffron-robed monks playing trumpets, cymbals, and drums. Much to their hosts' delight, Kate gamely tried her hand at archery, Bhutan's national sport. With William at her side and strong winds seemingly blowing from every direction, Kate, dressed in a purple-and-white dress inspired by native Bhutanese costumes, let fly with an arrow at a target nearly five hundred feet away. She missed, but it scarcely mattered—television captured a young woman clearly having the time of her life. News outlets in the United States and Britain could not resist comparing her to *Hunger Games* heroine Katniss Everdeen. "The Duchess of Cambridge," *Entertainment Tonight* host Kevin Frazier rhapsodized, "continues to surprise and delight us."

En route home, William and Kate made the requisite stop at the Taj Mahal in Agra, India, sitting on the same bench where Princess Diana had sat alone as her marriage to Charles fell apart. The last-minute decision to put their own spin on the iconic photo of Diana looking forlorn was William's. In contrast to Diana, Kate and her husband smiled brightly. "We wanted," the Heir said, "to make our own memories."

Inside the Taj Mahal itself, Kate became emotional when their guide told them it was built by the Mughal emperor Shah Jahan in memory of his wife Mumtaz Mahal. Moments later, Kate managed to make William laugh when she said the emperor's wife "really deserves this kind of building. Obviously they were *madly* in love with each other."

Later that April, Kate and William joined Harry in cohosting a dinner with Michelle and Barack Obama at Apartment 1A in Kensington Palace. No one noticed until the last minute before the presidential couple's arrival that the immense seventeenth-century painting by Dutch old master Aelbert Cuyp dominating the living room depicted a young Black servant holding the reins of two horses. There was no time to replace the artwork, but Kate enlisted the help of aides to hastily reposition a plant to hide the painting's potentially offensive title, *The Negro Page*.

The Obamas were too busy being charmed by Prince George to notice. Charlotte was already asleep, but Kate allowed George to stay up fifteen minutes past his 7 p.m. bedtime to meet the Obamas. When he walked into the room wearing pajamas and a monogrammed white bathrobe, their hearts melted. "Just adorable," Michelle said as President Obama knelt to shake the ruddy-cheeked prince's hand and have a brief eye-level to eye-level chat. Then Kate led her little boy over to the handcrafted rocking horse the Obamas had given him when he was born. Moments later, the adults looked on as George played with his new toy from the Obamas—a plush replica of their dog, Bo.

Once photos of the meeting were released, George proved that he too was a trendsetter. CNN dubbed him "the world's youngest fashion icon," pointing out that for once "nobody noticed what either Princess Kate or the American First Lady were wearing" because George "stole the show.

There's some bad news, though, for the young prince's fashion followers: the $39 bathrobe has already sold out."

A week later, President Obama used the encounter in his joke-filled speech at the White House Correspondents' Dinner—the last he would give before leaving the White House. "Even some foreign leaders have been looking ahead, anticipating my departure," he told his audience. "Last week, Prince George showed up to our meeting in his bathrobe. *That* was a slap in the face."

Harry had seemed unusually quiet during the royals' dinner with the Obamas, admitting to Michelle that he wanted to settle down but hadn't yet "found the right girl." Kate was so worried about Harry's uncharacteristically pensive state of mind that she reached out to one of the brothers' closest pals, only to discover that he hadn't seen Harry for months. To her astonishment, Kate learned that only recently had Harry begun to reconnect with friends—that for much of the previous year he had kept to himself, preferring to spend nights home alone at Nott Cott, eating over the sink with "*Friends* on low in the background."

By his own account, Harry had become agoraphobic—all in an effort to avoid the panic attacks that could still strike without warning. Just a few months before their cozy dinner with the Obamas, Harry was suddenly gripped by chest pains after being forced to give a speech. William, inexplicably, went backstage to needle his brother. "Harold!" he shouted. "Look at you! You're drenched!"

When she heard about the encounter, Kate knew it would do no good to ask William to apologize. Instead, she reached out directly to Harry, inviting him to join them in the exciting new cause they were championing: Heads Together, aimed at ending the stigma surrounding mental health. It became the trio's most important joint initiative.

Kate, the driving force behind Heads Together, staked out mental health in the schools as the area where she would concentrate her efforts. Given Harry's decade-long service in the military, it was only logical that he zero in on post-traumatic stress disorder (PTSD) among wounded warriors. William's focus was on the rapidly accelerating suicide rate among young men—something he had sadly witnessed firsthand.

In fact, it was Kate's concern over the state of William's mental health—far more than Harry's—that drove her to establish Heads Together. While Kate cared for the children and made the occasional public appearance, her husband was exposed to soul-searing tragedy on a daily basis from his very first day on the job as an air ambulance pilot. His first callout was to the home of a young man who had taken his own life—one of five suicides or attempted suicides that took place every day in East Anglia alone. From then on, William's work life consisted of ten- and twelve-hour days transporting the victims of falls, car crashes, strokes, heart attacks, gunshots, knifings, domestic violence, workplace mishaps—and, of course, suicides—to local emergency rooms.

"You're exposed to such high levels of sadness, trauma, and death that impacts our own life—and your family life," William admitted. "It's always there, and you're drawn into it. . . . You see the world as a much more depressed, darker, blacker place." Now that he had a family of his own, William was affected more deeply than ever. "We're all human beings with loved ones. It's only natural to become depressed when you're surrounded by such grief, such bereavement."

The Heir also allowed that he was often stricken with "some very dark moments. You try not to take it home, but sometimes . . . it can be quite difficult." After two years of constant exposure to "very dark moments," William conceded he was experiencing "a very negative feeling where you think death is just around the corner. . . . I could feel it brewing up inside me, and I could feel it was going to be a problem."

Kate was terrified. She no longer sat up nights imagining that the father of her children might crash into the side of a mist-shrouded mountain trying to airlift someone to a hospital. Now she was consumed with the fear that William, who had always been given to dark moods and long, brooding silences, was slowly sinking into a quagmire of depression.

Adding to the potential recipe for disaster was William's temper—not his father's hair-trigger, exactly, but formidable nonetheless. It was worth noting that, long before he met Kate, the Heir ran an elderly aristocrat off the road with his car and almost trampled a well-known press photographer with his horse. Harry, who admitted such outbursts ran in the family, called the brothers' bottled-up rage "red mist"—a fog of anger that momentarily blinded them to all reason. If William did indulge in the rare window-rattling tantrum, it was invariably aimed at the excesses of the UK's prying press or at Palace operatives demanding he do more on behalf of the Firm.

William was spending his pulse-pounding air ambulance workdays surrounded by gore, pain, suffering, death, and loss. But Kate knew that, no matter how overwhelming it all seemed, her husband would never act on thoughts of suicide; he was far too devoted to his family and to the Crown. Nor would he ever lash out at—or close himself off from—the children; he was too dedicated a father for that. But the twin burdens of his air ambulance and royal personage on-call jobs were taking their toll. It would take considerable prodding and cajoling on her part, but Kate eventually convinced William to set a deadline for exiting East Anglia Air. He agreed to climb out of the cockpit of the Eurocopter EC145 he normally flew once and for all and return to full-time royal life after George turned four and entered his second year of preschool.

William had, in fact, grown tired of the ceaseless chatter about the Cambridges not doing their share as royals. He acknowledged to Sky News during an interview marking the Queen's ninetieth birthday that her schedule was "packed," but insisted she understood "that I'm a family man, and I want to be around for my children as much as I can." He added that, as Kate had wished, he had plans to quit the air service and help out more around the palace once George and Charlotte were just "a bit older."

William's problematic job situation wasn't the only thing on Kate's mind in August 2016. Harry had accompanied Prince Charles and the Cambridges to France to mark the hundredth anniversary of World War I's Battle of the Somme, but they hadn't seen Harry since. It was so unlike him not to drop in from Nott Cott when they were just across the courtyard. Soon, Palace scuttlebutt had it that he was head over heels in love with a mysterious young woman.

Harry's path to finding his mystery lover was meandering, to say the least. Scrolling on Instagram, he stumbled upon a clip of his friend Violet von Westenholz and an unknown woman using a filter to give themselves dog tongues, ears, and noses. Nevertheless, he was instantly smitten with the stranger. Before long they were texting into the early morning hours, meeting clandestinely for drinks at London's exclusive Soho House (with three royal protection officers lurking nearby), getting to know each other over cozy dinners at Nott Cott. There were also the usual cloak-and-dagger outings—arriving separately at unexpected places, using assumed names, pretending not to know each other as they shopped in a supermarket.

The Spare and his new girlfriend also bonded over their shared love of Africa, and traveled there together in August after having only known each other a few weeks. "This beautiful woman just sort of tripped and fell into my life," Harry said. "I fell into her life." The speed with which they fell in love "so incredibly quickly was a confirmation to me that all the stars were aligned, and everything was just perfect."

There was a complication: she worked full-time in Toronto, and that meant to some extent that theirs was a long-distance relationship. But the absences just made their reunions that much more intense. "Is it . . . The One?" he asked himself. "Have I found her? At long, long last?"

Kate was eager to know as well. "Something is going on with your brother," Kate told William, "and I think we should find out what it is." Over dinner at KP, everyone played it coy at first. Kate knew from the gossip she was hearing that there was someone new in Harry's life, but was careful not to push too hard. For his part, Harry was reluctant to say anything at first. "I wasn't sure I was ready to tell them," he later wrote. But after he helped tuck George and Charlotte into bed and the adults settled themselves in the Cambridges' TV room, Harry spoke up. "There's a new person in my life," Harry said. Before he went any further, the Spare pleaded with them to keep the news top secret. "I'm sure this time, Willy. I have never met anyone like her. She is perfect. She is *the* one."

William's face fell slightly when Harry told them his new love was an American, divorced, biracial—and an actress. Kate, inscrutably joyful as ever, felt her heart skip a beat when she heard all these adjectives strung together, but she would never let it show. "Yes, Harold, go on," William continued. "Would we know her?"

She starred in a TV series that, until they met, Harry had never heard of. "*Suits*," he said.

"Fuck off!" William shot back, jumping out of his seat. "No way!"

"Impossible!" Kate chimed in. "Harry, it's one of our favorite shows! We watch it *all the time*—we're *completely* addicted. What's her name?"

"Her name is Meghan. Meghan Markle."

From the pit to the palace in three generations.

—Malcolm Ross, longtime courtier, on the rise of the Middletons

6

Flower Girls' Dresses

To Bully or Not to Bully

"Spitting Blood"

January 10, 2017

Meghan, barefoot and wearing ripped jeans, threw open the door to Nottingham Cottage and beckoned the Cambridges in. Kate, elegantly attired in a cocktail dress and flashing the iconic blue sapphire engagement ring that had once belonged to Diana, smiled demurely and stepped inside. How was it possible that we ever managed in such a tiny space? she thought. William followed closely, holding Princess Charlotte in his arms. It was a school day, Kate explained, so sadly George was at Anmer Hall with his nanny. It had been four months since Harry told them about the new woman in his life, and while Meghan had already met William—"I want to meet the girl who put that silly grin on my brother's face" was the Heir's opening line—she had yet to meet Kate. "It's so wonderful to finally meet you," she said as she wrapped her arms around Kate. It was at this moment that Kate seemed startled, then stiffened.

It should not have come as a surprise to Miss Markle. During that first meeting with William months earlier, he recoiled when she came in for a hug. This time, he was suffering from a cold—"the perfect excuse for a classic collision of cultures," Harry called it. "I was a hugger," Meghan later said. "Always been a hugger. I didn't realize that that is really jarring for a lot of Brits. I guess I started to understand very quickly that the formality on the outside carried through on the inside." For Americans, she explained, "there is the side one presents to the world and then you close the door and you go, 'Oh, great. Okay, we can relax now.' " Not so for the markedly more reserved upper-class Britons, said Markle, "and that was surprising to me." What also surprised her was that William and Kate acted as if they had never heard of *Suits*, even though Harry had told her they were die-hard fans of the series.

Incredibly, Meghan had gone undetected by the press throughout the summer and fall of 2016—in large part because so much else was happening. In the United States, Donald Trump squared off in a race for the presidency against heavily favored former First Lady, senator, and secretary of state Hillary Rodham Clinton—and won. The United Kingdom offered up a shocking upset of its own when voters chose to exit the European Union, forcing Prime Minister David Cameron to resign and coining a new term—"Brexit"—that would soon be tweaked for other purposes.

Also making a sizable splash were the traveling Cambridges—three-year-old George, his one-year-old sister Charlotte, and their parents—drawing thousands of cheering fans as they barnstormed Canada. It was their first foreign tour as a family of four and the high point for the royal offspring was a children's party in British Columbia complete with puppets. a petting zoo, and miniature horses named Honey and T.J. *Vanity Fair* dutifully reported that Charlotte kept yelling "pop" as she "obsessively" threw herself into a pile of balloons, and that George "picked up a fish-shaped bubble gun and cheekily fired at his little sister. All in all," continued the magazine, "there are going to be enough pictures . . . to populate at least four different George-and-Charlotte wall calendars."

Kate hit the ground running as soon as they returned home: a trip to a soccer match and then a children's hospice in Manchester that had been opened by Princess Diana twenty-five years earlier was followed by a lavish black-tie reception at Buckingham Palace to honor British medalists from the 2016 Rio Olympics and Paralympic Games.

While all this was going on, Meghan was quietly meeting Harry's friends and relatives. Even before her first awkward encounter with William, Meghan—who was already friends with Prince Andrew's daughter Eugenie—met Sarah Ferguson, Andrew, and the Queen. Later over tea at Clarence House, the couple had a lively chat with Charles and Camilla about Americanisms versus Britishisms and their shared love of dogs. (When Meghan mentioned her rescue beagle, Guy, and how the breed was frequently used for animal experiments and then euthanized, Charles and Camilla were visibly shaken.) Soon the conversation turned to the arts, acting, and Meghan's career. Charles was impressed, even delighted. Remembering William's reaction and cognizant of Charles's status as monarch-to-be, Meghan resisted the urge to hug her future father-in-law, demurely offering her cheek instead—something Charles "actually seemed to enjoy."

By the time she met Kate—even before she met William, in fact—Meghan had already been subjected to ruthless, often racist, attacks in the British press. Once the *Sunday Express* revealed that Harry and Meghan were an item, there were the inevitable comparisons with Wallis Simpson, that other American divorcée who sparked a constitutional crisis that ended with Edward VIII's abdication in 1936.

Most egregious of all the attacks was the *Daily Mail* piece headlined "Harry's Girl Is (Almost) Straight Outta Compton" and columnist Rachel Johnson's assertion that Meghan would "thicken" the royal family's "thin blue blood" and "pale skin" with "rich and exotic DNA."

The stories weren't all racist in nature. In addition to several essentially depicting Kate's family as bankrupt grifters, one hinted that Meghan was a porn star. "Harry's Girl's on Pornhub" blared the front-page story in the *Sun*. The story inside made no mention of the fact that someone had posted a *Suits* clip of Meghan's fully clothed character up against a filing cabinet on the X-rated website that came nowhere close to being pornographic.

What was more revealing about the *Sun*'s Pornhub story is how it was presented—right below a full-length photo of a broadly smiling Kate dressed in a floor-length white evening gown with a thigh-high slit up the side at the premiere of the film *A Street Cat Named Bob*. "The press," said one former Kensington Palace staffer, "was playing them off against each other from the very beginning, whether they were happy with that or not."

Kate had dealt with exposés laying bare her own family's shortcomings—from her gum-snapping mum's social climbing to photos of her naked brother to her uncle's drug-fueled buffoonery. So when Meghan's half sister, Samantha Markle, lambasted Meghan as a "shallow social climber" who had always dreamt of being a princess—the royal family would be "appalled by what Meghan's done to her own family"—Kate understandably sympathized with Harry's girlfriend. But what if it were all true?

Whatever doubts Kate and William harbored took a back seat to Harry's moral outrage. With William's backing and his father's consent, a furious Harry had the Palace issue a scathing statement claiming "a line had been crossed" by Fleet Street. The "wave of abuse and harassment" directed at Meghan included a "smear on the front page of a national newspaper, the racial undertones of comment pieces, and the outright sexism and racism of social media trolls." Harry compared the attacks to the "pressure, scrutiny, and harassment" endured by his mother, whose decision to date a Muslim man, Dodi Fayed, fueled the media frenzy and car chase that ultimately led to her death.

Still unsure of what to think—her big-sisterly instincts were telling her that the divorced American actress might not be the perfect fit for her Harry—Kate managed to put off meeting Meghan face-to-face for two full months after William made the effort. Now that she finally had Kate at Nott Cott, Meghan was determined to win her over despite the Duchess's aversion to hugs. "Happy belated birthday!" Meghan burbled—Kate had turned thirty-five the day before—and handed the birthday girl a gift Meghan had thoughtfully wrapped herself: a $295 Smythson Portobello leather notebook.

Meghan's charm offensive did not stop there. She served her guests a three-course dinner that she had prepared, and when William began coughing, Meghan darted into another room and returned with one of her favorite cold remedies: a homeopathic blend of turmeric, oil of oregano, vitamin C, and cayenne. William thanked her profusely and promised to down the concoction when they returned home to Apartment 1A, but Kate was unconvinced. "That's very kind of you," she said, "but my husband is quite conservative when it comes to medicine. Doesn't like home remedies. He will *never* take that!"

Meghan was eager to earn Kate's respect, if not her affection. She also appreciated, perhaps to a lesser degree than she should have, Kate's seemingly effortless ability to walk the royal tightrope. Without having to be asked, both Kate and William offered to do whatever they could to help make Meghan's transition into the royal family as seamless as possible. The Cambridges were turning out to be "amazing" partners, Harry and Meghan repeated as frequently and as publicly as possible in the ensuing months.

In truth, from the beginning each side harbored festering doubts about the other. Why, Meghan wondered, did Kate seem so hell-bent on delaying their first meeting? Kate, in turn, grew suspicious when Meghan complimented her style and asked the princess if she might recommend some of her favorite British designers—a request Kate instantly viewed as an attempt to poach her fashion contacts. William's wife was unaware that their soon-to-be sister-in-law already had, primarily through her Hollywood friends and long-standing British pals like designer Misha Nonoo and Princess Eugenie, carefully cultivated fashion contacts of her own on both sides of the Atlantic.

Much to her husband's chagrin, Kate and Carole Middleton grew increasingly concerned that Meghan would eclipse Pippa at her May wedding to billionaire hedge fund manager, former race car driver, and endurance athlete James Matthews. Matthews, heir to the feudal title of Laird of Glen

Affric and the ten-thousand-acre estate in the Scottish Highlands that goes with it, was the elder son of David Matthews, owner of the luxury Eden Rock resort on the Caribbean island of St. Barts.

Caught in the middle, William shrugged that there was nothing he could do; disinviting Harry and Meghan was not an option. A compromise was reached: Harry would attend the wedding ceremony at St. Mark's Church in Berkshire, and then he and Meghan would arrive together at the reception. It scarcely mattered that Meghan was absent from the church. That morning the *Sun* ran a front-page photo of Meghan's derriere in tight yoga pants next to the familiar close-up of Pippa's backside taken when she was Kate's maid of honor. The headline: "It's Meghan vs. Pippa in the Wedding of the Rears."

Kate was understandably outraged on her sister's behalf, and while she could not blame Meghan, the fact remained that Harry's girlfriend was dominating UK media in a way no American woman had since Wallis Simpson. Still, that summer had far more pressing matters to contend with, not the least of which was a major shift in the Cambridges' commitment to life as working royals representing the Crown full-time at countless events in the United Kingdom and abroad. On July 27, 2017, William made good on his promise to devote himself full-time to princely duties by pulling his last ten-hour night shift at East Anglian Air Ambulance. In a bizarre turn of events that underscored how emotionally taxing the job could be, his final assignment was to airlift a missing woman who had been struck by the very police van that had been dispatched to save her. She later died in the hospital.

Weeks later, Kate was facing a familiar health crisis of her own. Once again stricken with the debilitating symptoms of hyperemesis gravidarum, she pulled out of an appearance at London's Hornsey Road Children's Centre at the last minute. The next day, September 4, 2017, Kensington Palace announced that the Duke and Duchess of Cambridge were expecting their third child. "The Queen and members of both families," the statement continued, "are delighted with the news."

That same week, an ailing Kate stayed home while William accompanied four-year-old George to his first day at Thomas's Battersea, a $27,000-a-year coeducational day school. To avoid the sort of chaos that surrounded William's first day at school, the Cambridges stipulated that this time only one still photographer and one TV camera be present to capture the moment. Holding his father's hand and looking somewhat sheepish, George was formally introduced to the head of the lower school, Helen Haslem. Among other things, the school promised to teach George to "be kind," acquire "confidence, leadership, and humility," and to not have a best friend so that other children's feelings wouldn't be hurt. As unrealistic as that last rule may have seemed, Kate fully supported it. "She understood that of course everyone would want to be Prince George's best friend," a teacher at the school said. "Princess Catherine was all about not making the other students feel hurt or left out. She also wanted George to be treated just like the others, not like a star." Kate wanted George "to have a childhood more like the one she had."

As it became increasingly clear that Harry was headed to Balmoral to ask the Queen for permission to marry Meghan, Kate urged William to intervene. From the moment he learned of Meghan's unconventional background, William had discouraged his brother from even dating her on the grounds that she was simply too foreign, with too much of a backstory to ever be accepted into the royal family. Now Kate was weighing in, as well—and her opinion mattered to Harry. "Kate and I think Meghan seems like a lovely girl, but why rush things?" the Heir said. "Does she really know what she's getting into?" William never mentioned Meghan's biracial heritage, but there were two words he spat out with particular disdain: "American actress." While Prince Charles ostensibly objected on the grounds that he simply didn't want to add someone new to the royal payroll, it was clear to Harry that he and Camilla couldn't tolerate someone "shiny and new" seizing the limelight.

Kate was the first to throw up her hands in defeat. "Harry is not going to wait. He is going to marry her," she told her parents, "and there is nothing anyone can do about it." After announcing their engagement in November 2017 and posing for photos in Kensington Palace's Sunken Garden, the newly engaged couple sat down for a lengthy interview with the BBC. When asked how William and Kate felt about Meghan, Harry began to reply but was interrupted by his fiancée.

> *Harry: Catherine has been absolutely—*
> *Meghan: She's been wonderful.*
> *Harry: Amazing, as has William as well, you know, fantastic support.*

Harry went on to falsely claim that the "whole family have come together and have been a huge amount of solid support."

The charade continued the next day, when Kate was cornered by reporters as she arrived for a scheduled appearance at the Foundling Museum in London. "William and I are absolutely thrilled," she said, robotically reciting the script she had memorized and painstakingly rehearsed the night before. "It's such exciting news. It's really a happy time for any couple and we wish them all the best and hope they enjoy this happy moment."

By this time, Meghan had abandoned all hope that she and Kate would somehow bond over their shared "outsider" status. Notwithstanding their effusive praise of the Cambridges and the "fantastic support" they offered, none was in fact forthcoming. Harry's repeated pleas for Kate to essentially mentor her soon-to-be sister-in-law went unheeded. According to a friend from Meghan's acting days in Toronto, she came to believe "Kate was never going to reach out to her. Regardless of what they said publicly, William and Kate didn't think she was right for their Harry. They wanted a proper English rose."

Try as the Palace might to conceal behind-the-scenes tensions, Fleet Street was determined to pit Kate and Meghan against each other—like it or not. During the BAFTAs in mid-February 2018, Meghan, like most attendees, wore black in support of the anti-sexual harassment Me Too movement. Kate, who was now seven months pregnant and favoring empire-waisted gowns, preferred a more subtle approach that adhered to rules prohibiting members of the royal family from taking a political stand.

She wore dark green—but with a black sash tied around her waist. Predictably, Kate's shrewdly understated nod to Me Too was not enough to stop tabloids from running photos of Kate and Meghan side by side with stories that implied a rift between the two women. The faux controversy "put Kate on edge," Harry later recalled, because it signaled one inescapable thing: she and Meghan would forever be cast as rivals.

It came as no small irony that William, Kate, Harry, and Meghan were dubbed the "Fab Four" when, just ten days after BAFTA, they made their first public appearance together at the Royal Foundation Forum. Meghan was coming on board as a fellow foundation trustee, and was intent on making her voice heard. Backstage before the event, Meghan suddenly realized she had left her tube of lip gloss at home and asked to borrow Kate's. Slightly horrified at the request—sharing someone else's lip gloss was scarcely hygienic—Kate nevertheless obliged, then scowled disapprovingly as Meghan squeezed some gloss onto her finger and dabbed it on her lips. Later Kate, still not knowing what to make of the American in their midst, hung back during the question-and-answer session—fixing her gaze on Meghan's lips as the newest trustee shared equal time with the Heir and the Spare.

Seven weeks later, on April 23, 2018, church bells pealed and artillery roared as crowds of well-wishers gathered outside the Lindo Wing of St. Mary's Hospital to see Prince George and Princess Charlotte arrive to meet their new baby brother. At eight pounds, seven ounces, Louis Arthur Charles slightly outweighed both his siblings at birth. He was also named after some serious heavyweights, both mythical and real: Lord Louis Mountbatten, the legendary King Arthur of Camelot, and, of course, his grandfather Prince Charles. It was notable that Kate and William recycled one of George's middle names—Louis—to create a given name for their youngest child, and perhaps equally auspicious that the littlest prince was born on St. George's Day, the feast day honoring England's patron saint and the protector of Britain's royal family.

Louis's birth was, in fact, history-making in its own right. Under the centuries-old rules of royal primogeniture, he would have been fourth in line for the throne behind Prince George. Under the new Succession to the Crown Act 2013, Louis was now fifth behind big sister Charlotte.

Perhaps no one was more delighted than "Grandpa Wales," whose rivalry with Granny and Grandpa Middleton for the affections of George and Charlotte was already in full swing. (The Cambridge children settled on "Gan-Gan" for step-grandmother Camilla, although her own grandchildren called her "GaGa." Gan-Gan was also what George and Charlotte called their great-grandmother Queen Elizabeth II, and what William and Harry had called the Queen Mother.) "It is a great joy to have another grandchild," Prince Charles wrote to Kate and William that day. "The only trouble is—I don't know how I'm going to keep up with them!"

Not that he wasn't trying. Charles expanded the tree house that had originally been built at Highgrove for William and Harry, and added a playscape with slides, swings, and monkey bars. Despite Kate's best efforts to corral her high-spirited offspring, George and Charlotte could not be prevented from trampling the estate's painstakingly manicured gardens. Prince Charles "used to wince when he saw them run through the daffodils," Camilla told a visitor to Highgrove. "Now he thinks they're absolutely hysterical."

Kate, in particular, was touched by the lengths Grandpa Wales went to to spend time with his grandchildren—even though it sprang in part from his desire not to be outdone by his Middleton counterparts. Charles explained that he was following the example set by the Queen Mother—"the most magical grandmother you could possibly have."

As their May 19 nuptials at St. George's Chapel in Windsor Castle approached, it did not take long for Harry and Meghan to reclaim their place in the spotlight. Nor did it take long for petty slights and disagreements to become the order of the day. For starters, William bitterly resented the fact that, while he had been barred from sporting a beard or wearing the frock coat uniform of the Blues and Royals at his wedding, the Queen was permitting Harry to do both. (In fairness, at this point Meghan had never seen Harry in the flesh without a beard.)

Then there was the matter of the flower girls' dresses. When Charlotte tried hers on at Kensington Palace just four days before the wedding, she took one look in the mirror and burst into tears. Not only was her dress too big, but all the other girls' dresses were ill-fitting as well. Kate called Meghan, who told her that their tailor was standing by at Kensington Palace to make alterations. But that wasn't enough. Kate, who had given birth just three weeks earlier, stood her ground. She insisted that all the dresses had to be remade. Moreover, Kate disapproved of Meghan's plan for the flower girls to be barelegged rather than wear tights. London was in the middle of a hot spell, and Meghan "made the point of it being so hot," said an assistant who witnessed the argument, "and Princess Catherine kept saying, 'But it's just not done.' Both of them got very emotional."

When details of their contretemps eventually came to light, Meghan was blamed for making everyone's favorite duchess cry. But Meghan insisted the reverse was true—that she was so upset she collapsed on the floor, weeping. Kate realized she had pushed too hard, and dropped by the next day with a note of apology and flowers. Kate was "upset about something, but she owned it," Meghan recalled. "And she did what I would do if I knew that I hurt someone." There were other perceived slights that rankled Kate, but they would have to wait until after her brother-in-law and his betrothed celebrated their big day.

To the outside world, whatever drama surrounding the wedding of the newly minted Duke and Duchess of Sussex stemmed from the bride's problematic family. Thomas Markle Jr. joined Samantha in slamming their half sister as a "phony" who "thinks she's another Princess Diana. She is giving the performance of her life. . . . It's ugly to see." After a long string of embarrassing tabloid stories about Meghan's father, Thomas Sr., he decided not to show up. Instead, Prince Charles walked Meghan halfway down the aisle—a gesture of kindness that William and Kate nonetheless felt was going a step too far.

A month later, the Cambridges invited Harry and Meghan for tea—and a verbal thrashing. Kate was upset that, while she and William had given them an Easter present, none had been given in return. But what really stuck in Kate's craw was a comment made during one of their phone calls a week before the wedding, when she forgot a rehearsal date. "It's not a big deal," Meghan replied at the time, "it's baby brain. Because you'd just had a baby. It's hormones."

In another glaring example of culture clash, the comment infuriated Kate. "You talked about my hormones! We're not close enough for you to talk about my hormones!" Meghan's offhand remark was "rude," William added. "It's not what's done here in Britain."

Meghan explained that, in the United States, her reference to "baby brain" and postpartum hormones would have been considered commonplace. "That's the way I talk to my girlfriends," she protested, realizing as she finished the sentence that Kate did not put her in that category. But Meghan apologized anyway, making it clear to her sister-in-law that she would never knowingly "say anything to upset you."

If there was one thing the two women and their spouses could both agree on it was Donald Trump. During the 2016 presidential campaign, Meghan had denounced the Republican candidate as a dangerous misogynist. She was shooting *Suits* in Canada at the time, and promised that, if he won the election, that's where she would remain. While all members of the royal family were barred from taking political stands, everyone but the Queen managed to be unavailable when Trump, by then in the middle of his first term as president, arrived at Windsor Castle for tea in July 2018. Charles hosted a reception for Duchy of Cornwall employees at Highgrove, while William played in a charity polo match and Harry had a "prior engagement."

Kate and Meghan had the best excuse of all: they were both at Wimbledon, where the Duchess of Sussex cheered on her longtime friend Serena Williams in the women's singles final. Kate's presence was required: in 2016, she had taken over from her grandmother-in-law the Queen as royal patron of Wimbledon—a nod to Kate's own athletic prowess and her passion for sports. Sitting next to each other for two hours, the duchesses behaved for all intents and purposes like the best of friends, chatting, laughing, and cheering the players on throughout the match.

(A year later Her Majesty honored Trump with a glittering banquet at

Buckingham Palace, and this time only the Sussexes absented themselves. Kate wore white along with the famous Lover's Knot tiara and for the first time the blue, red, and white sash of the Royal Victorian Order. Camilla, the Queen, and First Lady Melania Trump also wore white. On the Cambridges' eighth wedding anniversary, the Queen made Kate a Dame Grand Cross of the Order—one of the highest honors the monarch can bestow—out of gratitude for her service to the sovereign.)

Over the coming months, Meghan—who had already been the target of overtly racist slurs in the British press—was raked over the coals in dozens of articles that depicted her as uncouth, demanding, and wantonly ambitious. Her bra strap was briefly visible at a royal reception. Her nail polish was black, she *wore* too much black. She violated royal protocol by crossing her legs in the presence of the Queen. She was "Hurricane Meghan," the "Duchess Difficult" who allegedly bullied her staff, reducing them to tears—a story that was leaked to the press by a member of the Cambridges' staff.

It soon became clear that many of the stories that were now driving Meghan to the brink of suicide had, in fact, been planted by Kensington Palace and Clarence House as part of an ongoing campaign to boost the Cambridges' public image at the expense of the Spare and his hapless American wife. When it was falsely reported that Meghan had made Kate cry during their row over the flower girls' dresses, Kate was the first to admit to the Sussexes that the opposite was true. But when it came to setting the record straight, Kate and William, adhering to the long-standing Palace rule that responding to such rumors only poured gasoline on the fire, refused to speak up.

Slanted comparisons between the two duchesses abounded. When Meghan was pregnant with the Sussexes' first child, the press jumped on the fact that her hand lingered on her baby bump for a few moments during a television appearance—an unconscious gesture that was instantly decried as being "too showy." Yet the year before when Kate was expecting Louis, she was widely applauded in the press for tenderly cradling her stomach in an even more obvious manner.

Kate sympathized with all that Meghan had gone through. But, like William, she believed much of what she was being told by their own Kensington Palace staff—that Meghan was pushy, bullying, demanding. At the same time, they knew that there were courtiers who were also willing to throw the Cambridges under the bus if it meant boosting the profiles of Charles and Camilla. When confronted by his sons, Charles admitted as much—that he, and even the Queen, looked the other way when loyal staffers planted stories in the press calculated to put other royals on the defensive.

In early 2019, Kate was having to deal with unfounded rumors that William was in the midst of a torrid affair with the couple's Norfolk neighbor and longtime friend Rose Hanbury, Marchioness of Cholmondeley. The baseless chatter subsided once William directed his lawyers to threaten legal action, but it would resurface periodically over the next several years. Kate believed that the so-called affair was pure fiction—gossip that had been planted by Palace sources to bring the high-flying Cambridges down a peg. But from now on, her encounters with the woman who had once been a member of her tight inner circle would be few and far between. "She knew if they were seen together," another Norfolk neighbor pointed out, "it would stir things up all over again."

Kate and William were both painfully aware that they, too, were the victims of Palace intrigue. They needed to make sure that their own team was on board to protect them, their charities, the causes they championed. Yet, according to what they were reading in the papers and hearing from certain advisors, Meghan had alienated half the Kensington Palace staff. "You must," Kate told her husband, "talk to Harry about Meghan."

William's confrontation with Harry did not go well. At Nott Cott, the brothers quarreled bitterly. William accused Meghan of causing friction in the royal household; she was imperious, difficult, texting demands at insane hours, and shrieking commands at quavering underlings. Something had to be done, the Heir insisted.

None of it was true, Harry replied, but even if it was, what did William expect Harry to do about it? Besides, the racist attacks, the unauthorized tabloid publication of a tearstained letter she had written to her mercurial father, the nonstop sniping, plotting, and backstabbing by the Palace, orders from on high that she stay locked up at Frogmore Cottage because she was "overexposed"—it was all taking an enormous toll. Meghan was thinking of taking her own life. She needed professional help—mental health was something the "Fab Four" had campaigned for, wasn't it?—but the Palace was refusing to provide any. By the way, Harry added, they had counted on guidance from William and Kate but none was forthcoming. Crickets.

Eyes bulging and jaw clenched, William, whose dark moods and periodic tantrums had long been of concern to Kate, lunged at his younger brother, ripping off the tiger's eye necklace Harry had been given by a friend in Botswana and shoving Harry to the floor. According to Harry, he fell backward onto his dog Guy's bowl, shattering it and leaving Harry with cuts, scrapes, and bruises on his back. Despite his brother's demand that Harry hit him back—after all, like so many other brothers they had tussled with each other many times over the years—Harry refused.

After cooling off, William begged his brother not to mention the incident to Meghan and Harry agreed, although the next day he recounted what had happened after she spotted the abrasions on his back. William, meanwhile, shared what had happened with Kate. She had always cautioned her hot-tempered husband never to lose control—over the years he had shouted obscenities (Harry was served an earful during their heated encounters), slammed doors, and even thrown objects in fits of pique—a side of the future king the public never saw. But in this case, she sympathized with William. By this point, Kate had heard directly from Palace staffers accusing the Los Angeles–born duchess of barking orders incessantly and, on at least one occasion, making a key aide cry. Kate was now completely convinced that Meghan was "impossible. But I do feel sorry for Harry."

Archie Harrison Mountbatten-Windsor was eight days old when Kate and William visited the Sussexes at their new home, Frogmore Cottage on the grounds of Windsor Castle. (Frogmore got its name from the massive population of frogs that flourished in its low-lying, marshy location.) The first multiracial child born into the Windsor dynasty had already triggered a flurry of offensive stories online and in the press—a BBC radio anchor posted a photo of a couple holding a chimpanzee's hand with the caption "Royal baby leaves hospital"—and Kate was eager to lend her support to the new parents. On her way to the Sussexes, Kate, who suddenly realized she had forgotten to bring a gift for Archie, was relieved when someone in the crowd handed her four stuffed animals: an owl, a squirrel, and a fox for the Cambridge children—and a rabbit for Archie.

Yet in reality, relations between the Cambridges and the Sussexes could scarcely be called warm and fuzzy. While Harry had spent a lifetime in his brother's shadow, Meghan saw no reason to join him there. She chafed at the notion that, whenever their projects and causes seemed to draw attention away from Kate and William, they were required to simply step aside. "You know how things work, Harold," William would say. "What is your problem?"

Speculation concerning the growing tension between William and Harry ran rampant, and Kate could only look on helplessly as the rift widened. In June 2019 the brothers split up the Royal Foundation that they had jointly run to keep their mother's philanthropic legacy alive by supporting twenty-six charities. The Queen was also creating a separate household for the Sussexes, and by way of amplifying their declaration of independence, Harry and Meghan waited until William's thirty-seventh birthday to officially establish their own Sussex Royal Foundation.

Whatever bitterness was roiling beneath the surface, none was apparent during Trooping the Colour ceremonies that marked the monarch's official birthday in June. For unforeseen reasons that would alter the lives of millions across the globe, another full-scale Trooping the Colour like this would not occur for another two years. On June 8, 2019, Kate, Camilla, Harry, and Meghan waved and smiled ear to ear as they rode through the streets of London in a horse-drawn carriage. Later, with the Queen and her family standing on the Buckingham Palace balcony to watch the traditional flyby of military aircraft, the Cambridge children stole the show. While an ennui-stricken George, five, glowered and four-year-old Charlotte dutifully waved to the throng, it was one-year-old Louis, making his balcony debut, who proved to be a royal handful. Squirming in his mother's arms, the littlest prince asked to be handed off to Papa, then turned to excitedly wave as his parents burst into laughter. Once the charade of togetherness was over, the Queen, Charles and Camilla, Harry and Meghan, and the Cambridges went back to their separate corners.

As distressing as the brothers' split may have been for the Queen, it wasn't the only steaming scandal on Her Majesty's plate. A string of allegations revolving around Prince Andrew's involvement in the Jeffrey Epstein underage sex scandal had left the Palace reeling. In November 2019, after Andrew gave a disastrous no-holds-barred interview to the BBC, calls for the Queen's favorite child to be stripped of his title and handed over to the FBI escalated.

Andrew's principal accuser was an American woman named Virginia Roberts Giuffre, who was suing the prince on the grounds that he had had sex with her on three occasions when she was underage—trysts that had been arranged by Andrew's longtime sex-offender pal, financier Epstein. The Queen doted on Andrew, Kate knew, but she also worried that her husband would eventually inherit a badly tarnished crown if something wasn't done. William agreed, and urged his father to pressure the Queen to act. Within days, Andrew was summoned to Sandringham for lunch with Charles and Prince Philip. There Andrew was told that he was "retiring" as a senior member of the royal family—removed from the Firm's lineup, banished. It would be an important first step in the direction of the less-wasteful, more cost-conscious, and sustainable slimmed-down monarchy Charles described for the future—but not the last.

That Christmas, the Queen was dealt another glancing blow—this time Harry and Meghan decided to skip the royal family's usual festivities at Sandringham, opting instead to spend the holidays with Meghan's mother, Doria Ragland, in British Columbia. Kate, relieved that she would not have to pretend all was well between the sisters-in-law, made sure the Cambridges would take up the slack. Rousting everyone out of bed at 5 a.m. on Christmas morning, she got six-year-old George and four-year-old Charlotte ready for their first walk with the Queen from Sandringham House to and from church. (Nineteen-month-old Louis stayed behind at Anmer Hall.) Holding their parents' hands and waving to well-wishers, the young royals delighted the crowd by stopping to chat with other churchgoers. At one point, Charlotte graciously accepted a gift from someone in the crowd—an inflatable pink flamingo that she happily walked off with.

On January 8, 2020, the Sussexes posted a statement on Instagram. After "many months of reflection and internal discussions," Harry and Meghan were going to "step back as 'senior' members of the royal family and work to become financially independent, while continuing to fully support Her Majesty the Queen." They also intended to split their time "between the United Kingdom and North America, continuing to honor our duty to the Queen, the Commonwealth, and our patronages."

Kate and William knew that negotiations with the Queen and her senior staff had indeed been going on for months, and that a carefully crafted statement of some sort was in the works. But Megxit, as the *Sun* shrewdly dubbed the Sussexes' decision to put one foot out the door, still left everyone inside and outside palace walls gobsmacked. "Harry and Meghan Quit the Firm," announced the *Daily Telegraph*, while the *Daily Mail* shouted "Queen's Fury as Harry and Meghan Say: We Quit!" from its front page. Normally a pillar of restraint, the venerable *Times* of London declared, "Harry and Meghan Quit Roles Amid Palace Split." While inaccurate, the *Daily Mirror*'s finger-wagging "They Didn't Even Tell the Queen" headline struck a chord with the vast majority of Britons. What ingrates! How could they?

At Anmer Hall, William was still aghast at his brother's impertinence. "What the fuck do Harry and Meghan think they're doing?" he asked a speechless aide. "My father will be furious." So will his grandfather, Kate added. Prince Philip and Charles in particular had welcomed Meghan into the family with open arms. Now, the Duke of Edinburgh asked, "What are they playing at?" A courtier described the monarch's ninety-eight-year-old husband, who had recently been in and out of the hospital with a variety of ailments, as "furious, deeply hurt, spitting blood." As for the Queen, Kate would tell a friend from St. Andrews that Her Majesty was "very hurt by all that's going on. Very hurt."

Five days later, the principal players—Harry, William, Charles, and of course the Queen—met, along with their key advisors, at Her Majesty's country estate in Norfolk to hammer out the details of the Sussexes' new bicontinental life. The unprecedented closed-door emergency session was promptly billed on front pages everywhere as the "Sandringham Summit."

Meghan had already returned to Canada with Archie but was given the opportunity to listen in on speakerphone—an offer she declined. Always knowing when to defer to her in-laws, Kate remained with the children just five minutes up tree-lined King's Road at Anmer Hall.

The Duke and Duchess of Cambridge had talked of little else since the Sussexes detonated their megaton bombshell, and they agreed that what Harry and Meghan were doing was unforgivable. At a time when Prince Andrew's involvement in the Epstein scandal was casting a shadow over the monarchy, now was hardly the time to bail. Moreover, Kate was especially worried that she and William would somehow be blamed for hounding the Spare, his wife, and their infant son out of the Firm altogether. Right before the summit, a story in the London *Sunday Times* claimed the Sussexes felt they were the victims of William's "bullying" attitude. According to a friend of the couple, Harry and Meghan were fed up after two years of "constantly being told your place . . . constant bullying . . . constantly told what you can and cannot do."

Having been bullied as a child, Kate was upset that anyone would use the term to describe her husband—and, by extension, her. "She has spent her whole life crusading against bullies," a Middleton family friend observed, "so it was very painful to hear someone apply that word to her family." At Kate's suggestion, the Palace drafted a joint statement for the brothers to sign refuting the bullying claims in the *Sunday Times* piece—a rare show of unity that nevertheless managed to ignore the deepening fissures in their relationship. Most important, Kate was aware that William was suffering pangs of loss, and that there was little she could do to comfort him. "I've put my arm around my brother all our lives," he said, "and I can't do that any more. We're separate entities. I'm sad about that."

Ultimately the Queen—bowing to pressure from senior advisors that Harry, William, and Kate derisively called the Bee and the Wasp—decided the Sussexes' plan to be part-time, self-sustaining royals was unworkable. Harry and Meghan would no longer be working members of the royal family—period. Her Majesty rescinded Harry's royal patronages—allowing him to keep the private charities he had started like Invictus and Sentebale, his home for AIDS orphans in Lesotho—and, most hurtfully, stripped him of his honorary military appointments. There was a caveat: the couple was given one year to change their minds. Presumably, the Sussexes would be welcomed with open arms—if they moved back to the United Kingdom and, in Harry's words, agreed to "do whatever we were told, surrender our autonomy, keep our hands and feet inside the gilded cage at all times. . . ." (In March 2025, Harry resigned from Sentebale in a dispute with its chair.)

"How awful for Harry," Kate said when she was told the ten-year combat veteran could no longer wear the ceremonial uniforms of captain general of the Royal Marines, honorary commodore-in-chief of the Royal Navy's Small Ships and Diving Operations, and honorary RAF commandant. Kate asked William if he couldn't intercede with the Queen to at least reclaim the military honorifics, but he told her his grandmother's mind was "made up. She thinks you're either all in or you're all out. Harry and Meghan want out, well, they're all the way out."

Kate was relieved to hear that Harry and Meghan were permitted to keep their titles and their HRH status, as long as they refrained from "actively" using their titles in the future. Harry had actually written to his father, offering to give up his title and Meghan's—if that meant they could still be part-time royals. But Kate agreed with William's claim that Princess Diana "would never have wanted that."

Nor would the late Princess of Wales want Harry and Meghan to give up their royal bodyguards. Diana's decision to rely on Dodi Fayed for security was a major contributing factor to her death. Haunted by that fact, Harry would press to have the Crown continue to provide protection for his small family whenever they visited the United Kingdom—a campaign in the courts that would last more than five years.

Kate found herself in the middle of a protocol dilemma in March 2020 when, during the nationally televised Commonwealth Day Service at Westminster Abbey, Harry and Meghan were told not to take their customary place behind the Queen when she made her entrance. Now that they were no longer working royals, they were excluded from the senior lineup. The two thousand printed programs listed the Cambridges as entering the abbey along with the Queen, but Kate didn't want to seem to be snubbing Harry and his wife. Although William resisted at first, he followed Kate's lead and took his seat before Her Majesty made her grand entrance. Unfortunately, their first-row seats were directly in front of the Sussexes, and William was in no mood to make nice with the Spare. When Harry leaned in, his unsmiling brother said, "Hello, Harry"—and that was it. "He didn't," a disappointed Harry told Meghan, "say anything more than that!"

That same day, Meghan took the last commercial flight back to Vancouver, and Harry joined her a few days later. In the predawn hours of March 14, they departed for Los Angeles aboard actor-producer Tyler Perry's $150 million Embraer E-190 jet. The renegade royals were about to take up temporary residence in Perry's $18 million Beverly Hills estate just as countries were beginning to close their borders to halt the spread of a deadly new strain of coronavirus, COVID-19. While the Sussexes were still in the air, William and Kate were coping with the news that Prince Charles had tested positive immediately after lunching with Monaco's Prince Albert, who also contracted the virus.

William was "quite concerned," he later admitted, pointing out that as a seventy-one-year-old, Charles "fit the profile" of someone for whom COVID was "risky. So I was a little bit worried." Kate reassured her husband that Charles was more than a match for any virus. William agreed. "My father has had many chest infections, colds, things like that over the years, and so I thought to myself, 'If anyone is going to beat this, it's going to be him.'"

Only a week earlier, while visiting a pub in Dublin, the Cambridges had shaken hands with scores of strangers and poked fun at what they then believed was an overblown reaction to COVID. "I bet everyone's, like, 'I've got coronavirus. I'm dying,'" he told a paramedic in the crowd, "and you're, like, 'No, you've just got a cough.'" William went on to say that people were being dramatic and that the global epidemic in the making was "hyped up in the media." Kate laughed when her husband, feigning horror, then joked, "By the way, the Duke and Duchess of Cambridge are spreading coronavirus! Sorry! Do tell us if we need to stop!"

Prince Charles's symptoms would turn out to be mild, but his eldest son was not so lucky. In April, one month after his father's COVID diagnosis, the Heir contracted the disease. Prince William "was hit pretty hard by the virus," a Kensington Palace staff member said. "It really knocked him for six." (This is a cricket reference, the British equivalent of the American phrase "knocked him for a loop.") At one point, Kate frantically summoned help when her husband began gasping. "He was struggling to breathe," the staffer recalled, "so obviously everyone around him was pretty panicked." One of the couple's security team—all trained to provide emergency first aid—administered oxygen to William until one of the doctors from Her Majesty's medical team arrived from nearby Sandringham House. At first it was suggested that the prince be hospitalized, but the patient said no. Instead, he canceled his schedule for two weeks while doctors treated him at home.

While Charles's COVID diagnosis was immediately made public, William's remained a secret for more than a year. The Heir felt "there were more important things going on," he later explained, "and I didn't want to worry anyone."

Like tens of millions of others, the Cambridges self-isolated, rarely straying from the confines of Anmer Hall. For the next two years, Kate and William would keep a busy schedule of remote appearances, usually appearing side by side FaceTiming masked groups that otherwise would have met them in the flesh. Inevitably, talk would turn to the pandemic that by 2026 would take more than seven million lives worldwide.

A month into Britain's COVID lockdown, the Queen gave a stirring speech designed to boost morale. She ended it with a reassuring reference to Vera Lynn's famous World War II song "We'll Meet Again." Yet it fell to the younger generation—specifically William and Kate—to be the front-line royals in the face of the pandemic. The Cambridges appeared numerous times to thank health care workers as well as encourage the wearing of masks, frequent handwashing, and other precautions. When it was finally rolled out in December 2020, William and Kate also championed the use of the first effective COVID vaccine.

As the mother of three youngsters, Kate reached out to families via FaceTime and on social media to share her lockdown experiences. She conceded it was "hard to explain what's going on" to her children. "You don't want to scare them or make it too overwhelming. But they are aware. . . . I'm always surprised."

Kate and William also struck a chord when they spoke candidly about the demands of homeschooling—and their own obvious shortcomings in that department. The Duke of Cambridge admitted that he couldn't help with George's second-grade math problems ("I have to admit, I'm a bit embarrassed"), but his wife claimed to be even worse. Asked to rate her math skills on a scale of one to ten, she replied, "Minus five." Kate raised her eyebrows when Will went on to claim that he still found homeschooling "fun. We make a good tag team. I chat with the children, get them to do some stuff, and then hand over to Catherine when frankly everything has gone wrong." Kate took advantage of the break she got when the children were doing their schoolwork during the day. "Don't tell the children," she whispered into the camera. "We've actually kept it going through the holidays. I feel very mean."

While she gave a nod to one person as being most helpful during the lockdown—William—Kate was certainly the ringmaster at Anmer Hall, making sure the children were busy with projects, playing outdoors, "not spending their entire day in front of a computer screen.

"I've become a hairdresser during this lockdown, much to my children's horror," Kate joked. But she also allowed that, even with the help of a nanny, she found the situation daunting. "I feel personally pulled in so many directions and you try to do your best with everything . . . but at the end of the day I do feel exhausted." With good reason. "You write down a list of all the things you've done: Let's see, pitch a tent, take the tent down, cook, bake. *They've* had a lovely time, but it's amazing how much you can cram into one day, that's for sure. And, listen," she said, referencing Louis, "it's hard with a two-year-old, I'm not going to lie."

As the pandemic stretched on into the fall, Harry and Meghan spent $14.65 million for an 18,671-square-foot mansion seventy-five miles north of Los Angeles in the chic Santa Barbara County enclave of Montecito. The hefty price tag was not going to be a problem. Harry had held on to nearly all the $12 million-plus he had inherited from his mother and an additional $20 million left to him by the Queen Mother, who felt the Spare would need the money a lot more than his brother, the future king. Moreover, the Sussexes signed a $20 million podcast contract with Spotify and a $100 million deal to produce scripted series, documentaries, movies, and children's programming for Netflix. They also teamed up with Oprah Winfrey, who was a friend of Meghan's and had been a guest at the Sussexes' wedding, to produce a mental health docuseries.

Understandably, William and his Windsor relatives were none too pleased when they learned of the Sussexes' plans to build their own brand by blatantly exploiting their connection to the royal family. Kate, whose parents had been raked over the coals for selling princess-themed party favors during her 2011 royal wedding, still felt warmly toward Harry. But she was especially disappointed. Now that they were off the royal payroll, the Sussexes had to start an income stream of their own—that was understood. "They need to make money, yes, I can see that," Kate mentioned to a Kensington Palace staffer, "but great *mountains* of it?"

As the yuletide holidays approached and the pandemic lockdown continued, Her Majesty announced that, for the first time in thirty-three years, she would be celebrating Christmas not at Sandringham but at Windsor Castle. Incredibly, neither the Queen nor her ninety-nine-year-old husband (the longest-living male member of a reigning family in British history) had contracted the virus, and she intended to keep it that way. The

Cambridges followed suit as the COVID crisis worsened, canceling plans to spend Christmas with Kate's family at Bucklebury Manor and instead hunkering down at Anmer Hall.

While Kate juggled her calendar and the demands of three small children stuck at home, Harry and Meghan were 5,520 miles away scrambling to keep up with a two-year-old of their own. On Valentine's Day 2021 they announced that a sibling was on the way for Archie Mountbatten-Windsor. The previous July, Meghan had suffered a miscarriage, and wrote about the harrowing experience in a *New York Times* op-ed piece. "Oh my God, how terrible," Kate said when she read the news. "So brave of Meghan to write about it. . . ." William was shocked and saddened—and disappointed that Harry hadn't confided in him or their father or even the Queen about what had happened. Rather than praise Meghan's courage for confronting such a sensitive issue head-on, Buckingham Palace issued the usual tone-deaf response. "This," read the official statement, "is a deeply personal matter for the couple."

This time, the royal family was quick to react to word that the Sussexes were expecting—albeit with a single terse announcement from Buckingham Palace: "Her Majesty, Duke of Edinburgh, Prince of Wales, and the entire family are delighted and wish them well."

Their happy news aside, Harry and Meghan were formally handed their walking papers five days later. With William and Kate's full backing—as well as that of Prince Charles—Her Majesty announced that the Spare and his wife had permanently and completely stepped down as full-time working royals.

The news came as no surprise to Kate and William. What they didn't know was that, while the Bee and the Wasp and other Palace officials were toasting each other for engineering the Sussexes' departure, Meghan and Harry were having a lively chat in a neighbor's shaded garden with a mutual friend.

Her name was Oprah.

The world does not know when it will see Kate Middleton again. But whenever that is, she'll wear an outfit that does all the talking.

—Elise Taylor, in *Vogue*

7

"London Bridge Is Down"

"I Felt Her Kindness and Energy Around Me"

March 8, 2021, a Monday
Anmer Hall

Kate could hear her husband retching in the bathroom. For a full week, William was too distracted to think of food, literally sick with worry over what Harry and Meghan might say to Oprah Winfrey. The interview had premiered in the United States the night before on CBS and would air in the United Kingdom twenty-four hours later, but the Cambridges were not about to wait. They had already read what was being posted online about what the Sussexes were saying, and now sat side by side at the massive oak table in their kitchen staring at the screen of Kate's laptop. They watched for two hours, as would a worldwide audience of more than sixty million, while Harry and Meghan lobbed one grenade after another over the battlements: Heartless Palace officials had pushed Meghan to thoughts of suicide with their demands. Harry's father had not only refused to speak to him for more than a year, he had stopped paying for the Sussexes' security, placing their family in danger. And, of course, it was Kate who made Meghan cry, not the other way around.

William? Well, the brothers needed—and were giving themselves—"space. And time heals all things . . . hopefully," Harry said. "There's a lot to work through here. There's a lot of hurt that's happened."

Not all the laundry being aired was dirty; there were a few pleasant, even upbeat, moments as well. Oprah squealed with glee when Harry revealed they were expecting a girl. Everyone agreed that the Queen was warm, thoughtful, and kind. Kate, Meghan went out of her way to say, was, despite all their differences, "a good person."

Yet one allegation above all others would shake the monarchy to its foundations. There were charges of racism among unnamed royals who, Meghan and Harry claimed, expressed concerns about what a child of theirs would look like—how dark-skinned he or she might turn out to be, and "what that means" for the monarchy.

It would later be revealed that a casual remark by Charles—a grandfather's innocent musings on what the couple's child might look like—was spun into something quite different and weaponized by competing camps inside the Palace. But for the moment, all Oprah and her audience could do was gasp in gape-mouthed disbelief. The Sussexes declined to name the culprit ("That would be very damaging to them," Meghan said), but were quick to rule out the Queen as well as Prince Philip, whose penchant for making cringeworthy remarks was legendary.

The Queen had chosen to wait and watch the bombshell interview Monday night, when the rest of Great Britain was watching it. By then, however, a reply to the Sussexes' accusations was already in the works. It was then that Kate, realizing that she and William were now prime suspects, swung into action. She pressed William to have a major voice in deciding how Her Majesty was going to react—insisting that they join a conference call with the Queen's private secretary, Sir Edward Young, to hammer out an official Palace response.

Incredibly, the idea was originally floated that the Queen should stay silent—that, as was the default approach in such cases, she simply not dignify the charges with any response at all. But Kate quickly shot that down. The Oprah interview was far too big and the allegations too sweeping to be ignored. There was no doubt that there had to be an official response, directly from the Queen herself, but what would she say?

It would take several hours before William and Kate were shown a first draft. "The whole family is saddened to learn the full extent of how challenging the last few years have been for Harry and Meghan," it read. "Harry, Meghan, and Archie will always be much-loved family members."

What about the charges of racism? Kate wanted to know. That issue had to be addressed. Back to the drawing board. Thirty minutes later, two sentences were added: "The issues raised, particularly that of race, are concerning. They are taken very seriously and will be addressed by the family privately."

William was about to sign off on this version, but Kate wasn't satisfied. She pointed out that the statement did not push back against the Sussexes' depiction of events at all. It was at this point that Kate suggested adding the phrase "While some recollections may vary"—making it clear that not everyone was on board with what Harry and Meghan were saying. Most of the senior staff thought this was going too far—that any such rebuttal, even one as subtle as Kate was suggesting, might provoke the Sussexes. "We don't want them firing back with more ugly charges," a deputy secretary argued, "or pointing fingers at members of the royal family."

Kate held firm. "History will judge this statement," she said, adding that without that key phrase, "everything that they said will be taken as true." The Queen agreed and signed off on Kate's "recollections may vary" version. The next day while visiting a school in East London, William was less equivocal when a reporter asked if the royal family was racist. "We're very much not a racist family," the prince shot back.

Tellingly, William had calmly told the same reporter that he had not yet spoken to his brother about the interview "but will do." Kate, knowing her husband's frame of mind, cautioned against him speaking with Harry—at least not now, in the heat of the moment. She had spent more than a year quietly working in the background to patch things up between the brothers, but for William the sense of betrayal ran too deep.

While William fretted over the fact that Harry was going public with his grievances, Kate focused on the Sussexes' charges of racism inside the royal family. She was right to. They spawned a heated debate not only about racism but about classism, entitlement, and how the world was still grappling with the pernicious vestiges of British colonialism. Birmingham City University professor Kehinde Andrews went so far as to call the Windsors "probably the primary symbol of whiteness that we have."

The monarchy was the Cambridge children's destiny, their future, and it was now being threatened by explosive charges leveled by a once-beloved uncle. Still, Kate harbored a soft spot in her heart for Harry. She was determined to exploit even the slightest breach in the wall that William and Harry had built between them.

In the meantime, there were other weighty matters that Kate felt deeply about, not the least of which was the issue of women's safety. On March 3, thirty-three-year-old London marketing executive Sarah Everard was abducted, raped, and murdered by Metropolitan police officer Wayne Couzens. Everard's death sparked outrage across the United Kingdom, and hit home with Kate, who remembered how, as a young single woman, she had at times felt menaced while walking the streets of the city alone. Without fanfare or advance notice of any kind, Kate unilaterally decided to break from royal protocol and show up alone to silently pay her respects at a memorial for Everard. Had she not been spotted in the crowd by a TV news cameraman covering the event, Kate's presence would have gone unnoticed.

More sad news arrived a few weeks later when, after going in and out of the hospital for a variety of ailments, the Queen's husband of seventy-three years passed away on April 9. Amid COVID restrictions, the family gathered at Windsor Castle for Prince Philip's funeral on April 17. William and his father had wanted to wear their military uniforms to the memorial service inside St. George's Chapel—a modest ceremony like all others conducted during the pandemic—but the Queen said no. She did not want Harry, who had been a particular favorite of Prince Philip, to feel excluded because he was barred from wearing military regalia at royal events. Mourners, the newly widowed monarch decreed, were to wear civilian attire—and masks. Kate took this as a signal that the Queen was also smoothing the way for some sort of rapprochement between the warring factions of Windsor men. It also helped that Meghan, who was seven months pregnant, stayed home in California with Archie.

After the small ceremony was over, Elizabeth II rode back up Castle Hill in her maroon Bentley state limousine while the mourners made their way up to the residence on foot. As the most empathetic member of the family, Kate saw that, of all the Windsors with the exception of the Queen, Prince Charles seemed most devastated by the loss of the father who had bullied and belittled him well into adulthood. As they left the church, she put her hand on his shoulder and whispered a few words of comfort before leaning in to kiss him on the cheek. The moment reflected what had become a genuine bond of affection between Kate and her congenitally stiff father-in-law.

Kate walked partway toward the castle a few steps behind William, but when she looked over and saw that the brothers appeared to be immersed in friendly conversation, she drifted off with Prince Edward's wife, Sophie, Countess of Wessex.

At that point, there was a glimmer of hope. William and Harry agreed that the funeral had come off without a hitch. The music, the readings, the dramatic exit of a royal bagpiper that signaled the end of the service, the army green Land Rover Defender TD5 130 that carried Philip's coffin to and from the chapel—all detailed by the Duke of Edinburgh nearly twenty years earlier and executed with military precision.

Funeral planners had arranged for the boys' cousin, Princess Anne's son Peter Phillips, to sit between the brothers as a sort of buffer. But that hardly seemed necessary. None of the fireworks that Kate, among others, had expected to see had been ignited—yet. She urged her husband to accept Prince Charles's invitation to meet with Harry—it would be just the three Windsor men—to try and make peace.

Harry and Meghan had spent $3.4 million out of their own pockets to refurbish Frogmore Cottage on the Windsor Castle grounds, and now

Princess Eugenie—"Euge" to her cousins—was temporarily living there with her husband, marketing executive Jack Brooksbank. It was doubtful that the Sussexes would ever be allowed to return, but at least Frogmore's lush gardens, originally designed for George III's wife Queen Charlotte in the late eighteenth century, could serve as the setting for yet another summit.

There was an added incentive for Charles and William on one side and Harry on the other to try and make amends. In just four days, the Queen was turning ninety-five. "Wouldn't it be a wonderful present for you and Harry to give your grandmother?" Kate asked. "You really have to try, William." At least on this, Meghan and her sister-in-law were in agreement. Coming so closely on the heels of Prince Philip's death, Her Majesty's birthday was bound to be bittersweet; it would help to have Harry stay in London a few extra days to help her get through it.

Late that afternoon, the three men met in Frogmore's gardens and within minutes were shouting at each other. Harry was especially incensed that unfounded bullying allegations had been leveled at Meghan right before the Oprah interview and that neither Kensington Palace nor Clarence House did anything to refute them. Conversely, William and Charles still felt betrayed by the Oprah interview itself. Accusations and epithets flew, father and sons talked over each other, and at least twice William angrily grabbed his brother by the shirt and spun Harry around to confront him.

William admitted to Harry what Kate had known and been dealing with all along—that the Sturm und Drang surrounding the brothers' rift was having a profound impact on the Heir's health. "I've felt properly sick and ill after everything that's happened," William told Harry, "and . . . I swear to you now on Mummy's life that I just want you to be happy!" Even though swearing on Princess Diana's life was a pledge invoked only under the rarest of circumstances, Harry was unconvinced. No inroads had been made, no positions had been changed. Charles and William conceded nothing, nor did Harry. Three days later—on the eve of the Queen's birthday—Harry boarded a plane for California.

Kate was distressed to hear William confess that he had lunged at his brother and grabbed him, and even more upset to learn that he had lost his temper with Harry earlier while talking about Meghan—specifically, the incident in 2019 when, William admitted, he had shoved his brother and sent him crashing to the floor as they quarreled about Meghan. "You cannot lose control like that," Kate scolded. "I understand why you're angry. I'm angry, too. But violence is never justified." As she had done in the past, Kate told her husband to seek help from his therapist. "Obviously, something else is going on here."

Harry was not the only family member subjected to William's unfortunate outbursts. The Heir was kind and considerate to a fault with servants, staffers, and strangers he might meet on his walkabouts—and was never heard to lose control with Kate or the children—but he often raised his voice at his father. "When he gets frustrated, he does resort to shouting at Prince Charles," said a former Highgrove staffer who witnessed several such scenes. "William has a huge, booming voice—much louder than his father's—so it's not something you soon forget. But Princess Catherine knows how to calm things down."

Over the years, Charles had come to regard Kate as the daughter he never had; on numerous occasions, he referred to her as "my beloved daughter-in-law." Therefore, it often fell to her to smooth things over between the two future kings when things got heated. "Her mother says Catherine rolls her eyes when she hears it," a Bucklebury neighbor of the Middletons said, "but she definitely is the peacemaker."

Keeping the peace among her own brood of three also proved challenging, although the surprise video they released on April 29 to mark their tenth wedding anniversary showed only family harmony. In the video, shot at the beach near Anmer Hall in Norfolk, the Cambridges are shown scampering hand in hand up and down the dunes, chasing one another—at one point William pops out of the brush to surprise Charlotte and Louis—taking turns on a seesaw, climbing a tree, and then finally roasting marshmallows over an open fire.

These moments spent enjoying nature were the ones that most resonated with Kate. When someone asked her what she wanted George,

Charlotte, and Louis to remember about their childhood, Kate mused, "Is it that I'm sitting down trying to do their maths and spelling homework over the weekend? Or is it the fact that we've gone out and lit a bonfire and sat around trying to cook sausages that hasn't worked because it's too wet?" She concluded that, in the end, she'd "rather we all be outside doing things—even if it doesn't always work out."

Eye roll or no, Kate had not yet given up on making peace with the Sussexes. She was now betting that the family might come together over the birth of Harry and Meghan's second child. After their daughter was born at 11:40 a.m. on June 4, 2021, at Santa Barbara Cottage Hospital—the first of Queen Elizabeth's grandchildren to be born outside the United Kingdom—Harry called the Queen directly and asked if she would mind if they named their new baby Lilibet after Her Majesty's childhood nickname. Lilibet ("Lili") Diana Mountbatten-Windsor would pay tribute to both the Queen and Princess Diana in much the same way the name Charlotte Elizabeth Diana did. The Queen was touched by the idea and gave her permission, but that scarcely mattered. The BBC ran a story criticizing Harry for making an end run around his grandmother, and once again the Spare asked his go-to law firm, Schillings, to threaten legal action.

Lili's Aunt Kate, for one, loved the name they had chosen and sent a note to Harry and Meghan telling them so. "We are all delighted by the happy news of the arrival of Baby Lili," William and Kate wrote on their Instagram account. Accompanying the note was a photo of Harry and Meghan holding their two-year-old son. "Congratulations to Harry, Meghan, and Archie."

It would be a solid week before Kate, who was touring a primary school in Cornwall with First Lady Jill Biden while President Joe Biden met with other G7 leaders, was asked about the newest Sussex. "I wish her all the very best. I can't wait to meet her," the princess said somewhat awkwardly, "because we haven't yet met her yet. So, hopefully, that will be soon." When asked if she had been able to see Lilibet through FaceTime or any other virtual means, she paused for a moment. "No," she replied, "no, I haven't." Privately, Kate was doing all she could to make that happen, sending flowers, cards, and gifts for the baby in hopes it would win over Lili's parents. Apparently, none of it worked.

Not that Kate didn't have enough on her plate. In addition to feeding carrots to bunnies with Jill Biden at the Connor Downs Academy in Cornwall—the American First Lady and Kate shared a keen interest in early childhood education—Kate joined William and Prince Charles in hosting a number of G7 events, including tea with the Queen at Windsor Castle. It was first time the Queen was meeting face-to-face with world leaders since the pandemic struck, and the fact that she was leaning so heavily on Kate to wield the monarchy's "soft diplomacy" spoke volumes. Certainly, when it came to Britain's brand, no one was having a greater impact. "The younger royals have re-energized interest in the UK. . . . and reignited the love affair with all things British," said marketing guru Penny Erricker. According to one study released in 2021, 76 percent of Americans credited Kate as being "the most powerful royal Influencer." So much so that at one point 53 percent of those Americans surveyed said they believed the United States should join the Commonwealth.

Not long after Kate charmed the Bidens and G7 leaders like German Chancellor Angela Merkel, Canada's Prime Minister Justin Trudeau, and UK Prime Minister Boris Johnson, she had her fingers crossed that another opportunity had arisen for the brothers. For four years, William and Harry had been working to get a statue honoring their mother installed in the Sunken Garden at Kensington Palace. The unveiling was to take place on July 1, 2021—what would have been Princess Diana's sixtieth birthday—but William was still so furious at his brother that initially he did not want to attend; Kate had to talk her husband into going.

Shoulder to shoulder as they entered the garden, the brothers convincingly engaged in cheerful banter, just as they had following Prince Philip's funeral. They graciously greeted the thirteen guests, including their Spencer uncle and aunts and a handful of others, but it was impossible to ignore the fact that no other members of the royal family were present—not the Queen, Charles, or Camilla, not another Windsor in sight.

At least the Duchess of Cambridge had an excuse. Since Meghan understandably chose to stay home in California with the not-quite-one-month-old Lili, Kate felt it was only fair that she lie low at Anmer Hall—although earlier she and William had discussed bringing along George, Charlotte, and even little Louis. After all, the Cambridges often spoke with the children about their late grandmother. On more than one occasion, Kate sat down with George and Charlotte and helped them write letters to their "Granny Diana." On Mother's Day, Charlotte wrote, "Dear Granny Diana, I am thinking of you. . . . I love you very much. Papa is missing you. Lots of love."

In the end, Kate decided that the focus at the unveiling should be entirely on Diana and her sons. Fittingly, the bronze Sunken Garden statue depicted Diana surrounded by three small children—two boys and a girl—symbolizing the impact she had, said the brothers, as "a force for good around the world."

That summer, Kate was zeroing in on her own humanitarian causes. Wearing blue jeans, a sleeveless top, and a mask, she looked the other way while she received her first dose of the new COVID vaccine at London's Science Museum. "I'm hugely grateful to everyone who is playing a part in the rollout," she wrote on the official Duke and Duchess of Cambridge social media accounts. "Thank you for everything you are doing." An avid amateur photographer, Kate also launched her Hold Still campaign, which invited people to submit images of themselves as a way of documenting life during the pandemic lockdown. Out of 31,000 submissions, several hundred were included in a book published by England's prestigious National Portrait Gallery.

Kate also continued her work championing early childhood education, drug treatment (as royal patron of the newly merged Forward Trust and Action on Addiction), and mental health—stopping in July to once again preside over Wimbledon as patron of the All England Lawn Tennis and Croquet Club. Kate also teamed up with William to try to assuage a public still coping with life under COVID restrictions. While visiting a nursing home, William and Kate stopped to chat with an elderly patient in a wheelchair. "We have to wear masks because of the virus," he told her, "but it's difficult to hear sometimes when you can't see someone's mouth." The woman then pointed to Kate and asked William, "Is that your assistant?"

"Well." Kate laughed and, turning to her husband, added, "I *am* your assistant! I have been for a long time!"

In addition to humor, Kate injected youth, energy, natural beauty, and unforced glamour into every public appearance. At the world premiere of the new James Bond film *No Time to Die* in late September, onlookers gasped, cameras flashed, and journalists reached for superlatives to describe Kate's tastefully diaphanous, bejeweled gold gown. Three weeks later, the Duchess of Cambridge caused another commotion when she accompanied William to the awarding of the first Earthshot prizes at Alexandra Palace in North London. The Heir established the awards, and in keeping with the environmentally conscious theme, guests were asked to wear something they had worn at least once before. Kate fished around in her closet before selecting a lilac Grecian column gown by Alexander McQueen—the same dress that had caused a stir when she first wore it a decade earlier during the couple's visit to Los Angeles. Ed Sheeran, Coldplay, and Shawn Mendes performed at the Earthshot Prize ceremonies, and the five award recipients each took home £1 million. Yet once again, Kate and what she wore dominated the news cycle.

As the holidays approached, Kate had another surprise up her designer sleeve. The world had been in the grips of the COVID pandemic for eighteen months, and she wanted to do something to thank frontline health care workers. Toward that end she organized a concert, "Royal Carols: Together at Christmas," to be recorded at Westminster Abbey and broadcast on ITV Christmas Eve.

In the process of picking the performers, Kate reached out to British singer-songwriter Tom Walker after he performed his hit "Leave a Light On" at one of her charity events. Walker suggested he sing "For Those Who Can't Be There," a new song he had written about losing his grandfather during the pandemic. The Duchess, who had studied piano as a child and taken it up again during the pandemic, asked if she could accompany him. "I had never heard her play. . . . I had no idea if she was any good," admitted Walker, who made a practice track for her to rehearse with. By the time the concert aired, audiences were stunned to see the always-poised princess at the keyboard—her first performance in public.

"The duchess was unbelievable," Walker said. "To pick up a song she'd only heard for the first time five days before, join a band she'd never played with, in front of loads of cameras, a director, a whole team of people on set, and just absolutely nail it—really impressive. She blew my mind."

No one was more impressed than the Queen. "How absolutely marvelous," Her Majesty said to the butler as she watched the televised concert in her private sitting room at Windsor Castle. Her Majesty plucked a Bendicks Bittermint chocolate from one of the three Fortnum & Mason candy boxes she always kept within arm's reach. "Did anyone know she could play? That girl . . . she never fails to amaze me."

Elizabeth II's respect for the woman who would one day carry the title of queen consort had grown exponentially over the years. Any criticism of Kate for not taking on a heavy enough schedule of royal events was now decidedly a thing of the past. "Princess Catherine wasn't playing a numbers game," said a former Kensington Palace press officer. "She is always very selective about what causes she embraces and how she does the job—and as a result everything she does counts. The people love her. The Queen feels William could not have made a better choice."

There were more mind-blowing events ahead in the new year. To mark her fortieth birthday on January 9, Kate, remembering that Princess Diana had hired fashion photographer Mario Testino to take the iconic final portraits of her that appeared in *Vanity Fair*, turned to another Italian master lensman to do the same for her. Paolo Roversi had taken glamorous, cutting-edge fashion shots of everyone from Rihanna to Kate Moss for *Vanity Fair* and *Vogue*, but Kate had ideas of her own. At St. Andrews, she had done her dissertation on Victorian photography, and turned to the photos of royal women from that era to emulate—most notably Edward VII's wife, Alexandra of Denmark. Alexandra was, like Kate, a great beauty who not coincidentally was also an incredibly popular, even beloved queen of England.

Wearing a dress designed by Sarah Burton for Alexander McQueen, Kate posed for two hundred and fifty pictures, nearly all black-and-white. The photos were supposed to show Kate's regal, informal, and glamorous sides, and at one point she even danced for the camera. Kate, who as patron of the National Portrait Gallery agreed to have the photos displayed there, let George, Charlotte, and Louis pick one shot out to be the centerpiece of the exhibit. The black-and-white close-up they picked showed Mummy smiling straight into the camera.

"In years past, the family has opted for more informal portraits—a 2018 Christmas card, for example, showed the duchess in jeans," wrote *Vogue*'s Elise Taylor, who pointed out that Kate had shrewdly paid homage to both Diana and Queen Elizabeth by wearing their jewelry in many of the fortieth birthday images. "These, however, exuded an ethereal glamour and formality: these were not photos of Kate Middleton, as she's more colloquially known, but of the future queen consort of the United Kingdom."

Still recovering from her husband's death, the Queen was now preparing to celebrate her Platinum Jubilee marking an unprecedented seventy years on the throne—seven years longer than the previous record holder, Queen Victoria. But first the sovereign had to dig into her own deep pockets to help her favorite child, Prince Andrew, settle the sex abuse case brought against him by Virginia Giuffre as part of the Epstein scandal.

If that weren't enough, Charles intensified the pressure on his mother to pave the way for Camilla—the perennial mistress she had once reviled—to eventually become queen. The monarch relented, and on February 6—the anniversary of her father George VI's death—declared that it was her "wish that, when the time comes, Camilla will be known as Queen Consort as she continues her own loyal service."

Both of Granny's actions fell with a thud at Kensington Palace and Anmer Hall. William shared his father's disgust over Andrew's connection to child predator Epstein, and opposed bailing Andrew out. In fact, despite his genuine fondness for his cousins Beatrice and Eugenie, William wanted his uncle Andrew turned over to the FBI for questioning. Kate, however, was more sympathetic to the Queen—not only because she was protecting her child as any mother would, but because settling the lawsuit erased a dark cloud that hung over her jubilee.

From William's standpoint, the rise of Camilla was equally irksome. Charles had promised the British people that his wife would never be queen—that she would have the title Princess Consort. Now his sons, who had both begged Charles not to marry Camilla in the first place, felt betrayed. Kate, whose seventeen-year relationship with Camilla had evolved from frosty to cordial, understood why her husband felt so strongly about the Duchess of Cornwall. William was, after all, still coping with the psychological scars inflicted by his parents' stormy marriage and his mother's untimely death—both, many argued, a direct result of Charles's affair with Camilla. Now the Queen had given Camilla her blessing, and it stung. Kate, always the pragmatist, ultimately thought it best to remain silent on the issue.

There were other things going on in the world, not the least of which was Russia's invasion of Ukraine on February 24. In 2020, William and Kate had hosted Ukrainian President Volodymyr Zelenskyy and his wife, Olena, at Buckingham Palace. Now, in a major departure from the royals' usual policy of not speaking out on political issues, they posted on Twitter that they were "privileged to learn of the Zelenskyys' hope and optimism for Ukraine's future. Today we stand with the President and all of Ukraine's people as they bravely fight for that future." To show their support, both Kate and William began wearing blue and yellow—Ukraine's national colors—during their public outings.

William and Kate were not alone. Visiting London's Ukrainian Catholic Cathedral of the Holy Family on Ash Wednesday with Camilla, Charles denounced Russia's "terrible aggression" as "unconscionable." The Queen had to be more subtle: she contributed what the Palace called a "generous donation" to Ukrainian relief and made a point of welcoming world leaders in front of a massive display of blue hydrangeas and yellow tulips. She also took to wearing blue and yellow to several jubilee events, including the opening of a new Underground line in London.

It was around this time that the ninety-six-year-old monarch really began showing her age. William and Kate had watched as Prince Charles began taking on more and more of his mother's duties—accepting diplomatic credentials, filling in on trips to the shires, presiding at investitures, and more. But everyone grew increasingly concerned when, on May 10, last-minute mobility issues forced her to miss the State Opening of Parliament for only the third time in her long reign. Instead, Charles filled in, speaking from the consort's chair while the Imperial State Crown, with its 317-carat Cullinan II diamond, sat majestically on the slightly taller throne where the Queen would normally sit. William and Camilla flanked him, symbols of what the future held in store.

Noticeably absent was Kate, who still had something important to do that day. Immediately after the State Opening, she and William traveled 211 miles north to Manchester. There, they officially opened the Glade of Light memorial honoring the twenty-two people who had lost their lives when an Islamic suicide bomber attacked Manchester Arena following an Ariana Grande concert. After laying flowers at the memorial, the Cambridges also met with bereaved families of the victims in a private ceremony at the city's six-hundred-year-old cathedral.

Nine days later, Kate and William were launched on an eight-day Platinum Jubilee tour to Belize, Jamaica, and the Bahamas—their first overseas trip as a couple since the COVID-19 pandemic began. From the couple's perspective, the tour was yet another triumph. Photos from the trip posted on Instagram showed the Cambridges charming their hosts as they always did—visiting farms, markets, and businesses; kicking a ball around with teenage soccer players; touring ancient Mayan ruins; gamely showing off their dance moves; playing drums in a reggae band; scuba diving along Belize's spectacular barrier reef. In Kingston, the duke and duchess actually seemed a little starstruck themselves as they posed for photos with the Jamaican bobsled team of *Cool Runnings* fame.

Yet, for the first time, they found what was supposed to be a pro forma goodwill trip mired in controversy. Six months earlier Barbados—another Caribbean Commonwealth nation that was one of fourteen countries that recognized Queen Elizabeth as its head of state—announced that it was severing ties with the British monarch. In his speech at the ceremony that saw Barbados become a republic, Prince Charles conceded Britain's part in the "appalling atrocity of slavery, which forever stains our history." At the same time, he was roundly criticized for even being present at the ceremony.

In Belize, a visit to a cocoa farm had to be canceled because of protests, and when Kate and William visited Belize's prime minister, he went out of his way to make it clear that Belize would soon be following in Barbados's footsteps. The blowback was even worse in Jamaica, where there were calls for the British monarchy to pay reparations for centuries of slavery and exploitation.

"We will not participate in your Platinum Jubilee celebration!" a coalition of Jamaican human rights groups called the Advocates Network wrote in an open letter to William and Kate. "We see no reason to celebrate seventy years of the ascension of your grandmother to the British throne because her leadership, and that of her predecessors, has perpetuated the greatest human rights tragedy in the history of humankind." By the time the Cambridges departed for home, the movement to ditch Her Majesty and make Jamaica a republic was more energized than ever.

Controversy aside, Trooping the Colour officially kicked off the Platinum Jubilee on June 2, with Her Majesty now only able to summon enough strength to appear on the Buckingham Palace balcony. Only "working royals" were permitted to join the monarch, which meant that Harry and Meghan, who had flown to London with Archie and Lilibet for the first time since Megxit, were excluded. Instead, they headed straight for their old digs at Windsor, Frogmore Cottage.

Meanwhile, Kate had her hands full corralling the Cambridge children as everyone waited in breathless anticipation for the traditional Royal Air Force flyby. As expected, four-year-old Louis, dressed in a blue-and-white sailor outfit, created havoc by squirming, pointing, making faces, and covering his ears as the RAF squadrons shrieked overhead.

Immediately afterward, the Queen returned to Windsor, where she met her great-granddaughter and namesake, Lilibet, for the first time. Harry later recalled that Baby Lili hugged the monarch's shins and her brother, Archie, practiced making "deep, chivalrous bows." Charles, who was also meeting Lili for the first time, was no less smitten with his half-American grandchildren.

The Queen was too exhausted to attend a Thanksgiving service at St. Paul's Cathedral the next day, but Harry and Meghan were there—as were William and Kate. It was the first time in two years that the two couples had been seen at the same royal event, but despite hopes for a reconciliation, they did not interact at all. The Cambridges and Sussexes arrived separately, were seated far apart, and departed separately.

This was not by accident. Reportedly fearing that anything they said or did might end up in the Sussexes' planned Netflix series or Harry's upcoming memoir, William and Kate made sure that Netflix cameras were barred from all palaces. They also ordered Palace officials to keep the battling brothers and their spouses far apart.

The Queen skipped several major Jubilee events, most notably the star-packed Party at the Palace pop concert. She was also too under the weather to join the Sussexes when they celebrated Lili's first birthday with a backyard picnic at Frogmore Cottage. The next day, they packed up and left for Los Angeles. Apparently no one told the Queen, who tried to invite the Sussexes for tea but was told they'd gone. "What do you mean, 'They've gone'?" she asked.

"They've gone back to America."

"Oh no," the crestfallen queen replied. "They never said goodbye." According to her former footman Paul Burrell, Her Majesty "had a birthday cake made with one candle in it. And they never turned up. That candle was never lit."

The rest of Kate's summer schedule was packed. As royal patron, she turned up several times at Wimbledon—usually with fellow tennis fan Charlotte—cheered her husband on from the sidelines during a charity polo match, then gave polka dots a boost when she showed up at Royal Ascot in a black-and-white dress by London-based designer Alessandra Rich. She also attended the Commonwealth Games and took part in the

Sail Grand Prix, hopping aboard a catamaran to help out in a race against New Zealand. The Cambridges still made room for some family time. They celebrated George's ninth birthday with a trip to the surprisingly subtropical Isles of Scilly off the southwestern tip of England, and in mid-August spent several days with the Queen at Balmoral.

Few photo ops could match what the Cambridges delivered on September 7, when they arrived hand in hand for all three children's "settling-in afternoon" at Lambrook School near Windsor—one day prior to the official first day of school. Lambrook, which would cost the family roughly $70,000 a year for the three children, was part of the family's decision to relocate from Anmer Hall to Adelaide College at Windsor. Now that the Queen was ninety-six and increasingly frail, the Heir understandably wanted to be close to her and Prince Charles.

Outfitted in the school summer uniform (blue shorts, white shirts, and blue socks for the boys, a light blue shirtwaist dress with blue socks for the girls), George, nine, Charlotte, seven, and four-year-old Louis walked up to headmaster Jonathan Perry. Perry addressed each by name as he bent over to shake their hands: "Welcome, George. Welcome, Louis. Welcome, Charlotte. Lovely to have you with us." Asked if they were excited, all three said yes. Papa added that they were "all looking forward to it" and had "lots of questions." As they marched up the steps and someone opened the door, William announced, "We brought the gang!"

Their first day of school, September 8, 2022, would be memorable for other, sadder, more historic reasons. Just two days earlier, the Queen had been photographed at Balmoral looking happy and well as she invited her fifteenth prime minister, Liz Truss, to form a new government. But there was concern that the monarch's health was rapidly deteriorating. Charles, Camilla, and the Princess Royal—Elizabeth's only daughter Anne—were already at Balmoral. Now, moments after the Lambrook photo op, William was being summoned to Scotland.

While Kate stayed home at Adelaide Cottage with the children, William joined his uncles Andrew and Edward at RAF Northolt and boarded a royal jet for Aberdeen. Unbeknownst to them, the Queen was pronounced dead at 3:10 p.m. UK time, while they were still in the air. With William at the wheel, the princes drove the hour and ten minutes to Balmoral. In the meantime Harry, who, coincidentally, was in London with Meghan to attend the WellChild Awards that day, was inexplicably left behind and had to catch a separate private jet. Charles told the Spare that, since Kate was not coming to Balmoral, Meghan shouldn't either.

Determined that George, Charlotte, and Louis not learn about the passing of their Gan-Gan from someone else, Kate picked the children up at school, drove them home, and sat them down at the kitchen table. They knew Gan-Gan had not been well, and news of her death did not come as a shock. George and Charlotte wanted to make sure their father wasn't "too sad," and Louis tried to cheer Mummy up by saying that at least "Granny is with Great-Grandpa now."

As earthshaking events go, this was one of history's most well rehearsed. Yet it still had the power to shock. The world was riveted by the spectacle, solemnity, pageantry, and poignancy surrounding the death of England's longest-reigning monarch. An estimated 90 percent of the earth's population had only known a world with the Queen in it. She had been, by any measure, the most instantly recognizable human alive. When people referred to the queen, they were talking about Elizabeth II.

Now that she was gone, her subjects needed time to absorb the news. Those in charge at the Palace were not so fortunate. The first outside the family was Prime Minister Truss. She and other top government officials were all initially told "London Bridge is down." Operation London Bridge was the code name given to the detailed funeral plans for the monarch.

Kate was surprised when she was told that these had been drawn up ten years earlier. "Oh really? The reality of it must be very different," she said. "It's time-specific, isn't it?" Indeed, William pointed out that no one expected London Bridge to fall in Scotland. Balmoral was, he observed, "the least planned-for plan."

Every few years, under cover of predawn darkness so as not to alarm the general public, there was a trial run of the Queen's cortege through the streets of London. Each senior royal had a code-named funeral plan: for Charles, Operation Menai Bridge, after the bridge that links mainland Wales to the island of Anglesey; for William, Operation Clare Bridge, after the bridge over the River Cam in Cambridge; and for Kate, Operation Reading Bridge, chosen by William to honor the city of her birth in Berkshire.

Now that lineup would change. Since he became king, Charles's funeral plan became Operation London Bridge; as the new Prince of Wales, William's became Operation Menai Bridge; Kate's Operation Reading Bridge designation remained.

The Queen lay in state at St. Giles' Cathedral in Edinburgh from September 12 to 13 before being flown to London, where more than a quarter million people filed past her body as it lay in state in Westminster Hall. For the first time, the monarch's grandchildren took part in the Vigil of the Princes, each taking turn standing at the four corners of Her Majesty's coffin. William wore the uniform of the Blue and Royals, as did Harry; even though the Spare and Prince Andrew were no longer working royals, King Charles insisted that the two combat veterans both be allowed to wear military garb.

In his first televised address to the nation as king, Charles III paid tribute to his late mother, and then stated it was "a time of change for my family." He went on to first proclaim that Camilla would become Queen Consort, and then, accompanied by footage of Kate and William walking hand in hand with their children on the way to their first day at school, declared that William (who remained Duke of Cambridge) was now inheriting all Charles's previous titles: Duke of Cornwall—which came with an annual income somewhere in the neighborhood of $40 million—Duke of Rothesay, Earl of Carrick, Baron of Renfrew, Lord of the Isles, and Prince and Great Steward of Scotland. The Welsh titles were not inherited but bestowed, so Charles wasted no time announcing that William and Kate were the new Prince and Princess of Wales. The couple would, Charles said, "continue to inspire and lead our national conversation." It was a relief to Kate, still holding out hope that somehow the brothers might reunite, when her father-in-law said he wanted "to express my love for Harry and Meghan as they continue to build their lives overseas."

Charles appeared composed, thoughtful, even kind as he delivered his first speech to his subjects. Earlier in the day, however, he had reverted to his old habits, snapping at one aide for not clearing his desk promptly enough as he signed the ascension papers that officially proclaimed him king—an unflattering display of regal pique that was caught on camera and instantly went viral. "It's his first day [as king] and the entire world is watching," marveled William, who to some extent shared his father's volatile temper but never bullied underlings the way some other members of the royal family did. Kate had little tolerance for tantrum throwers, but in this case, she spoke up in the King's defense. "He's just lost his mother and he's very stressed, as we all are," she said. "I think we have to consider that."

Not long after, while signing documents at Northern Ireland's Hillsborough Castle, Charles III threw another hissy fit—this time over getting the date wrong on the papers he'd just signed and then over a leaky pen. "Oh God, I hate this!" he said, leaping to his feet. "I can't bear this *bloody* thing!" he added as he stormed out of the room. "What they [fountain pens] do every *stinking time*!" Another viral moment only days into Charles's reign, and again Kate was sympathetic: "He's right about the pens." (That same year saw the beginning of a minirebellion at Highgrove, where eleven out of a gardening staff of twelve quit, claiming they were understaffed, underpaid, and treated "like dirt" by Charles.)

During the days before the state funeral—Britain's first since Winston Churchill's in 1965—preparations were underway at Windsor Castle for the Queen's eventual interment alongside the Queen Mother, her sister Margaret, and predecessors such as Henry VIII, Charles I (without his head), George III, William's namesake William IV, Edward VII, and Elizabeth II's adored father George VI.

Kate and William agreed that it was best not to disrupt the children's schedule. Dropping them off at school the day after the Queen's death, the new Prince of Wales explained to teachers that he and Kate wanted to "keep some sense of continuity for them at school and keep things as normal as possible." Teacher Elaine Gee echoed the faculty's opinion of the Cambridges. "Kate and William," she said, "were both very kind and gentle and genuine."

The frenzied activity at Windsor gave Kate an opportunity to distract her children and ease them into the realization that their great-grandmother was gone. Kate told volunteers that, while doing what she called the "school run" to Lambrook, she and the children were "able to see the preparations going up. We've seen it growing. It's quite the undertaking." All three children made a game of spotting security drones that hovered over Frogmore, Adelaide Cottage, and the other residences at Windsor. "George, Charlotte, and Louis," Kate said, "*they're* the beady-eyed ones!"

In a scene reminiscent of the days following Princess Diana's death, waves of flowers lapped at the gates of the royal palaces and other official buildings. "It's very strange being here without Her Majesty," Kate admitted while mingling with the crowd outside Windsor Castle. "She's touched everyone's lives globally." At Sandringham, cameras caught a touching moment when Kate plucked an eight-year-old girl clutching flowers and a stuffed corgi from the crowd and led her by the hand to the palace gates. As they knelt to place the bouquet and the corgi among the other items left by mourners, the little girl burst into tears.

BBC television commentators covering the comings and goings at Windsor were taken by surprise when a black Audi sedan with William at the wheel and Kate at his side drove from the castle toward the front gates with Harry and Meghan in the back seat. The brothers and their wives, all dressed in black and walking side by side, remained somber faced as they headed toward the cheering crowd. While Kate and William never touched, Harry and Meghan, unsure of the crowd's reaction, clung to each other for reassurance. They perused the floral tributes and worked the rope line, sparking speculation that their feud was at last at an end. But their body language spoke volumes as the two couples walked off in separate directions before returning to their waiting car.

At the Queen's Westminster Abbey funeral service a few days later, the Cambridges and the Sussexes continued to put on a united front out of

As the female half of the powerhouse "Fab Four" who were supposedly going to reshape the monarchy, Kate and Harry's then-fiancée, Meghan, seemed to hit it off when they got together to launch their Royal Foundation Forum in late February 2018. But just before Harry and Meghan's wedding that May, both women were driven to tears during a dispute over the dresses to be worn by Charlotte and the other flower girls. A year later, Kate dazzled at the BAFTA Awards in a white Alexander McQueen gown, but behind the scenes tensions between her husband and Harry over Meghan's alleged bullying had reached the boiling point.

Even before he became king, Charles bonded with his "beloved daughter-in-law" over their shared sense of humor—something even Camilla, who had initially disapproved of Kate marrying William, came to appreciate. The duo made each other laugh during a visit to a physical rehabilitation center in 2020 and warmly greeted each other at the world premiere of the prophetically titled James Bond film *No Time to Die* the following year.

Headmaster Jonathan Perry greets all three Cambridge children—George, Louis, and Charlotte—on their first day at Lambrook School. Sadly, their great-grandmother Queen Elizabeth II died at Balmoral Castle the next day. In a stunning gesture before the queen's state funeral, Kate, William, Harry, and Meghan reunited to greet crowds gathered outside Windsor Castle.

Always there to cheer on her husband, Kate congratulates the Prince of Wales when he wins the couple's annual Royal Charity Polo Cup. Founded in 2011 by the then-newlyweds, the match has earned nearly $20 million for their charities.

Walking the green carpet on their way to the Earthshot Prize ceremonies in Boston in December 2022, Kate made the right color choice and a statement about recycling in a slinky kelly green, bare-shouldered gown she rented off the internet for $100.

May 6, 2023—Coronation Day. Standing alongside the Duchess of Edinburgh and Princess Anne on the Buckingham Palace balcony, Kate, William, Charlotte, and Louis wait for the traditional (and very noisy) RAF flypast. Page of Honor George, meanwhile, was literally holding up the rear of the newly crowned king's ermine robes as Charles III turned to leave.

Shy at first, Kate has flourished on her own, often surpassing William in the polls as the most-loved royal. From top: Kate reacts to a life vest going off, deploying faster than expected during a visit to the Royal Naval Air Station in Yeovil on England's southwestern coast in September 2023. A few weeks later, she sent the ball flying during a game of wheelchair rugby in Hull. An honorary colonel of the Irish Guards, camo-wearing Kate practiced treating a wounded soldier while training with the regiment on a snowy day in Wiltshire.

Started by Kate in 2021 to honor front line workers, caregivers, and the medical community for the work they did during the COVID-19 pandemic, televised "Together at Christmas" carol services at Westminster Abbey quickly became a holiday tradition in Britain. Mummy looks on warily as Louis mischievously blows out this sister's candle at the 2023 service.

March 22, 2024: Looking calm and poised but also wan, Kate brought a halt to rampant online conspiracy theories and shocked the world by announcing via video that she had been diagnosed with cancer—just weeks after the king's diagnosis. By late June, she poses in another bucolic setting—by a willow tree at Windsor—to give the public an encouraging update.

A year after her own diagnosis, Kate spends time sharing treatment experiences with other cancer patients at London's Royal Marsden Hospital, where she was treated secretly before going public with the news.

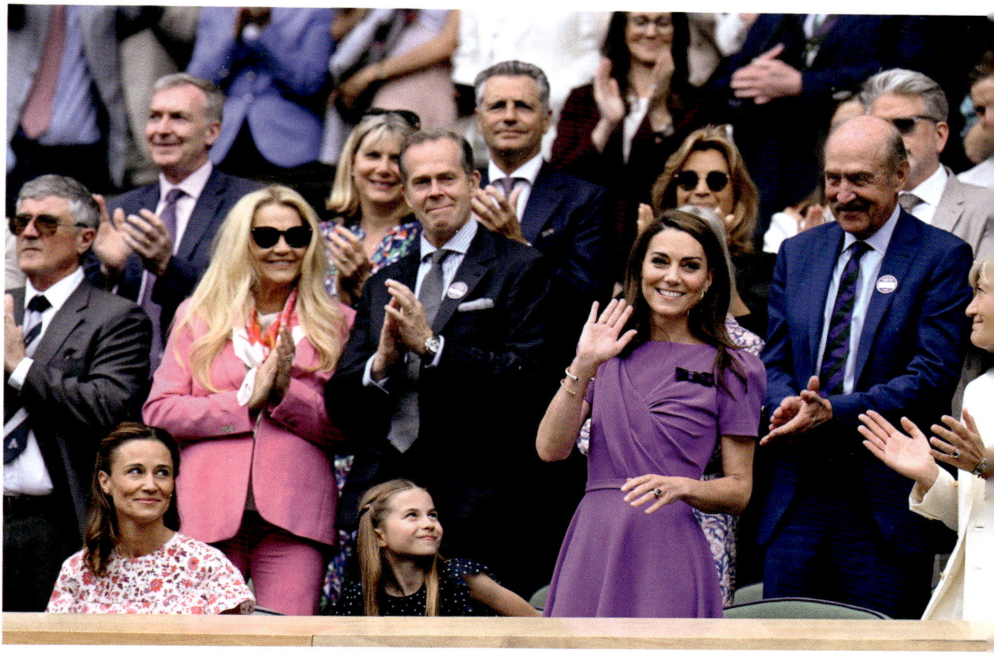

From top: Kate is genuinely moved when, as patron of Wimbledon, she returns to her place at Centre Court and 15,000 spectators give her a standing ovation on July 14, 2024. Charlotte looks on admiringly as her mother takes the unusual step of pausing to soak up the love. The crowds were no less enthusiastic when Kate and family showed up for Christmas morning services at Sandringham.

Here's looking at you, kid. During Trooping the Colour in June 2025, Kate looks daggers at Louis, who, true to character, is acting up on the Buckingham Palace balcony. A month later, the Prince and Princess of Wales are a head-turning couple at a state banquet at Windsor Castle for French President Emmanuel Macron, the first since her diagnosis. Proving that Louis isn't the only naughty boy she has to deal with, Macron gives Kate a sly wink when everyone stands to toast "Anglo-French relations." Next page: Kate is cheered as she arrives at Trooping the Colour ceremonies on June 15, 2024—her first public appearance after being diagnosed with cancer.

deference to the King. Meghan had to borrow a tissue from Edward's wife, Sophie, but again, few words if any were exchanged between the warring brothers and their spouses. Both duchesses paid tribute to the Queen with their jewelry, although Kate's access to the royal jewelry collection gave her a distinct advantage. While Meghan wore pearl earrings that had been given to her by the Queen, Kate wore Her Majesty's favorite four-strand pearl choker and the pearl drop earrings that had been given as a wedding present to the Queen by the King of Bahrain in 1947.

To her credit, Kate was busy holding it together while simultaneously keeping a watchful parental eye on George and Charlotte. (Mummy and Papa wisely decided to have Louis stay home.) Throughout the service, Kate's face was etched with grief. Yet she remained ramrod straight, never losing her composure as the family made its way to the abbey's center aisle to sit next to the Queen's flag-draped coffin. As they left the service, the emotion of the moment finally got to Charlotte, who began sobbing. Kate, on the verge of tears herself, took her little girl's hand and gave it a consoling squeeze.

Chatting with staff and volunteers later in the day, William pointed out that five rainbows had broken through the clouds at Balmoral the day after she died. "You hardly ever see rainbows up there, but there were five." Oddly enough, just before the Queen's death was announced, a double rainbow appeared over Buckingham Palace, and yet another materialized over Westminster when Elizabeth II was lying in state there. Her Majesty "was looking down on us," Kate replied.

Whatever signs of hope there were regarding a truce between the warring brothers vanished when William showed up at the funeral wearing his uniform while Harry was once again under strict orders not to. It also did not help that the Sussexes were seated in the second row, behind the rest of the royals and far from William and Kate. After reportedly being denied a request to hitch a ride back to the United States aboard Air Force One with President Joe Biden and First Lady Jill Biden, the Sussexes departed the day after the funeral aboard a British Airways flight.

While she and William now faced the sobering fact that they were one giant step closer to the crown, Kate discovered that for her not much had really changed. There were visits to Wales and Northern Ireland, where the newly titled Baroness of Carrickfergus shook the hand of a woman who told her, "It would be better if you were in your own country." Kate took a long look at the heckler, laughed heartily, and moved on.

There were no such awkward incidents to mar their three-day visit that December to Boston, where they presided over the second Earthshot Prize award ceremony. Since the Earthshot Prize was inspired by President John F. Kenney's iconic Moonshot challenge, they were greeted at the Kennedy Library by the late president's daughter Caroline, her husband Edwin Schlossberg, and two of their children, Tatiana and Jack. Still, the most electrifying moment of the visit was provided by the Princess of Wales when she stepped onto the traditional green carpet wearing a floor-length, off-the-shoulders, green gown by Solace London, rented for $100 from the website HURR. By wearing a recycled dress, Kate sent a powerful environmental message, albeit one that was contradicted by the emerald-and-diamond choker she also wore. Handed down from Queen Mary, the choker was once one of Princess Diana's favorite pieces and worth an estimated $20 million.

Even before they left for home aboard a commercial British Airways flight, Kate and William were dodging questions about the six-part Netflix documentary series *Harry & Meghan*. Much of the series was devoted to a treacly telling of their love story and an annoyingly repetitive skewering of Britain's tabloid press. But the series hurled plenty of accusations at the royal family, describing it as dysfunctional at best and diabolically dystopian at worst. Once again, there were charges of scheming and backstabbing and racism within the family that allegedly drove Meghan to the brink of suicide.

Neither Kate nor William watched the series, instead relying on aides to monitor it and report back to them. Instead, they concentrated on getting through their Christmas without the Queen. Kate planned her second "Royal Carols: Together at Christmas" concert at Westminster Abbey as a tribute to the late monarch. "Her Late Majesty's strongly held values of duty, compassion, and faith," Kate wrote in the program, "have guided the creation of this service." As an added touch, Kate asked that the Christmas tree at Westminster Abbey be decorated with Paddington Bear stuffed toys. During her Platinum Jubilee celebrations just three months before her death, the Queen costarred with Paddington in a filmed skit that preceded the Platinum Party at the Palace pop concert. At one point during the skit, Her Majesty pulled a marmalade sandwich out of her famously ever-present purse "for later." After her death, more than a thousand Paddingtons were left by mourners outside the Queen's residences. (The stuffed bears, again at Kate's suggestion, were later cleaned and sent to children's hospitals in and around London.)

Getting through Christmas at Sandringham without the Queen was hard for the family to bear. So was the release, just two weeks later, of Harry's explosive memoir, *Spare*. Refreshingly candid and insightful, but also overflowing with vitriol and self-pity, the book was the most searing indictment of the family yet. Racism and the recklessly ravenous press were central issues, along with duplicity and treachery among family members themselves. According to Harry, Charles was pathetically needy and covetous of any attention any other royal might receive. William was a bullying, sometimes violent older brother—"my archnemesis," the Spare called him—and his once-beloved sister-in-law Kate had turned aloof and petty. Nor did Harry mince words about Camilla: the new queen consort was, bluntly, "the villain."

As was the case with the Netflix documentary that preceded it, there would be no reaction from the Palace—official or otherwise. Technically, William and Kate hadn't even read it cover to cover. Instead, they, like the King, relied on aides to summarize *Spare*'s contents. The gist was enough to send tempers soaring. Harry's royal relatives were repeatedly and accurately described as livid, but none more than William. The Spare spared nothing in his campaign to humiliate his brother—right down to claiming the Heir's "alarming baldness" robbed him of his resemblance to their mother.

Understandably, Kate viewed *Spare*, with its overtly mean-spirited attacks on her and her husband, the royal family, and the institution of the monarchy itself, as an outright betrayal—and the final straw. After three years spent quietly working behind the scenes to repair the rupture in the brothers' relationship, the Princess of Wales was throwing up her hands in defeat.

Meanwhile, Harry was telling CNN's Anderson Cooper that "the ball is very much in their court." But Dickie Arbiter, Queen Elizabeth's former press spokesman, echoed the general consensus that this time the Spare had gone too far. "Once again Harry has crucified his family," he said. "The wedge has gone so deep, the chasm so wide that it's unbridgeable."

Over the next several months, Kate had plenty to keep her occupied. There were visits to food banks, nurseries, schools, hospitals, recycling centers, and rehabilitation centers. She played wheelchair rugby in the northeast city of Hull and, despite wearing a skirt and heels, won a spin-cycling contest in Wales. She also donned camouflage to train in the snow with the Irish Guards (Kate became an honorary colonel on the death of Queen Elizabeth) and rappelled down a cliff with volunteers of Wales's Central Beacons Mountain Rescue Team.

There were also appearances at the BAFTA Awards, on Commonwealth Day, and on St. Patrick's Day. In March, the Prince and Princess of Wales hosted their Norwegian counterparts—Crown Prince Haakon and Crown Princess Mette-Marit—at Windsor Castle. But for Kate, nothing was more moving than the Waleses' visit to the Welsh town of Aberfan, where a 1966 avalanche of coal waste from a mine killed 144 people, including 116 schoolchildren.

All was mere prelude to one of the most important dates in history: May 6, Coronation Day. Eight months after the world had been transfixed by the state funeral of Elizabeth II, they were going to be served up another epic display of pomp and ceremony as Charles and Camilla were crowned king and queen consort.

Kate and her husband had appeared happy and relaxed during rehearsals three days earlier, and even though they arrived late, King Charles was thrilled that such a complicated operation seemed to be running like clockwork. But at the coronation itself, Charles and Camilla arrived early, stalling traffic and making the Waleses, who were supposed to get there eight minutes before the King and Queen, ninety seconds late. After Charles could be seen fuming in the Diamond Jubilee State Coach, he and Camilla decided to make their entrance anyway. In an awkward breach of royal protocol, William, Charlotte, Louis, and a very sheepish-looking Kate were left to bring up the rear. George missed the drama. The first future monarch ever to play a part in a coronation ceremony, he was already on site as one of eight pages of honor assigned the task of helping King Charles with his unwieldy royal robes.

The timing snafu aside, the rest of the ceremony went off without a hitch. One of the most poignant moments came when, after Charles was crowned by the Archbishop of Canterbury, William knelt before his father and pledged his allegiance: "I, William, Prince of Wales, pledge my loyalty to you, and faith and truth I will bear unto you as your liege man of life and limb, so help me God." Then he rose, touched his father's crown, and bent down to kiss the monarch's left cheek. "Thank you, William," Charles III said gently to his son.

Kate, with Charlotte at her side, registered no emotion as they watched this profound moment in history unfold before their eyes. Yet even with priceless crowns, scepters, and diamond-encrusted orbs glittering practically within reach, heads in the abbey swiveled Kate's way. *Vogue* and *Newsweek* both hailed her as the master of coronation style, meaning that what she wore had, well, meaning. In this case, a rich blue satin mantle signifying her rank as Dame Grand Cross of the Royal Victorian Order. Beneath that, an ivory silk and silver bullion Alexander McQueen gown embroidered with floral emblems of the realm: rose, daffodil, shamrock, and thistle. In a nod to Charles's love of nature, Kate had wanted to wear a crown of real flowers, but instead she and Charlotte wore matching silver and crystal leaf headpieces. Kate's South Seas pearl and diamond earrings paid tribute to their original owner, Diana, and the three-strand diamond "George VI Festoon Necklace" she wore had been a gift from George VI to his daughter Princess Elizabeth.

Hundreds of thousands of wildly cheering, Union Jack–waving spectators jammed the Mall outside Buckingham Palace to get a glimpse of the new royal lineup in full royal regalia. Once again, Harry was barred from the balcony; since the coronation was taking place on Archie's fourth birthday, Meghan chose to stay stateside with him and Lilibet. The Spare, virtually ignored by his Windsor relatives, returned home to California as soon as the coronation ceremony was over.

All eyes were on the new Waleses that evening, when yet again the monarchy pulled out all the stops to throw a star-studded Coronation Concert against the stunning, up-lit backdrop of Windsor Castle. With the newly crowned king and queen looking on, William took to the microphone to praise his father before a crowd of more than twenty thousand. But it was Kate's reaction to William's promise not to follow concert headliner Lionel Richie's lead and go on "all night long" that made headlines the next day. "The Look of Love!" gushed the *Daily Mail*. "Royal fans went wild," wrote reporter Harriet Johnston, "over the moment the Princess of Wales was caught on camera swooning over her husband's speech." Prince George and Princess Charlotte, seated next to their mother, did not appear nearly as impressed.

More than 160 million television viewers throughout Europe were certainly impressed—and stunned—one week later, when Kate once again showed her musical chops during the opening sequence of the Eurovision Song Contest's grand finale. This time the new Princess of Wales, wearing an off-the-shoulder cobalt blue chiffon evening gown, sat at a grand piano in the Crimson Drawing Room at Windsor Castle. For ten seconds, Kate accompanied Ukraine's Kalush Orchestra in a specially crafted riff off the previous year's winning song, "Stefania." Normally, the previous year's winner hosts the contest, but that was not an option for war-torn Ukraine. So in 2023, the United Kingdom volunteered to step in to host Eurovision. Kate's performance, though brief, was billed as the Princess's personal tribute to the embattled nation.

Six days earlier, King Charles and Queen Camilla had done an awkward cameo for Palace favorite Lionel Richie on *American Idol* at the very same time Kate was down the hall recording her Eurovision piece. But it was Kate's surprise appearance that made international headlines—which did not sit well with Clarence House. "King Charles does not like to be overshadowed," a courtier observed, "*ever*." The Palace went out of its way to point out that the King and Queen had actually traveled to Liverpool to press the button that unveiled the huge Eurovision stage prior to the competition. In truth, it was Camilla who pressed the red button that did the job—Charles, standing beside her, reached out but somehow missed it.

The following month, everybody was back up on the balcony for the finale of Charles III's first Trooping the Colour as king—and William and Kate's first as Prince and Princess of Wales. Ironically, now that she was honorary colonel of the Irish Guards, Kate was entitled to wear a ceremonial uniform—something Harry, who served for ten years in the British Army and fought in Afghanistan, was now banned from doing. When it was suggested she wear a military-inspired outfit like the one Camilla wore as honorary colonel of the Grenadier Guards, Kate declined. "No," she replied, "I wouldn't feel right . . . not if Harry can't do it." Instead, Kate opted for a green outfit, matching broad-brimmed hat, and her signature gold-and-emerald shamrock broach.

There were other firsts that summer of 2023: Kate's first appearance at Ascot as Princess of Wales—particularly poignant since this had been one of the horse-loving late queen's favorite events—and her first time as Princess of Wales at Wimbledon. In typical fashion, Kate recorded a video paying tribute to Wimbledon's "unsung heroes"—the tournament's inexhaustible ball girls and ball boys—and in the process gave tennis great Roger Federer a run for his money on the court.

At Wimbledon that year, the Princess of Wales also broke royal protocol—but for a typically Kate reason. As a member of the royal family and patron of Wimbledon, she was allowed to shake winners' hands when presenting them with a trophy. But when Tunisian tennis star Ons Jabeur became emotional after becoming runner-up in two hard-fought consecutive finals, losing to Markéta Vondroušová, Kate approached Jabeur after the match to offer her a hug and some words of encouragement. "She kept asking me if she could hug me," Jabeur later recalled, "and I was, like, Who doesn't want a hug from a princess, you know? For me, it was such an amazing moment. And not just that, I felt her kindness and energy around me."

Kate would rack up 128 engagements during the year, including meetings with billionaire philanthropist Melinda Gates on behalf of the Royal Foundation of the Prince and Princess of Wales and Apple CEO Tim Cook to support the Earthshot Prize. Nothing drew more attention than what Kate wore to glamorous outings like the South Korean State Banquet (caped white gown topped with the rare Strathmore Rose Tiara, which has only been worn by the Queen Mother and now Kate), the Royal Variety Performance at the Royal Albert Hall (a striking floor-length Poseidon blue gown by Safiyaa London), and the annual Diplomatic Corps reception held for more than one thousand ambassadors and emissaries at Buckingham Palace (a pink, rose-gold sequin- and crystal-embellished "Georgia" gown by Kate favorite Jenny Packham).

Yet Kate claimed she got true satisfaction out of more down-to-earth engagements. She showed up at a prison with bandaged fingers—injured while jumping on a trampoline at home with the kids—to shake hands with scores of inmates battling addiction. She donned a khaki wax jacket for a visit to a seaweed farm in Wales, a navy blue tracksuit to a rugby event in Hull, combat boots and jeans to help girls build campfires and dens at a forest school, and more camo and full-body armor—this time for a training mission with the Queen's Dragoon Guards in Norfolk. During a visit to a royal navy base in Somerset, the princess gamely climbed into a helicopter flight simulator and later burst into fits of giggles when a life vest she tried on suddenly inflated, catching her by surprise.

None of this prepared her for the onslaught that lay ahead. Just one week after Kate charmed South Korean President Yoon Suk-Yeol at the state banquet in his honor, there was bombshell news concerning Omid Scobie's new book, *Endgame*. There were reports that the Dutch edition contained the names of the "royal racists" alluded to but not named by Harry and Meghan in their infamous Oprah interview. The author flatly denied that there had ever been such a mention of names in any of the versions of his manuscript—English or otherwise—and the Dutch publisher, explaining that there had been a translation error, scrambled to retrieve copies of the book.

But there was no putting the genie back in the bottle. Before long, news outlets were reporting that Charles and Kate were the royals who commented on how dark a child of Harry and Meghan's might turn out to be. Since it was already known that Charles had made a wholly innocent comment musing about what physical characteristics a Sussex child—his grandchild—might have, the mention of Kate's name came as a shock.

And no one was more shocked than the Princess of Wales, who had fought so hard to refute the racist claim against the royal family when it had first been made nearly three years earlier. As they arrived at the Royal Variety Performance, William and Kate smiled for photographers but said nothing when asked about the reignited charges of racism. Instead, William, who seldom indulged in public displays of affection, took his wife's hand and held it protectively. Throughout the evening's performance, the normally ebullient Kate was subdued, the stress of the previous week etched on her face. As they left two hours later, Kate quietly said to her prince, "I'm not feeling well, William. Not at all well."

From a personal family point of view,
it's been, yeah, it's been brutal.

—William

The body is amazing at telling us
"You need to take time out."

—Kate

They always made sure that they had to have time to be parents.
For both of them, the children mean everything.

—Jason Knauf, former aide and confidante

8

"It's Such a Shock"

"I'm So Proud of My Wife, I'm Proud of My Father"

PG Tips, Lottie, and Lou Lou

June 14, 2024
Windsor Castle

She leans against an ivy-covered willow on the banks of the River Thames, arms folded against her chest, gazing pensively up at the sky. "I have been blown away by all the kind messages of support and encouragement," begins her first message to the world in months. "It really has made the world of difference to William and me and has helped us both through some of the harder times."

Kate goes on to say that she is "making good progress, but, as anyone going through chemotherapy will know, there are good days and bad days. On those bad days you feel weak, tired, and you have to give in to your body resting. But on the good days, when you feel stronger, you want to make the most of feeling well." Her treatment was "going well," she said, and would continue for a "few more months." In the meantime, on the days she was feeling well enough, it was "a joy" to drive her children to and from school and do "a little work from home."

The Princess of Wales struck a positive note by saying she would attend Trooping the Colour—her first appearance since she shocked the world with news of her cancer diagnosis—but then sounded an alarm by admitting she was "equally knowing I'm not out of the woods yet." She went on to say she was learning to be patient, "especially with uncertainty," taking "each day as it comes, listening to my body, and allowing myself this much-needed time to heal." Kate ended by thanking "all of you who have so bravely shared your stories with me."

The next day, as promised, Kate made her triumphant return to public life. Spectators lining the streets applauded while William, wearing the customary eighteen-inch bearskin hat and his uniform as honorary colonel of the Welsh Guards, rode down the Mall on horseback. Cheers went up when his father, who was also undergoing chemotherapy for his undisclosed form of cancer, passed by with Queen Camilla in the Scottish State Coach. But nothing compared to the crowd's ecstatic reaction when the Glass Coach—the same horse-drawn carriage Diana and Charles had left their wedding in—now carrying Kate and all three Wales children—pulled into view.

Realizing the importance of this moment, Kate wore a white Jenny Packham dress with a large black-and-white bow and a wide-brimmed hat. She chose the outfit for two reasons: white is the universal color of hope, and—Kate always follows the late Queen's famous dictum: "I must be seen to be believed"—white is visible from a distance.

The volume was pumped up at the end of the ceremonies, when Kate stepped out onto the Buckingham Palace balcony with her husband and children. Kate laughed as Louis moved to the music of the regimental band, and, in a particularly tender moment, stroked Charlotte's hair. Throughout it all George and Charlotte, unamused by Louis's antics, tried to keep their little brother in check. When Louis turned to talk to his father, George admonished him to pivot and face the crowd. Later, during the playing of

"God Save the King," Charlotte instructed Louis to stand up straight with his hands at his sides. In every case, Louis obeyed.

Once the event was over and they returned to Adelaide Cottage, Kate collapsed from exhaustion. "Unless they've been through it," she said, "people don't realize how much chemo takes out of you. There's only so much you can do."

Just two days after her balcony appearance, she was still too weak to join William and her Windsor in-laws at the colorful Order of the Garter ceremonies, where senior royals don blue velvet robes, glistening insignia, and, much to their chagrin, floppy hats with ostrich plumes. Kate had been attending the over-the-top ceremony since she and William had been dating in 2008, and was invariably spotted trying—unsuccessfully—not to be photographed laughing.

Although Kate was not yet a member of the Order, just two months earlier she had been given a historic honor. On April 23, 2024, Kate was at Adelaide Cottage with her husband and children celebrating Louis's sixth birthday when the King announced he was naming her Royal Companion of the Order of the Companions of Honor—a historic first, since no member of the royal family had ever been named to the order. Founded by King George V in 1917 to recognize outstanding achievements in the arts, sciences, medicine, and public service, it has a strict membership limit of sixty-five. Specifically, the honor was bestowed on Kate for her service as a member of the royal family, and for her support of the arts as patron of the Victoria and Albert Museum, the National Portrait Gallery, and the Royal Photographic Society.

At the same time, William was also being given a promotion—to Great Master of the Most Honorable Order of the Bath, the spot Charles had occupied from 1974 until Queen Elizabeth's death in 2022. The fourth most senior of the orders of chivalry—behind the Order of the Garter, the Order of the Thistle, and the now-dormant Order of St. Patrick—the Order of the Bath gets its name from the bath the knights were once (but no longer) required to take as part of a purification ritual. Just as the title of Prince of

Wales does not automatically go to the first in line to the throne—it must be bestowed by the sovereign—the Great Master honor is not automatically inherited. King Charles wanted to mark the three hundredth anniversary of the order by appointing his son to the post.

Such singular honors aside, Kate's bad days—days when she was sapped of energy and could barely get out of bed—were still far outnumbering the good ones. Most alarming to Swifties the world over was the news that Kate couldn't muster enough energy to join William when, to celebrate his forty-second birthday, he took George and Charlotte to see Taylor Swift's Eras Tour concert at London's Wembley Stadium. (All three went backstage to take a selfie with the megastar.) Four days later, Kate remained at Anmer Hall trying to shake off the debilitating side effects of chemotherapy while Charles, Camilla, and William hosted a state dinner at Buckingham Palace for Japan's Emperor Naruhito and Empress Masako.

Princess Kate "will only go back to work when doctors give her the green light," was Kensington Palace's oft-repeated explanation for the Princess's frequent absences from events where attendance was invariably regarded as compulsory. "You can only imagine how sick she must have been," a courtier observed, "to miss a state dinner for the Emperor and Empress of Japan."

Contributing to Kate's stress was the collapse of the Middleton family business. Party Pieces had been dealt a mortal blow by Brexit and the COVID pandemic lockdowns that restricted social gatherings, leaving Kate's parents saddled with nearly $3 million in debt. Even after filing for bankruptcy that summer, they owed hundreds of thousands of dollars—although creditors, perhaps mindful of what Kate was facing, did not seem particularly eager to collect.

Obviously, given the enviable financial positions of both their daughters, there was little for Carole and Michael to worry about. Still, they were both proud, self-reliant people who worried about embarrassing their royal counterparts. Moreover, they had played an outsize role in helping Kate through her cancer experience—driving her to and from appointments, helping with the children, and buoying Kate's spirits however and whenever they could. Kate "hated to see them sad," a onetime Party Pieces employee said. "Especially Carole. She was very upset she couldn't save the company."

Fortunately, Kate's siblings were doing fine. In addition to being happily married to billionaire Scottish nobleman James Matthews, Pippa was now the mother of Arthur, Grace, and Rose. Brother James, who had overcome crippling depression with the help of his dog, Ella, now ran his own company selling organic freeze-dried dog food. James married French financial analyst Alizée Thevenet in 2018, and their son, Inigo, was born two years later. Both Kate and Pippa immediately sent their little brother hand-me-down baby clothes. "They are milestones," James explained, "because my sisters remember when their child was wearing something, and how old they were. It takes them back. It's been a lovely thing for them—and for us."

Kate managed to summon enough strength the following month to attend Wimbledon. Since marrying into the royal family in 2011, she had missed Wimbledon only once—in 2013 when she was desperately sick with hyperemesis gravidarum and just weeks away from giving birth to Prince George. This time, wearing an eye-catching purple dress, she took Charlotte behind the scenes to meet several female players, then they made their way with Pippa to the royal box at Center Court.

As soon as Kate appeared, the crowd of fifteen thousand erupted into thunderous applause and leapt to its feet. The princess, who often seemed embarrassed by all the attention she received and usually just took her seat, stayed standing for a moment. Clearly surprised and moved by the outpouring of affection, she smiled and waved at the crowd while Charlotte looked up at her with loving admiration. "When she usually comes in, Kate walks down the steps and into her seat," said photographer Karwai Tang. "She doesn't normally stand and wave. But she stood for a while and took it all in." This time—only her second public appearance since making her cancer announcement—Kate found the experience "sustaining." Veteran London *Evening Standard* royals editor Robert Jobson observed that her appearance "showed a lot of courage and character. She knows the world is watching."

That summer, Kate and family carved out some time to spend at Balmoral with the King, Queen Camilla, and some other royal children their age. There the family indulged in its usual nonstop schedule of hiking, fly-fishing for salmon and trout in the River Dee, horseback riding, raucous family board games, and picnics by a campfire. That August 25, approaching the twenty-seventh anniversary of Diana's death, Kate ventured out to attend Sunday church service at Crathie Kirk, the same stone church where every monarch since Victoria has worshipped—and the church where the devastated William and Harry attended services just hours after learning of their mother's death.

For Kate, time spent with the family at Balmoral was restorative. She took the time to reflect on her cancer journey, and was now ready to share some good news with the world at large. Several weeks earlier, the couple's go-to videographer, Will Warr, had shot a three-minute video on the grounds of Anmer Hall. As an accomplished photographer with an impressive grasp of all things visual, Kate was always heavily involved in polishing the final product. "I'm drawn to intimate, honest stories," Warr said. "There's something so powerful in the simplicity of those everyday moments. I'm a bit obsessed!"

When the video was released on September 9, those "powerful everyday moments" underscored a stunning new update from the Princess of Wales: that she was "cancer free."

"As the summer comes to an end," Kate begins as the entire family is shown happily making its way through the dense forest surrounding Anmer Hall and Sandringham, "I cannot tell you what a relief it is to have finally completed my chemotherapy treatment. The last nine months have been incredibly tough for us as a family," she continues in a video narrative fraught with symbolism. "Life as you know it can change in an instant and we have had to find a way to navigate the stormy waters and the road unknown."

Throughout, there are intimate Hallmark card moments conveying faith, hope, joy, and of course love. In the beginning, Kate is shown at the manual controls of a Land Rover, sending the clear message that she is back in the driver's seat. Kate and William are then shown sitting on a log, her head resting on his shoulder as he gently caresses her hands. "The cancer journey is complex, scary, and unpredictable for everyone," Kate says before the entire family starts climbing a steep hill, "especially those closest to you.

"With humility, it also brings you face-to-face with your own vulnerabilities . . ." she continues as once again she stands beneath a colossal tree, staring up through the leaves at a cloudless sky, "and with that, a new perspective on everything." That new perspective meant being "grateful for the simple yet important things in life, which so many of us often take for granted. Of simply loving and being loved.

"Doing what I can to stay cancer free is now my focus," Kate goes on as she strolls pensively, gliding her hand over shafts of wheat. Meanwhile, the children are playing on swings, leaping onto hay bales, and clambering over logs. At one point—in a nod to the Middleton grandparents for their love and support—the family is in the garden room, playing one of their usual take-no-prisoners card games. "Although I have finished chemotherapy, my path to healing and full recovery is long and I must continue to take each day as it comes."

Kate makes it clear she is looking forward to getting back to work and making more public engagements in the coming months "when I can. Despite all that has gone before, I enter this new phase of recovery with a renewed sense of hope and appreciation of life."

The princess thanks the public for their support, claiming she and William drew "great strength from . . . everyone's kindness, empathy, and compassion . . . all those who are continuing their own cancer journey," Kate concludes as a butterfly flies from her hand, "I remain with you, side by side, hand in hand. Out of darkness can come light, so let that light shine bright." The gauzy, windblown confection ends with everyone running happily through the surf as music swells in the background.

The glossy video was widely hailed as positive and uplifting. "It is an intimate portrayal of an apparently everyday family: close, loving, playful," wrote Harriet Sherwood in the *Guardian*. "The children climb trees and play cards with their parents and grandparents. Mum and Dad are affectionate, a little wistful. But this is no ordinary family."

It was certainly one thing, as the London *Times* pointed out—groundbreaking. "One of the most consequential changes to royal communications since the invention of the printing press," wrote Hilary Rose in a particularly hyperbolic moment, "and certainly the most intimate." Pointing out that Kate and William are "generally more formal than other members of the family" and that there has "always been a marked avoidance of hand-holding and adoring gazes," Rose conceded that the couple has "thawed a little, just occasionally" to reflect "our values and aspirations as a nation in a less formal and less deferential age—real people as well as constitutional ciphers in crowns and robes. A real woman with an all-too-real disease."

"It's Kate as the millennial everymum," agreed Rose's colleague Harriet Walker. This is a family "who lean on each other, tumble together and haul themselves back up again. . . . It is immediately obvious that the Waleses have weathered this together, as affectionately and openly as parents can when the stakes are so high and the children so young."

Although Walker rightly concluded that the video was "the informal view of the royals the nation seems to crave: hugs, hand-holding . . . Kate hanging off William the way she once did at St. Andrews—Kate and her loved ones are bathed in warm harvest gold." But not everyone was a fan. The video sparked a media debate over whether Kate had stepped over the line in an effort to manipulate viewers' emotions. There were many who felt the video was too gauzy, too saccharine, too slick, too self-serving, too contrived.

"Kate's recovery is great news," wrote Hilary Osborne in the *Guardian*, herself a cancer survivor. "But be wary of a soft-focus view of life after chemo." Osborne claimed that a video of her postchemo life would look more "like a trailer for a new zombie film," and that of course Kate wasn't going to release a video showing her "sobbing on a beach as she wonders if her cancer would come back."

Variously described by UK columnists and commentators as "cringy," "clichéd," "sugary," and "manipulative," Kate's "I'm cancer free" video was also compared to the sort of soft-focus content Meghan and Harry were churning out in Montecito. Still, the video resonated with the vast majority of people on both sides of the Atlantic. A *Newsweek* poll of two thousand Americans who had viewed the video showed that 80 percent strongly approved of it. Quickly dissected for brief clips on TikTok and other platforms—mostly happy family scenes highlighting the children—it would become an online phenomenon and one of the most-watched videos of the decade.

What Kate did not reveal in her video was what Hilary Osborne and every other cancer patient undergoing chemotherapy knew: even after it was over, exhaustion, frustration, and sometimes a mental fog were just a few of the common side effects that could persist for months. In fact, it would be another month before Kate ventured out into public again—and this time it took all the strength she could muster.

In the meantime, there were still things she could do privately. Always eager to encourage other aspiring photographers, Kate invited sixteen-year-old Harrowgate resident Liz Hatton to Windsor to shoot an investiture ceremony being presided over by William. Hatton was battling a rare and aggressive form of cancer, and covering the ceremony was one of the things on her "photography bucket list." A photo of Kate greeting Hatton with a warm hug promptly went viral. Later, after posing with the entire Hatton family, the Waleses wrote on social media: "A pleasure to meet with Liz at Windsor today. A talented young photographer whose creativity and strength has inspired us both." They signed with a heart emoji and *W & C*, using the initials they use only when the message comes directly from them.

"Such lovely, genuine, and kind people," Liz wrote on her Instagram account under the photo of being hugged by Kate. "I'm over the moon that my family and I had this experience." Liz Hatton died seven weeks later, leaving Kate "shattered" over the loss she described as "unimaginable."

For her first public appearance since the release of her history-making video, Kate chose to confront another unimaginable tragedy. She insisted on accompanying William on his trip to Southport in northwest England.

There, he was to visit with the families of three little girls aged six, seven, and nine stabbed to death with an eight-inch kitchen knife during a Taylor Swift–themed dance class. The teenaged assailant stabbed ten others, including eight more children, and was eventually sentenced to a minimum of fifty-two years in prison.

The senseless attacks triggered riots in several cities, spurred on by the false story that the assailant, who was born in Wales and was Christian, was a Muslim asylum seeker. Weeks after the murders, King Charles visited Southport to spend time with survivors and first responders, and later met privately with the victims' families at Clarence House.

Taylor Swift, who was "in shock" when she heard the news, met with two survivors of the knife attack backstage at one of her Eras Tour concerts. Kate, who had positioned herself as the chief advocate for young children inside the monarchy, broke down when she heard the news. "As parents," she and William said in a statement at the time, "we cannot begin to imagine what the families, friends, and loved ones of those killed and injured today in Southport are going through."

In Southport, the Waleses spent a half hour with the survivors and each of the families of the victims. To protect their privacy, the surprise visit was not made public until after William and Kate departed. They visited the first responders as well, talking to them about the day of the attacks and the long-term impact on their mental health—another issue with which the prince and princess were both strongly identified.

At one point, an emergency medical worker who had been on the scene the day of the attacks asked Kate how the families of the three dead girls were faring. The princess took a moment to compose herself. "They're okay," she replied. "They're managing it differently . . . processing this tragic event in very different ways . . . sharing their experience I think is massively helpful." She went on to tell the first responders "how grateful they all are for your support. On behalf of them, thank you."

As the royal couple walked toward their car, Kate paused and turned around. "The Princess of Wales broke off and came back into the building to give a hug to the people who responded," said firefighter Phil Garrigan, "because she could see the emotion in them—how difficult it was for them to share their feelings. . . . I think that just shows a really caring side and is very, very touching."

Throughout all their public encounters, Kate and William kept the stiffest of upper lips whenever her health battle—or the King's—was mentioned. But, during a solo trip to South Africa for the presentation of the Earthshot Prize, the Prince of Wales finally let down his guard. At the opening ceremonies in Cape Town, William admitted that he nearly broke down watching a prerecorded performance of "The Circle of Life" from *The Lion King* by Lebo M and the Ndlovu Youth Choir atop South Africa's iconic Table Mountain. "Hearing things like that gets me quite emotional," conceded the future king. "So, when they started singing and . . . we were all there . . . I did feel quite emotional."

When a reporter asked about his year, William was surprisingly quick to answer. "Honestly, it's been dreadful. It's probably been the hardest year in my life." Although it certainly offered an unvarnished view of what the future held for him as king, having to fill in while his father underwent weekly cancer treatments added to the Heir's stress level. "Trying to get through everything else and keep everything on track has been really difficult," he said. "But I'm so proud of my wife, I'm proud of my father for handling the things that they have done. But from a personal family point of view, it's been, yeah, it's been brutal."

Told that he looked relaxed, a quizzical look came over William's face. "I couldn't be *less* relaxed this year," he replied. "But it's more a case of just crack on and you've got to keep going," he continued. "I enjoy my work and I enjoy pacing myself and keeping sure that I have got time for my family, too."

Did he like the freedom and responsibility that came with his relatively new role as Prince of Wales? "It's a tricky one," he answered. "Do I like more responsibility? No. Do I like the freedom that I can build something like Earthshot? Then, yes." He wanted to spend his life, he added, "doing something good. . . . It's important that I'm helping people's lives and I'm doing something that is genuinely meaningful."

Kate hadn't missed a Remembrance Day event since she became a working royal, and she wasn't about to now. The back-to-back events she attended—the Remembrance Day Festival at Royal Albert Hall and the wreath laying at the Cenotaph the following day—marked the eightieth anniversary of D-Day, and she wanted to honor her grandparents' service during World War II. Although she followed protocol and wore black at both events, Kate also paid subtle tribute to her immediate predecessor Diana—Camilla had declined to be called Princess of Wales for fear of riling up public sentiment against her—by wearing the late Princess of Wales's Collingwood pearl drop earrings.

Kate came close to being upstaged by her husband, who had grown back his beard. The Princess of Wales always seemed to be tolerant of the look, but not so Charlotte. When William had tried to grow a beard earlier in the year, her reaction surprised him. "Well, Charlotte didn't like it the first time. I got floods of tears, so I had to shave it off," the prince said. Realizing that his little girl took comfort in the familiar when so many things around her were in a state of upheaval, William waited until cooler autumn temperatures began to kick in to give it another try. "And then I grew it back. I thought, hang on a second, and I convinced her it was going to be okay." For whatever reason, Papa's facial hair no longer upset Charlotte. "She just needed," William said, "a little reassurance."

After each major appearance, Kate withdrew from public view—this time for another month, when she reappeared to join with her husband and the King—Camilla was recovering from a chest infection—in welcoming the Emir of Qatar for a state visit. Wearing deep burgundy and white to mirror the colors of the Qatari flag, Kate paused for a moment to perform a flawless curtsy before her father-in-law—a gesture of respect that, like many of her other curtsies over the years, instantly went viral.

The Princess of Wales had little time to catch her breath before hosting her annual televised "Together at Christmas" carol service at Westminster Abbey just three days later. The theme was a nod to the year William described as "brutal." When one of the performers at the concert, English pop star Paloma Faith, inquired about Kate's health, she smiled. "I didn't know this year was going to be the year I've just had," she answered.

"The unplanned," Faith said.

"The *unplanned*, exactly," Kate replied, nodding in agreement. "But I think lots of people this year have had such challenging times, and many who are here today." In an official statement, Kensington Palace explained that Kate "wanted to celebrate the many people supporting those in need—individuals who have inspired, counselled, comforted, and above all else shown that love is the greatest gift we can receive." Kate personally reminded guests inside the abbey that "we must all shine for each other. Because in times of joy and sadness, we are all each other's light."

On Christmas morning, she went out of her way to thank caregivers directly. During the royal family's walk to church at Sandringham, Kate spoke to Rachel Anvil, twenty-four, a worker at Cambridge's Royal Papworth Hospital. When Anvil, who worked with cancer patients, told Kate she was "an inspiration to all the patients," the princess stopped, visibly moved. "Thank you, honestly," she replied, "for doing all the hard work. . . . I'm hugely grateful."

"We're all behind you," Anvil said. "Never forget that."

Kate lingered for a moment, letting it all sink in, then thanked Anvil for her "kind words."

For Anvil and so many others, Kate was "an inspiration. There is a consensus that what she is doing is very courageous. By sharing her story, it makes cancer patients feel less alone. The general consensus is she is really brave and has done an incredible thing. She is a remarkable woman."

It had indeed been a brutal year for Kate, and she was eager for a new beginning. But it fast became clear that 2025 would also hold heartache for the royal family when Edward Pettifer, the thirty-one-year-old stepson of William and Harry's nanny Tiggy Legge-Bourke Pettifer, was killed in a New Year's Day terrorist attack. Ed Pettifer had been celebrating on New Orleans's famous Bourbon Street when ISIS supporter Shamsud-Din Jabbar drove his rented pickup truck down the crowded street, killing fourteen and injuring thirty others before being killed in a shootout with police. King Charles had remained close to Tiggy, as has had William and Harry, and all three reached out to her directly to express their condolences.

"Catherine and I have been shocked and saddened by the tragic death of Ed Pettifer," Prince William posted in a rare personal message on X. "Our thoughts and prayers remain with the Pettifer family and all those innocent people who have been tragically impacted by this horrific attack."

As unexpected and sad as Ed Pettifer's death was, there would soon be happy news to report. There were plans afoot for a big announcement, but first William scooped up his wife and children and flew them all to the Alps for a ski vacation—all by way of celebrating Kate's forty-third birthday on January 9. The princess, said a skier who witnessed the Waleses cavorting on the slopes, looked like she was having a lovely time." In fact, the whole family "seemed to be really happy."

For her first royal engagement of 2025, Kate decided to make a surprise visit to the place where her cancer journey began: Royal Marsden Hospital. But rather than sneak in a back entrance for fear of being spotted by the press, this time Kate walked unannounced straight through the front door. "Coming in the front entrance here, having made so many quiet, private visits," she said, "actually it's quite nice."

Wearing a long brown plaid coat over a burgundy maxi dress, Kate thanked doctors and nurses for giving her "such amazing care and support" and then sat to chat with patients who were in the process of receiving their chemo. "Cancer makes you appreciate all the small things in life that you take for granted," Kate said as she listened to other patients describe their experiences and shared some of her own. Two of those everyday things that made "such a difference" in her recovery: "Loads of water and loads of sunlight."

Kate connected with her fellow cancer patients over the initial diagnosis ("It's such a shock. It's the uncertainty . . . understanding the diagnosis, it's a massive amount of information to take on as a patient."), the treatment ("It's incredibly tough. Everyone said to me, 'Please keep a positive mindset, it makes such a difference.' "), and the aftermath. "You think the treatment has finished and you can crack on and get back to normal," the Princess of Wales said, "but that's still a real challenge." She went on to say that doctors warn patients at the very beginning that side effects from chemo can linger for months, even years. For most patients who are just eager to get the treatments over with, those warnings "totally disappear—they just fly right out of your head." It's only later, she said, that the patient comes to realize that "yes, there are side effects during treatment, but actually there are more long-term side effects."

There were plenty of hugs and words of hope and encouragement ("Keep doing what gives you joy"), and bonding over some of the peculiarities of chemotherapy—like the port implanted in the chest through which drugs flowed. "I got so attached to it," Kate said with a laugh, confessing that she hesitated to let her port go even "after they said to me, 'But you can have it taken out now!' "

There were moments during the visit when emotions ran high. Kate hugged Tina Adumou, who cried as she told the princess her nineteen-year-old daughter was in intensive care. "I'm sorry, I wish there was more I could do to help," Kate said, putting her arm around Adumou. "There is light at the end of that tunnel. . . . You are in the best of hands." The next day, Kate followed up her visit to Royal Marsden by dropping a bombshell of her own. "It is a relief to now be in remission," she wrote on X, "and I remain focused on recovery. As anyone who has experienced a cancer diagnosis will know, it takes time to adjust to a new normal."

The "new normal" did not remotely mean that the Princess of Wales was about to resume her precancer life. There would be no full-blown foreign tours, or the sorts of back-to-back-to-back engagements that Princess Anne, King Charles, and the late Queen Elizabeth thrived on. Kate carefully curated her own return to public life, making sure to carve out time for her first priority—family.

In the coming months, Kate would continue to create the sort of Diana-like moments that made her the most beloved member of the royal family. In London, at a ceremony commemorating the eightieth anniversary of the liberation of Auschwitz, Kate spotted Holocaust survivors she had photographed years earlier and rushed up to them. "I want to give you a big cuddle," she told eighty-nine-year-old Steven Frank before she wrapped him in her arms. "Such a treat for me, an old friend," she said, sitting down with Yvonne Bernstein, also eighty-nine. Photos showed Bernstein, clearly moved, reaching up to gently stroke Kate's face.

Kate continued to touch hearts and make news during visits to another children's hospice, a prison mother-and-baby unit, and to the Welsh town of Pontypridd that had been devastated by a flood. On World Cancer Day in February, she enlisted the help of another budding photographer in the family to make a powerful visual statement. In a striking image credited to Prince Louis and released by Kensington Palace, Kate is shown bundled up, standing on a log in a frosty woodland scene, arms outstretched and smiling. "Don't forget to nurture all that which lies beyond the disease," read the caption, which was signed simply *C*.

Heeding her own advice, Kate convinced her husband that they could skip the BAFTAs this year. Not surprisingly, rumors about Kate's health flew when the most stylish woman in the world and her prince failed to walk the red carpet. This time, however, Britain's answer to the Oscars conflicted with the children's half-term break from school. So, the entire family opted to holiday with Granny and Grandpa Middleton on Mustique.

In the ensuing months, Kate came under pressure to pick up the pace, particularly when it came to those events that were the touchstones of the royal calendar. Both Kate and the King, deep in the middle of their cancer regimens at the time, had missed the previous year's Commonwealth Day service at Westminster Abbey; but this year both showed—Kate making her usual sartorial splash in a scarlet dress by Catherine Walker, who also happened to have designed the black cocktail dress Princess Diana was buried in.

A week later, Kate, who had been too sick and weak to attend the St. Patrick's Day parade with her Irish Guards the previous year, returned to hand out shamrocks, pet the regiment's mascot Seamus the Irish Wolfhound, and chat with the Mini Micks, cadets from Northern Ireland ranging in age from twelve to eighteen. "Within the military, there are so many career paths you can take," she told one young boy. "It's so exciting." Later, after meeting with the families of some of the soldiers, she hoisted a pint of Guinness while the regiment gave three cheers for their colonel. Then, as she had arranged to have done the year before when she was unable to make it to the parade, Kate left money of her own behind the regimental bar for the annual St. Patrick's Day after-party. (There were only three other members of the royal family known to be so thoughtful when it came to picking up the tab: Diana and her sons. As a rule, Windsors carry no money or credit cards and were accustomed to being the recipients of others' largesse.)

There would be other outings that spring, like the Six Nationals Rugby match between Wales and England, with William rooting for Wales while Kate, having taken over as patron of the Rugby Football Union from Prince Harry, rooted for England. (England won, 68–14.) After the game, Kate went to the locker room to congratulate the winning team and tell them that watching George, Charlotte, and Louis play rugby is part of their weekend routine—although Charlotte preferred soccer and excelled at the sport.

Kate's most far-flung excursion since finishing chemo—her first overnight stay hundreds of miles away from home—was a two-day trip in April with William to the picturesque isles of Mull and Iona off the coast of Scotland in the Inner Hebrides. It was, in part, to celebrate their fourteenth wedding anniversary in the country where they fell in love. There they smiled and shook hands and endlessly asked questions at farms, schools, community centers, and nature preserves. With their work finally over, the Duke and Duchess of Rothesay—their official titles in Scotland—withdrew to a small rented cottage on the remote, wooded Isle of Mull to spend their anniversary in privacy. To mark the occasion, they posted a photo of themselves taken at a distance and from the back, soaking in the island's spectacular scenery.

No sooner did they return to London than Kate and William—along with the rest of the royal family—took incoming from Montecito. Harry, who had just lost his drawn-out legal bid for royal protection, told the BBC that he no longer could see a way he would ever return to the United Kingdom with his family. "I'm pretty gutted by this decision," he said. "I love my country . . . and I think that it's really quite sad that I won't be able to show my children my homeland." He went on to accuse the Royal Household of exerting undue influence on the Court of Appeal, and called its ruling against him a "good old-fashioned establishment stitch up." There was "no way," he concluded, "to win this through the courts."

In the interview, Harry conceded that he was still estranged from the King, whom he hadn't spoken to since his brief visit to London after he learned of his father's cancer diagnosis. The Spare also said he had "forgiven" his family, although he believed "some members of my family will never forgive me" for writing his memoir. "They will never forgive me for a lot of things." In the end, all the legal turmoil was "at the heart of it . . . a family dispute, and it makes me really, really sad," Harry admitted. "I would love reconciliation with my family. There's no point in continuing to fight anymore."

Then came the megaton remark that would explode on front pages across the globe. "Life is precious," Harry said. "*I don't know how much longer my father has.*"

Harry's jaw-dropping statement came just days after King Charles spoke publicly about the "daunting" and "frightening" experience of "being told you have cancer." Given the persistent gossip concerning the King's medical condition—what type of cancer he had, how far it had spread, what the prognosis was—the Duke of Sussex's nine-word sentence packed an outsize wallop. Was the situation more dire than the King's still-robust appearance led us to believe? Was he closer to death's door than we had ever imagined?

King Charles had always held out hope for some sort of truce with Harry, but now that seemed impossible. With his focus on doing the job he had waited seventy years to start, His Majesty had neither the time nor the patience to deal with his prodigal son. He had not shared the details of his cancer with Harry, but the damage was done: seeds of doubt concerning the King's chances for a full recovery had been sown.

For William, who was so protective of both his wife's feelings and his father's, Harry's words seemed crushingly insensitive, thoughtless, callous. No one battling cancer wants to hear someone—especially his own child—hint that death might be imminent. And what of Kate? Hadn't Harry considered how upsetting those words might be to her? Not only was Kate worried about how deflating those words would inevitably be for the King to hear, but she had to consider that they applied equally to her.

Kate was more disappointed than angry with Harry for making such reckless remarks. But William, who had already slammed the door shut on his brother over what Harry wrote in *Spare*, was, in the words of a courtier, "apoplectic" with rage. Now it was time to nail the door shut once and for all, and for the first time Kate, who had worked harder than anyone to mend the rift between the brothers, willingly handed her husband a hammer. Kate promised William that now she, too, was done with Harry. Princess Catherine is "the sweetest, most loving person you could ever know," said a Sandringham staffer, "but like everyone else, she has her limits."

Kate pulled herself together three days later to cohost a tea party at Buckingham Palace commemorating the eightieth anniversary of VE Day. It was an important first foray into the world of royal mingling for Prince George, who listened with rapt attention to veterans sharing their memories of World War II. "What was it like when you were coming in?" George asked 101-year-old D-Day survivor Alfred Littlefield from Portchester. "Pretty awful," Littlefield replied. Later, Littlefield turned to Prince William and pointed to his son. "You should be very proud," he said of George.

Video of the eleven-year-old future king interacting with centenarians in wheelchairs—"Did you ever get shot at?" "Did you ever see a U-boat?"—went viral, and soon Prince George was being praised in the press for his "empathy and confidence." British TV personality Jo Frost observed that he was getting on-the-job training from Papa. "Notice how he's leaning in just like William, dropping his chin and making sure his eyes are on the person he's listening to," Frost said. "He's a spitting image of his dad." And not just his dad. "Here we get to witness two parents with royal duty who have been an incredible example to their young children." Frost believed Kate's recent cancer struggle—and their grandfather's—had much to do with it. "Already the children have experienced so much emotional vulnerability witnessing their parent go through difficult circumstances—and yet they are resilient."

Resilience was something Kate continued to show as she hosted a garden party at Buckingham Palace, attended a London fashion show, and returned to Scotland to smash a bottle of whiskey across the bow of the Royal Navy's first Type 26 anti-submarine frigate HMS *Glasgow*. But the really big events still lay ahead. Five months after Kate announced her cancer was in remission, she and Charlotte rode in an open carriage to Trooping the Colour ceremonies wearing matching aquamarine outfits—done to balance out George and Louis, who wore matching blue blazers and red ties. For the first time, Kate was given the singular honor of being the only person to sit on the dais next to the King and Queen during Trooping the Colour at Horse Guards Parade.

"It was highly significant," said former BBC royals correspondent Jennie Bond. "It was a very powerful image of our next queen alongside her father-in-law who has made no secret of the respect he has for Catherine, especially after the cancer journey they have shared"—a shared experience "neither wanted, but which has brought them closer than ever. Cancer, the great leveler, is something they have been going through together, and it has made their relationship curiously unique."

The grand finale was the Buckingham Palace flyby, of course, and this year the Wales children had their balcony decorum down pat, mostly. At one point, Mummy leaned down and said two words—"National anthem"—which had George, Charlotte, and Louis instantly snapping to attention with their hands glued to their sides. Later, George had to tell Louis to stop waving because the adult royals had stopped, and it was time to go. But as the royal family made its exit, Louis turned around to give one last, parting wave—much to the delight of the crowd.

Soon Kate returned to another event she had missed during her cancer treatments the year before—Garter Day ceremonies at St. George's Chapel in Windsor. The Order of the Garter is the oldest order of chivalry in Great Britain and limited to a handful of members chosen by the monarch, and hundreds of people—some bringing camp chairs—stake out a spot outside the castle to see the berobed royals and dignitaries pass by in carriages. The event held special significance for William and Kate: Miss Middleton had made her debut as someone being welcomed into the royal fold when she attended William's induction into the Order of the Garter in 2008.

To mark her return to this over-the-top display of aristocratic finery, she wore what may have been her favorite outfit—a white boucle and lace blazer dress topped with a crisp white "hatinator" (a hat-fascinator hybrid) and pearls. Kate had already worn the ensemble to three high-profile events, most recently to a VE Day concert just a few weeks before.

Any other figure of her stature in the fashion world might have been raked over the coals for continually recycling outfits, but not the Princess of Wales. "Kate is angelic in white," raved Joel Calfee in *Harper's Bazaar*, while *Vogue*'s Hannah Jackson praised Kate for "reminding us there are infinite ways of rewearing our clothes, and we should all make the most of the pieces we love."

The press did plenty of recycling of its own, hyperventilating with the usual adjectives like "dazzling," "timeless," and "effortlessly elegant" to describe the princess. Most important, she looked stronger, healthier, and more vigorous than she had all year. Kate also looked like she was genuinely having fun; as with previous Order of the Garter ceremonies, she could not conceal her laughter when William and the others passed by in their cumbersome robes and poufy ostrich-plumed hats.

Appearances were deceiving. Immediately after returning to Adelaide Cottage, Kate began to crumble. Forty-eight hours later, although she was already listed on the program as being part of the royal carriage procession at Ascot, Kate abruptly canceled without explanation. The result was pandemonium at the palace. "Everyone was wandering around going, 'What is going on,'" a courtier said. "This is one of the biggest days of the year in the royal calendar; you don't just miss Ascot on a whim, so there was a real sense of panic." Even more troubling, he continued, "the chaotic nature of the announcement was eerily reminiscent of the dark days of last year. People were bewildered and worried."

Kate later apologized for canceling, but made it clear she was carefully pacing herself so as not to set back her recovery. "She's being sensible, listening to what her body is telling her, and easing back into public life," Queen Elizabeth's former spokeswoman Ailsa Anderson said.

Kate offered some words of explanation herself, opening up to cancer patients and staff during a visit to Colchester Hospital in Essex. "You put on a sort of brave face, stoicism through treatment," she said. "Treatment's done, then it's, like . . . You're not necessarily under the clinical team any longer, but you're not able to function normally at home as you perhaps once used to." She went on to say the experience is "life-changing. You have to find your new normal and that takes time. And it's a roller coaster, it's not smooth, like you expect it to be. But the reality is you go through hard times."

Even when she was, as she told friends, "recharging my batteries," Kate worked from home on the projects that were near and dear to her. She also made her opinions known—and felt—on some of the major issues affecting the monarchy. As the Jeffrey Epstein sex scandal heated up again in the United States there was a renewed and unwelcome focus on one of his closest friends, Prince Andrew.

As hard as she had worked behind the scenes to debunk any notion that the royal family was racist or, even worse, that she along with the King were the notorious "royal racists," Kate declined to criticize the Queen for standing by her favorite son. Now, however, she urged William to lobby with the King to banish Andrew even further. Andrew had already been stripped of his patronages, his charities, and his ceremonial military titles. He had also agreed to give up using his HRH title, and was essentially banished from much of royal life. But despite public outrage—especially in the city of York—the monarch was reluctant to unilaterally strip the Duke of York of his dukedom. That could be done through an act of Parliament, and although legislation to make that happen had been introduced, it was stalled in committee. Kate made it clear where she stood by banning Prince Andrew from all her functions, most notably the televised "Together at Christmas" carol service she hosted each year at Westminster Abbey—not even, as an aide inquired, if he snuck in a side door and watched "discreetly." The Princess of Wales "has no interest in having Prince Andrew's face appear on camera," said a volunteer staffer. "She is a very kind and forgiving person, but not when it comes to abusing children."

Kate's animosity toward her husband's uncle extended to their private encounters. She refused to speak to Andrew, even during family holiday get-togethers. William, one of the Duke of York's fiercest critics, followed suit. (The question of what to do about Prince Andrew had been mounting since his principal accuser, Virginia Giuffre, had committed suicide the previous April at age forty-one. The posthumous publication of Giuffre's memoir in the fall of 2025 yielded new details about Andrew's alleged participation in the Epstein sex trafficking case, as did newly released emails between the two men in which Andrew reportedly promised they would "play some more soon" long after he claimed to have severed ties with Epstein. Eventually, King Charles used his "Royal Prerogative," the sovereign's extra-parliamentary power to unilaterally manage titles and honors through the issuance of royal warrants and letters patent, to strip Andrew not only of his dukedom, but of the title "Prince." While his daughters Beatrice and Eugenie held on to their titles as princesses and he remained eighth in the line of succession behind Princess Lilibet of Sussex, Andrew would henceforth simply be known as Andrew Mountbatten-Windsor. He was also evicted from Royal Lodge, his stately thirty-room mansion in Windsor Great Park, and reassigned to a significantly more modest abode on the grounds of King Charles's privately owned Sandringham estate. The King's stunning statement stripping his brother of his royal status tellingly mentioned that both he and his wife sided with all victims of sexual abuse—a nod to Her Majesty's role in the historic decision. On this one issue, the current queen and the next one were unified. Camilla had campaigned for more than a decade against domestic violence and the sexual abuse of women, and Kate told friends she was physically "sickened" by the damage Andrew's actions were doing to the institution her children would one day inherit. Working in tandem, Camilla and Kate—along with William—actively lobbied to have King Charles banish Andrew from the

Firm once and for all. No one was prepared when Andrew was arrested on the morning of his sixty-sixth birthday; emails showed that he allegedly shared state secrets with Epstein.)

Now hailed as the monarchy's reigning queen of "soft diplomacy," Kate wore Christian Dior for the very first time to welcome French President Emmanuel Macron and his wife, Brigitte, when they arrived for a state visit on July 8. After the visiting couple stepped off the plane, Kate appeared mildly flustered when Macron bent down to kiss her hand—triggering a debate in royal circles about whether the distinctly French gesture was an egregious breach of protocol (apparently it was not).

The kiss to Kate's hand was not the state visit's most memorable moment, however. At the customary, mind-blowingly opulent state banquet for 160 dignitaries at Windsor Castle, Kate blended the two cultures, wearing a dramatic caped gown designed by Sarah Burton for Givenchy—along with her go-to Lover's Knot tiara. Macron sat to her immediate left, as all male guests of honor did, and when it came time for toasts he clinked the Princess's glass—and boldly winked at her while fellow guests Sir Mick Jagger and Sir Elton John looked on.

With a blazing sun beating down on Wimbledon, temperatures soaring into the nineties, and fans collapsing in the stands, there were serious doubts that the Princess of Wales would—or even should—make it to the tournament this year. The Macrons' state visit had left her wrung out physically—so much so that she had to skip William's annual charity polo match. So when she did appear at Wimbledon in traditional tennis whites to take her place in the royal box, the entire stadium showed no less enthusiasm than it had the year before—and Kate was no less moved.

Energized by her reception, Kate was back the next day for the men's finals—this time with William, George, and Charlotte in tow. (Louis, it was agreed, did not yet have the patience to sit through four or more hours of tennis.) While the Princess of Wales sat on the edge of her seat, applauding and cheering throughout the game, her daughter excitedly clapped her hands over her face whenever the match got too heated. Her brother reacted differently. During one particularly tense moment, Prince George rose from his seat, both hands pressed on the table in front of him, glowering intensely. Caught on camera, the future king's strangely fierce expression lit up the internet.

Louis was back in the equation when the entire family—joined by Kate's parents—sailed off for a secret vacation in Greece aboard United Arab Emirates Sheikh Abdullah bin Zayed Al Nahyan's $450 million, 479-foot superyacht *Opera*. Among other things, the family was given a private tour of the famous Melissani Cave on the island of Kefalonia, and swam in the turquoise waters of the Ionian Sea. Once back home in the United Kingdom, it wasn't long before they packed up again to join King Charles and Queen Camilla for what may be the family's most favorite summer vacation spot of all: the Scottish Highlands.

Superyacht adventures and Scottish castles notwithstanding, the Waleses stuck firmly to their oft-repeated vow to give their children something approximating a normal life. They no longer had live-in help, but nanny Maria Teresa Borrallo was still very much in the picture, especially after Kate's cancer diagnosis. One strange rule laid down by Borrallo early on: the word "kid" was never to be spoken in the house. Apparently in nanny circles, the word is considered to be an insult.

Still, her health and stamina permitting, it was Kate—often along with her husband—who drove them to and from school, helped them with their homework, kicked a soccer ball around with them in the backyard, participated in parents' sports day at school, and picked out their Halloween costumes at Sainsbury's supermarket. Like any parents, Kate and William played referee whenever the kids bickered—which was frequently. When the children kept quarreling over what music to listen to on their brief ride to school, Kate came up with a schedule that had them taking turns.

In fact, the highly organized Princess of Wales ran a fairly tight ship at home. The children all had chores that the no-nonsense mom kept track of with detailed written schedules: all three made their beds every morning and helped with every meal. Kate's go-to dish was roasted chicken, but the children pitched in when pasta or homemade pizzas were on the menu.

Then there were the pets. Their black cocker spaniel, Orla, and her newborn litter of puppies had to be fed, along with the guinea pigs. Gold stars were handed out accordingly.

As daunting as Middleton family game nights were, William still could match his wife's competitive streak on occasion. "I don't think we've actually been able to finish a game of tennis," Kate confessed. It's a trait all three of their offspring have inherited. George was a ferocious soccer player and, like his father, a die-hard Aston Villa fan. Charlotte rooted for England's Lionesses soccer team, but she also rode horses, played tennis, rugby, and netball, and began to show a talent for gymnastics. One thing she and all the children shared with both parents—and with their grandmother Diana—was a love of dancing; on any typical day, George and Charlotte, both of whom took ballet in preschool, could be seen bouncing around the kitchen with Louis. Meanwhile, William claimed Louis was "mad about" soccer, but, rather than commit to Aston Villa, was supporting "five different teams."

Stepping more and more into the public eye, it became increasingly clear that each Wales child had a distinctly different personality—and a nickname to go with it. After being called "Little Grape" by his doting mother for years, George was now known almost exclusively as PG to his friends. Around the house, he was PG Tips (or just Tips), a riff on the British tea brand. Like his father, PG Tips was more quiet, thoughtful, serious, at times oversensitive. His love of nature, imbued by both parents, was so intense that when a documentary on extinction by family friend David Attenborough was airing on television, George was so disturbed, he asked his father to turn it off.

"George is his father's son," Kate was fond of saying, and in their case that was particularly true. Like his father, PG Tips knew from an early age that he was destined to occupy a unique place in history. "You can see the way he searches both his parents' faces for clues on the right way to behave," a teacher at Lambrook School remarked. "He's a hard worker, and you get the feeling he knows he's got a big job to do up ahead." Added one of the other parents: "Prince George is very popular and has lots of friends, and there's little fuss made about who he is."

By the summer of 2025, a fuss was certainly being made about which boarding school George might attend after he turned thirteen the following year. A full-scale tug-of-war was happening between George's parents, as one or the other seemed to have the upper hand from week to week. Kate argued for her alma mater, Marlborough College, on the grounds that it was coed and that all Wales children could go there, just as they had all gone to Lambrook. But Marlborough was an hour and a half drive from Windsor and Adelaide Cottage, while William's old boys-only school, Eton College, was a brief stroll from the castle. There were security considerations, not to mention Eton's unparalleled stature among boys' boarding schools, that made it the logical choice.

Certainly "Poppet" or "Lottie," as Charlotte was called, wasn't about to make a fuss over George. Bolder, more outgoing, more willing to take chances than her older brother, Charlotte earned another nickname at nursery school for her tree-climbing tomboy antics: "Warrior Princess." The feisty four-year-old famously stuck out her tongue at the King's Cup regatta in 2019. When she turned six she confused her new milestone with England's emancipation age of sixteen and declared to her parents, "I'm six now. I'll do what I want!"

It turned out what she wanted to do most was order her brothers around. During the Platinum Jubilee, Charlotte was so insistent on repeatedly correcting their etiquette that even Queen Elizabeth was impressed. "She's quite bossy," Gan-Gan said admiringly to one of her ladies in waiting, "but they seem to do what she wants."

Well, not always. At the Platinum Jubilee Pageant, Louis (Kate alternates between the nicknames "Lou Bugs" and "Lou Lou") tested Mummy's patience by mugging outrageously—waving his arms, squirming, pointing his fingers, grabbing his mother's head, and, in a move that any parent would find humiliating, putting his hand over her mouth while she was speaking to him. Later that year, he stood on the Buckingham Palace balcony right next to his great-grandmother, once again clasping his hands over his ears and screaming as RAF jets flew overhead. Her Majesty was decidedly not amused.

Things changed after Kate's diagnosis. Dramatically. Even Lou Bugs, still widely regarded as the family's irrepressible scamp, toned down his act to make things easier for everyone. There was a genuine appreciation of all that their mother had endured on her harrowing cancer journey—and equally genuine apprehension about what lay ahead.

Although they did not ever betray their own fears to the children, William and Kate had to face not only Kate's potentially life-threatening health issues but those of the King as well. That meant reassuring George, Charlotte, and Louis that Grandpa Wales was also making strides in his treatment and that all would be well.

But would it? Just as the precise nature of Kate's cancer remained a tightly guarded secret, William and Kate were among a handful of people who knew the whole truth. Because of the Palace's passion for secrecy—it is important to remember that officials did not even tell King George VI that he was suffering from lung cancer—the rest of the world was left to guess, or at best try to connect the dots.

Shortly after King Charles's cancer diagnosis was announced, a former prime minister let slip that he knew the monarch was suffering from pancreatic cancer and "did not have long to live." Indeed, since for some reason Clarence House felt it was wise to rule out prostate cancer even though the cancer was discovered during a prostate procedure, this information ran like wildfire through the back halls of Westminster. And while Prince Harry had certainly not been given the salient details for fear they might leak, the dire-sounding description from the former prime minister gained some traction.

Yet as time passed, the notion that Charles III was battling one of the deadliest cancers began to fade. Instead, another prevailing theory emerged—that the King might be suffering from bladder cancer. By mid-2025 doctors were describing their approach as "managing the disease" rather than curing it. By the same token, they stressed that the King was not dying from cancer, but he was "living with cancer."

Whatever the precise diagnosis, the fact remained that any man in his mid-seventies suffering from any form of cancer that required weekly treatments was a man in crisis. And so was the monarchy. It was inevitable that Charles's reign would be only a fraction the length of his mother's seventy years on the throne. But that it might be cut so short and in such a manner seemed not just unspeakably unfair but cruel. Certainly His Majesty was not going quietly. Like his mother, who had refused to abdicate despite her age and failing health, Charles III has made it clear he will remain until the bitter end. Only the specter of being completely incapacitated would prompt the King's inner circle to invoke the Regency Act of 1937, making William Regent and giving him all the powers of an acting king.

Nevertheless, the Prince and Princess of Wales were forced to brace themselves for the probability that the burdens they thought were far in the distance might be thrust upon them at any time. With an eye toward the future, in the summer of 2025 they announced plans to move out of comparatively cramped Adelaide Cottage into Forest Lodge, just four miles away in a more secluded part of Windsor Great Park. With eight bedrooms, six bathrooms, a ballroom, six chimneys, tennis courts, a paddock, and even its own small lake, the $21 million redbrick Georgian manor was billed as the Waleses' "forever home"—a place where, after a "brutal year," the family could, in the words of a Kensington Palace spokesman, get "a fresh start." Presumably, when the time came for William to take what Princess Diana used to call the "top job," Kate and the family would not move to any of the other palaces but keep Forest Lodge as their principal full-time residence.

As king, William would also inherit Sandringham and Balmoral Castle, properties privately owned by the monarch. Nor would William pay the United Kingdom's 40 percent inheritance tax on Charles's $850 million estate, due to the "sovereign to sovereign" agreement reached with the British government in 1993. (Assets of the Crown, which are essentially held in trust for the nation by the reigning monarch and are not part of his private estate, are valued in excess of $42 billion.)

For now, Kate and the King continued to speak on the phone several times a week and when they did get together in private or in public, the bond they shared was palpable. Even Queen Camilla, who for years had tried to use her influence with Charles to steer William away from the girl with working-class roots, now had a deep appreciation for Kate's dedication to the family—and the magic she could work on the King's mood. "No one can cheer Charles up like Catherine can," Camilla confessed to William within earshot of an aide. "They make each other laugh, which is amazing when you think of what they're going through."

Kate, along with the rest of the royal family, took pains to put on a happy face when Donald Trump arrived in mid-September 2025 for his second state visit to the United Kingdom—a historic first for an American president. With tensions running high between the US and the UK over economic and foreign policy issues, Britain rolled out the red carpet to impress their pomp-and-pageantry-obsessed guest. Kate and William were on the front lines, walking out onto the lawn of Windsor Castle to greet the President and First Lady Melania as their helicopter landed—"You're beautiful, so beautiful," Trump said as he shook the Princess's hand—then escorting the Trumps to meet the King and Queen. There was a ride with the King and Queen through the streets of Windsor in a horse-drawn state carriage, and inspection of a guard of honor made up of the Coldstream Guards, the Grenadier Guards, and the Scots Guards—the first time all three regiments had been assembled for a state visit.

The high point of the two-day visit was a state banquet at Windsor Castle, where a radiant Kate was strategically seated at the right hand of the guest of honor. The Princess of Wales was well aware of President Trump's passion for all things gold and dressed accordingly: she wore a shimmering couture design by Phillipa Lepley that featured a gold Chantilly lace evening coat over an ivory silk gown. Queen Mary's iconic Lover's Knot Tiara, diamond pendant earrings that had belonged to Elizabeth II, and the blue sash that denoted her status as a Dame Grand Cross of the Royal Victorian Order completed the look.

Whether or not either Trump or Kate remembered that he had once publicly chastised her for sunbathing in the nude on a private estate hardly mattered. She went out of her way to win over the President, and he in turn periodically grinned at the princess like a smitten schoolboy. During Trump's speech, she smiled graciously as he described her as "so radiant and so healthy and so beautiful"—a clear reference to how she seemed to be thriving in the wake of her cancer battle.

The following day Kate continued her charm offensive, this time with the American First Lady. Melania seemed equally taken with the princess. In Frogmore Gardens on the Windsor estate, they helped a group of four-to-six-year-old "Squirrel Scouts" earn their "Go Wild" merit badges by, among other things, gathering and then painting leaves. At one point, the two women joined children in playing the "parachute game"—shaking a large, colorful parachute with balls as the children ran underneath the canopy to push the balls out. They clearly bonded as mothers, both happily interacting with the children while the notoriously stone-faced Melania smiled throughout the event. The scouts were handed their badges in an impromptu ceremony, and at one point one of them asked the First Lady, "Are you the next princess?" It struck Chief Scout Dwayne Fields that Kate and Melania were "amazingly warm with each other."

While it remained to be seen whether or not the Trump state visit had garnered the United Kingdom the kind of economic concessions Prime Minister Kier Starmer had been seeking, no one doubted that Kate had emerged once again as the monarchy's leading exemplar of soft power. When asked if Kate was the royal family's secret weapon, *Majesty* magazine editor-in-chief Ingrid Seward replied, "She is *the* weapon, not a secret one."

The Prince and Princess of Wales had long known that their personal likes and dislikes mattered little; they were willing to do whatever was asked of them to promote the interests of king and country. Yet it all took a personal toll, and in the coming weeks Prince William would open up—at least a little—in ways he hadn't before. During a mostly lighthearted interview for *Schitt's Creek* star Eugene Levy's Apple TV+ series *The Reluctant Traveler*, William arrived on a motor scooter, hoisted a few with Levy at a pub, and offered viewers a tour of Windsor Castle. He talked about ways he intended to shake up the monarchy once he became king—"It's safe to say that change is on my agenda"—and about his intention to maintain a zone of privacy around his family. The main takeaway, however, was William's admission that 2024—the year both his father and wife were diagnosed with cancer—was, in his words, "the hardest year I've ever had."

Not long after, in a video to coincide with World Mental Health Day, William sat down with Rhian Mannings, whose husband had committed suicide after the unexpected death of their one-year-old son. At one point, the Prince looked away and struggled to fight back tears. "Are you okay?" Mannings asked. "I'm sorry," he answered once he regained his composure. "It's hard to ask you the questions. . . ."

In the game of chess, no piece is more useful than the queen. She can move horizontally, vertically, and diagonally, and—like all the pieces on the board—her sole purpose is to protect the king. The last Princess of Wales, Diana, knew this better than anyone—and the future king she chose to protect was William.

Young, stunning, gracious, and smart, the woman known simply as Kate captured the world's imagination before she could officially lay claim to her royal lover's heart. She may have lacked the bloodline, but she proved beyond doubt to be extraordinarily patient—a cunning survivor of court intrigue and royal chicanery. As has often been said, Kate hasn't put a foot wrong.

"Stop comparing the current Princess of Wales to Diana," said Queen Elizabeth's former spokesman Dickie Arbiter, "and accept her as an asset to the royal family in her own right." But comparisons between Kate and her predecessor are inevitable and, to a certain extent, entirely legitimate. Both Diana and Kate were glamorous, beautiful, intelligent, stylish, compassionate, self-deprecating, and disarmingly down-to-earth. They were relatable young mothers. But there were defining differences, too. Unlike Diana, whose ties to English aristocracy run deep, Kate was destined to be a queen like no other—not merely the United Kingdom's first commoner queen, but its first working-class queen, *and* its first university-educated queen.

Perhaps even more important, Kate was no rebel princess. She was happily married to a man who loved her, and she carried with her none of the heartache, drama, and tragedy that were the hallmarks of Diana's enduring fame.

By marrying her Prince Charming and producing three heirs, Kate had already propelled the monarchy into the next century. Along the way, she proved to be the royal family's brightest and most beguiling star—lending new luster to a musty institution that was becoming increasingly out of touch with the modern world.

When the time comes, Kate will without doubt become a queen unlike any who has gone before—and not simply because of her relatively modest background. Until now, British monarchs have made one thing their top priority: self-preservation. For all her finer qualities, Queen Elizabeth II was a creature from another age. When she was born in 1926, Britain still ruled over a vast empire covering roughly a quarter of the world's land mass inhabited by four hundred million people—the largest empire in history. As queen, she followed in her father's footsteps to preserve what was left of the empire by nurturing the Commonwealth; and by the time she died in 2022, that association of former British colonies included fifty-six nations and more than one-quarter of the world's population. At home, she was more symbol than person, clutching her ever-present pocketbook as she stiffly went about the business of being queen. With his interest in art, architecture, organic farming, and especially the environment, Charles showed less interest in holding on to dreams of empire than addressing pressing issues of the day. Yet by virtue of a tweedy, foxhunting persona and his own innately strangulated personality, the man who waited seventy years to become king still seemed to have one foot firmly planted in the past.

William is—whether he likes it or not—along with Harry heir to their mother's particular brand of magic. He will use that blend of compassion and charisma to advance not only the charities and causes that Diana and Charles pursued, but the issues that matter deeply to him and to Kate as well.

"Every generation of the royal family has to reinvent the role for the generation that they serve," the couple's close aide Jason Knauf said of William and Kate. They "are going to bring down-to-earth wisdom and connection" to the role. In the meantime, Knauf added, in the case of both the Prince and the Princess of Wales, "what you see is what you get."

In the ongoing endeavor to drag the monarchy kicking and screaming into the future, it is impossible to imagine a better life partner for the new king. Unlike previous generations of royals, they both decided to put their family first, and that is not going to change. From the outset, they have made no secret that George, Charlotte, and Louis take precedence over everything—including royal obligations. At the same time, Kate, who had to overcome her own natural shyness just as Diana did, has discovered that she is more than up to the formidable task of being queen. It is a responsibility she does not take lightly. She understands that, beyond the glittering state banquets, the receptions, premieres, and whirlwind foreign tours, there is an unparalleled opportunity for her to do some real good in the world—to touch people's lives and maybe even change them for the better. Here is where family, fortune, and fate intersect, for in striving to keep the monarchy strong, Kate is paving the way for her children to fulfill their destinies.

If Kate was the brightest star in the royal firmament before, cancer only boosted the amperage. Facing her own mortality with dignity, grace, courage, and a kind of gallantry, she has proven herself to be more than just a queen in the making. She has been called a force of nature, larger than life, an icon. But now, Kate is something else, something even more important: an inspiration.

Acknowledgments

Hers has always been the classic Cinderella story: the shyly beautiful descendant of coal miners who persevered for nearly a decade to finally win the heart of her handsome prince. None of this is metaphorical. We are talking real coal miners and a real, born-to-be-king prince of the realm.

None of this was remotely imaginable when I began writing about the royal family in earnest more than a half century ago. When I covered the Queen's Silver Jubilee marking her twenty-fifth anniversary on the throne back in 1977, the Windsors were—with the notable exception of Elizabeth's rambunctiously hedonistic sister, Princess Margaret—more cardboard cutout than human. At the time, speculation was rampant about who would marry Charles, the Prince of Wales, and the list of possibilities was truly yawn-inspiring. Only the names of aristocratic young women with the bluest of blood were in the running, and when a nineteen-year-old no one had ever heard of—Lady Diana Spencer—made it into the winner's circle, no one was particularly surprised. Of course, at the time no one had the slightest inkling that Charles's callow young bride would, in life and in death, bring the monarchy to its knees.

By the time Kate Middleton entered the picture in 2001, the royal family had been churning out one headline-making scandal after another for over a decade. William's college girlfriend stepped onto the world stage totally unschooled in the ways of Britain's uber-upper classes. Nor was she exposed to Palace intrigue, yet somehow "Waity Katie" intuitively knew how to wend her way around countless obstacles strewn in her path.

The oft-cited similarities between William's mother and his wife—their status as trendsetting style icons, their intelligence, humor, and their innate ability to connect with the person in the street—are undeniable. But as I have noted before, so, too, are the differences. Where Diana was propelled by justifiable grievance—primarily against an unfaithful husband and unfeeling monarchal system—Kate was, as corny as it sounds, fueled by love. Simply by being her caring, preternaturally sunny self and never allowing pressures from either the press or the Palace's plotting Men in Gray to derail or defeat her, Kate now seems—barring yet another plot twist, of course—destined to be queen. Having covered the coronation of King Charles, I can say that no one inside Westminster Abbey looked more regal—and at the same time more human—than Kate.

To the many adjectives that have been used to describe Catherine, Princess of Wales, we can now add "brave." As perhaps the world's most famous mother of young children, Kate has handled her cancer battle with a quiet grace and even joyful optimism—along the way becoming a symbol of hope for millions. As was once said of the way Jacqueline Kennedy handled the many tragedies that befell her, "There is a kind of gallantry about her."

For the eighth time, I have had the opportunity to work with the amazing folks at Gallery Books. I am particularly indebted to the marvelous Aimee Bell, my consummately talented editor, whose fascination with the most high-profile family in history mirrors my own. I'm also grateful to my many other friends who make up the Gallery/Simon & Schuster team, especially Jennifer Bergstrom, Jonathan Karp, Jennifer Long, Jennifer Robinson, Abby Knudsen, Lisa Litwack, John Vairo, Paul O'Halloran, Felice Javit, Caroline Pallotta, Emily Arzeno, and Angel Musyimi.

My God, Ellen Levine—can it be we have been agent and author (not to mention dear friends) for forty-three years? And amazingly we haven't aged a bit! I'm sure Ellen has grown tired of my thanking her in the pages of thirty-four books, but she'll just have to put up with it again. My thanks to Ellen's wonderful team at Trident Media Group, including Lauren Champlin, Martha Wydysh, Audrey Crooks, and Miles Temel.

I am reliably told that another person I've thanked in all of my books is perfectly thrilled to once again be the recipient of effusive praise. Valerie has been my wife for fifty-three years and my best friend even longer. An international banker by profession, as well as a pillar of Washington, Connecticut (the real Stars Hollow of *Gilmore Girls* fame), Valerie has also played a key part in the publishing process as first reader and editorial advisor—an important role she also fulfills for our daughter Kate Andersen Brower. A former White House correspondent for Bloomberg News and CNN contributor, our Kate has written six nonfiction bestsellers of her own, including one No.1 book—*The Residence*—that was made into a highly rated Netflix miniseries. Valerie has had to put up with a lot, having two high-strung writers in the family—a fact she has repeatedly shared with her wide circle of family and friends.

Kate has her hands full as well, raising our amazing grandchildren—Graham, Charlotte, and Teddy—as she pursues her own literary career. (We are "Mema" and "Pa" to the grandkids. Don't ask.) Our son-in-law, Brooke Brower, is also a universally respected veteran of the journalism game, having worked as a top producer at MSNBC, CNN, and ABC News. More important, he is a great guy.

Our younger daughter, Kelly, has charted her own course, earning a master's degree in contemporary art at the Sotheby's Institute of Art in London and working at Christie's and the Guggenheim Museum before deciding to embark on a career in finance in New York. My own parents, Commander Edward F. Andersen and Jeanette Andersen, instilled in me a deep interest in both history and history in the making that we've passed along to our children and grandchildren.

Additional thanks to Alan Hamilton, Jules Knight, Lord Mishcon, Richard Kay, Mimi Massy-Birch, Lady Margaret Rhodes, the 2nd Countess Mountbatten, Janet Jenkins, Delissa Needham, Mark Shand, Peter Archer, Dr. Frederic Mailliez, Tom Sykes, Lady Elsa Bowker, Philip Higgs, Hugh Massy-Birch, Lady Yolanda Joseph, Guy Pelly, Hamish Barne,

Andrew Gailey, Thierry Meresse, Beatrice Hubert, Elizabeth d'Erlanger, Tara Palmer-Tomkinson, Andy Radford, Joan Rivers, Vivienne Parry, Lucia Flecha de Lima, Barry Dennen, Jules de Rosee, Richard Greene, Alexandra ("Tiggy") Legge-Bourke Pettifer, Adrian Munsey, Josy Duclos, Jeanne Lecorcher, the Countess of Romanones, Ezra Zilkha, Laura Watts, Lord Carnarvon, Harold Brooks-Baker, Mark Butt, Winston Spencer Churchill, Duncan Larcombe, John Kaufman, Max Clifford, Geoffrey Bignell, Regina Feiler, Remi Gaston-Dreyfus, Natalie Symonds, Wendy Leigh, Tom Freeman, Rachel Whitburn, Elizabeth Whiddett, Raine Spencer, Penny Russell-Smith, Lord Bathurst, Kitty Carlisle Hart, Miriam Lefort, Pierre Trudeau, Penny Walker, Claude Garreck, Rosemary McClure, Dee Ennifer, Patrick Demarchelier, Dudley Freeman, Janet Lizop, Elizabeth Longman, Peter Allen, Alfred Eisenstaedt, John Marion, Fred Hauptfuhrer, Jessica Hogan, Betty Kelly Sargent, James Whitaker, Alain-Phillipe Feutre, Mary Robertson, Gered Mankowitz, Tom Wolfe, Jeanette Peterson, Lord Olivier, Vivian Simon, the Earl of Powis, Lynn Redgrave, Michelle Lapautre, Tom Corby, Lord Glenconner, Cecile Zilkha, Kevin Lemarque, Pierre Suu, Hazel Southam, Norman Parkinson, Farris Rookstool, Ray Whelan Jr., Matthew Lutts, Tim Graham, Vincent Martin, Everett Raymond Kinstler, Sharman Douglas, Valerie Wimmer, Malcom Forbes, Angela Lansbury, Cathy Cesario Tardosky, Nicole Robson, Katrina Kochneva, Julie Grahame, Oleg Cassini, Tiffney Sanford, Amber Weitz, Andy Rouvalis, Michael Pintauro, Yvette Reyes, Scott Burkhead, Bill Diehl, Ron Galella, Richard Grant, Tiffany Miller, Christopher Plummer, Simone Dibley, Tom McShane, Daniel Taylor, Ray Whelan Sr., Paula Dranov, Claire Roberts, Brad Darrach, Mark Halpern, Rhoda Prelic, Liz Miller, Diana Finch, Govert Deketh, Steve Stylandoudis, Julie Cammer, Michael Cantlebury, Marcel Turgot, Louise Quayle, Cranston Jones, Nicolas Monaglio, Manuel Ribeiro, Mary Beth Whelan, Chris Helgren, Dominika Klimek, Joe Greensted, Kyle Cowser, David McGough, Charles Furneaux, Connie Erickson, Mel Lyons, Lindsay Sutton, Andy Rouvalis, Francis Specker, Scott Burkhead, John Stillwell, James Price, Jesse Birnbaum, Debbie Goodsite, Larry King, Elizabeth Loth, Ian Walde, Stuart Scheinman, Toby Anthony,

Wolfgang Rattay, Lindsay Potenza, Jasen Cook, Evelyn Phillips, Kinsey Schofield, Mick Magsino, Emma Salle, Tasha Hanna, Richard Anthony, Lawrence R. Mulligan, Tobias Markowitz, Jane Clucas, David Bergeron, Stefano Rellandini, Hilary Hard, Michael Crabtree, Art Kaligos, Kyle Tannler, Ala Diment, Tucker Di Edwardo, Agnieszka Mejri, Gary Gunderson, Gabriel Marshall, the Press Association, Buckingham Palace, Kensington Palace, St. James's Palace, Windsor Castle, Clarence House, Sandringham House, Marlborough College, Downe House, St. Andrew's school, Eton College, Ludgrove School, Lambrook School, Westacre Montessori School, Thomas's Battersea School, Willcocks Nursery School, University of St. Andrews, Houghton Hall, the Royal Military Academy Sandhurst, the BBC, Sky Television, Channel Four Television, *Times* of London, *Daily Mail*, *Guardian*, *Daily Telegraph*, *Sunday Times*, *Express*, *Financial Times*, *Mail on Sunday*, *Sun*, *New York Times*, *London Evening Standard*, *Time*, *Newsweek*, *People*, *Town & Country*, *Vanity Fair*, *Vogue*, *Washington Post*, *Wall Street Journal*, *Huffpost*, *Daily Beast*, *New York Post*, *USA Today*, *Forbes*, Associated Press, Bloomberg, Reuters, CNN, MSNBC, CBS, ABC, Bodleian Library Oxford, Holyhead Library, British Museum Reading Room, New York Public Library, Yale Center for British Art, Yale University Beinecke Rare Book and Manuscript Library, Bancroft Library of the University of California at Berkeley, Gunn Memorial Library, Brookfield Library, Silas Bronson Library, Litchfield Library, St. James's Club, Reform Club, Atheneum, Lotos Club, Lansdowne Club, East India Club, Rex USA, Capital Art, Alpha-Globe Photos, Shutterstock, and Zuma Press.

Sources and Chapter Notes

The chapter notes have been compiled to give a general overview of the sources drawn upon in the writing of *Kate!*, and are by no means to be considered all-inclusive. Certain key sources at Kensington Palace, Buckingham Palace, Windsor Castle, St. James's Palace, Highgrove, Balmoral Castle, Clarence House, and Sandringham House, as well as Marlborough College, Eton College, the University of St. Andrews, Sandhurst, Scotland Yard, Ludgrove School, Lambrook School, the London Clinic, and Royal Marsden Hospital—relatives, close friends and acquaintances, former classmates, professional colleagues, advisors, employees, employers, and government officials among them—agreed to cooperate only if they were allowed to remain anonymous. These are, in many cases, the same unimpeachable inside sources I have relied on over the decades to provide precise, highly detailed, and impeccably accurate information on the inner workings of the Firm. The author has respected their wishes and therefore has not listed them here or elsewhere in the text. It is worth pointing out that with comparatively few exceptions, everything in *Kate!* is on the record.

No family in the history of the world has had more written about it than Britain's royal family. Oceans of ink have been devoted to chronicling the Windsors' every move in such British newspapers as the *Times* and the *Sunday Times*, the *Daily Mail* and the *Mail on Sunday*, the *Guardian*, the *Daily Telegraph*, the *Financial Times*, the *Sun*, the *Economist*, and the *Daily Express*; while in the United States, the *New York Times*, the *Washington Post*, the

Wall Street Journal, *Newsweek*, *Time*, *People*, the *Boston Globe*, the *Los Angeles Times*, the *Chicago Tribune*, the *Detroit News*, the New York *Daily News*, *Vanity Fair*, and the *New Yorker*—not to mention the foreign press (*Le Monde*, *Paris Match*, *Bild*, *Stern*, to name a few) and wire services like Bloomberg, Reuters, and the Associated Press—cover the royal family as obsessively as if it were our own. By way of turning up the volume, broadcast and social media coverage have made it impossible for the children, grandchildren, and great-grandchildren of the late Elizabeth II to escape public scrutiny. Such is the price of unparalleled global fame—and, in Kate's case, a unique opportunity to better people's lives, not to mention shape history.

Chapters 1, 2, and 3

Interviews and conversations for these chapters included Richard Kay, Lady Margaret Rhodes, Alan Hamilton, Dr. Frederic Mailliez, Jules Knight, Richard Greene, Lord Mishcon, Alexandra ("Tiggy") Legge-Bourke Pettifer, 2nd Countess Mountbatten, Béatrice Humbert, Tom Sykes, Lady Elsa Bowker, Janet Lizop, Guy Pelly, Josy Duclos, Peter Archer, Jeanne Lecorcher, Janet Jenkins, Tess Rock, Barry Schenck, Mimi Massy-Birch, Judy Wade, the Duchess of Alba, Claude Garreck, Lady Yolanda Joseph, Andy Radford, Cecile Zilkha, Oonagh Shanley-Toffolo, Terry O'Neill, Lynn Redgrave, Rémi Gaston-Dreyfus, Prince Rupert Loewenstein, Harold Brooks-Baker, Miriam Lefort, Robin Leach, Alex Shirley-Smith, Aileen Mehle, Natalie Symonds, Christopher Plummer, Gered Mankowitz, Penny Walker, and Emma Sayle.

Published sources included Harry Howard, "Inside the London Clinic," *Daily Mail*, January 17, 2024; Georgia Brown, "Kate's Five-Star Hospital Where She's Recovering from Abdominal Surgery Has Its Own Concierge Service," *Hello!*, January 17, 2024; Erin Vanderhoof, "Kate Middleton Gets a Visit from Prince William on Her Third Day at the London Clinic," *Vanity Fair*, January 18, 2024; Victoria Murphy, "King Charles Visits Kate Middleton in Hospital as He Is Admitted for His Own Treatment," *Town & Country*, January 26, 2024; Danica Kirka, "King Charles Has Been Released from the Hospital," Associated Press, January 29, 2024; Dani Di Placido, "The 'Kate Middleton Is Missing' Conspiracy Theory, Explained," *Forbes*, February 28, 2024; Will Lloyd, "The Kate Conspiracy," *New Statesman*, March 12, 2024; Jane Clinton, "Staff at Hospital Where Kate Had Surgery 'Tried to Access Her Medical Records,'" *Guardian*, March 20, 2024; Jessica Winter, "The Kate Middleton Photo That Was Too Good to Be True: A Doctored Image of the Princess of Wales and Her Children Has Become the Most Captivating Episode of Her Entire Public Career," *New Yorker*, March 14, 2024; Rob Picheta, "Princess of Wales Apologizes for Editing Mother's Day Photograph," CNN, March 11, 2024; Erum Salam, "Where Is Catherine, Princess of Wales? The Internet Is Rife with 'Katespiracies,'" *Guardian*, March 16, 2024; Anna Russell, "The Kate Middleton Conspiracy-Theory Swirl," *New Yorker*, March 8, 2024; A. J. Willingham, "The Princess of Wales Controversy Has Only Gotten Worse," CNN, March 16, 2024; Sean Coughlan, "Kate, Princess of Wales: I Am Having Cancer

Treatment," BBC News, March 22, 2024; Kate Mansey, "The Princess of Wales Has Cancer," *Times*, March 22, 2024; Mark Landler, "Catherine, the Princess of Wales, Reveals She Has Cancer," *New York Times*, March 22, 2024; Isaac Bickerstaff, "Who Is in the Princess of Wales's Core Circle of Friends?," *Tatler*, March 25, 2024; Mark Landler, "Kate's Cancer Diagnosis Puts U.K. Royals on Even More Uncertain Terrain," *New York Times*, March 22, 2024; Sean Coughlan and Marianna Spring, "Kate Rumours Linked to Russian Disinformation," BBC News, March 26, 2024; Robert Jobson, *Catherine, the Princess of Wales: A Biography of the Future Queen* (New York: Pegasus Books, 2024); Alan Hamilton, Andrew Pierce, and Philip Webster, "Royal Family Is Deeply Touched by Public Support," *Times*, September 4, 1997; Anthony Holden, "Why Royals Must Express Remorse," *Express*, September 3, 1997; Robert Hardman, "Princes' Last Minutes with Mother," *Daily Telegraph*, September 3, 1997; Christopher Andersen, *The Day Diana Died* (New York: William Morrow, 1998); Brian Dakss,"Ex-Guard Speaks Out About Di Tapes," CBS News, November 30, 2004; Lord Stevens of Kirkwhelpington, *The Operation Paget Inquiry Report Into the Allegation of Conspiracy to Murder Diana, Princess of Wales, and Emad El-Din Mohamed Abdel Moneim Fayed*, December 14, 2006; Caroline Graham, *Camilla and Charles: The Love Story* (London: John Blake, 2005); Simone Simmons, *Diana: The Last Word* (New York: St. Martin's Press, 2005); Angela Levin, "Exclusive: Prince Harry on Chaos After Diana's Death and Why the World Needs 'the Magic' of the Royal Family," *Newsweek*, June 21, 2017; Wendy Berry, *The Housekeeper's Diary: Charles and Diana Before the Breakup* (New York: Barricade Books, 1995); Danny Danziger, *Eton Voices: Interviews* (London: Viking, 1989); Associated Press, "William Injured by Golf Club," June 4, 1991; Anna Pasternak, *Princess in Love* (London: Bloomsbury, 1994); "An Interview with HRH The Princess of Wales," *Panorama*, BBC One, November 20, 1995; "Earl Spencer 'Lied to' Over Princes Following Diana's Coffin," BBC News, July 26, 2017; *Diana, 7 Days*, directed by Henry Singer, BBC Television Documentary Special, aired August 27, 2017; "Diana, Princess of Wales 1961–1997," *The Week*, September 6, 1997; Mark Landler, "25 Years Later, BBC Apologizes for Diana Interview," *New York Times*, May 20, 2021; "Balmoral: Why the Royals Love Spending Time There," *Hello!*, September 7, 2016; John Simpson, "Goodbye England's Rose: A Nation Says Farewell," *Sunday Telegraph*, September 7, 1997; "The Nation Unites Against Tradition," *Observer*, September 7, 1997; Tess Rock and Natalie Symonds, "Our Diana Diaries," *Sunday Mirror*, November 16, 1997; "Driver Was Drunk," *Le Monde*, September 3, 1997; Max Clifford and Angela Levin, *Max Clifford: Read All About It.* (London: Virgin Books, 2005); Robert Jobson and Greg Swift, "Look After William and Harry," *Daily Express*, December 22, 1997; Jo Thomas, "The Early Education of a Future King," *New York Times*, April 13, 1986; Nicholas Davies, *William: The Inside Story of the Man Who Will Be King* (New York: St. Martin's Griffin, 1998); Marianne Macdonald, "A Rift Death Can't Heal," *Observer*, September 14, 1997; David Ward, "Prince's Pride in His Sons," *Guardian*, September 20, 1997; Sally Bedell Smith, *Diana in Search of Herself: Portrait of a Troubled Princess* (New York: Times Books, 1999); Sue Ryan, "Here's Harry!," *Mail on Sunday*, October 14, 1984; James Hewitt, *Love and War* (London: John Blake, 1999); William E. Schmidt, "Charles and Diana Are Separating 'Amicably,'" *New York Times*, December 10, 1992; Paul Burrell, *A Royal Duty* (New York: Signet, 2004); Ken Wharfe with Robert Jobson, *Diana: Closely Guarded Secret* (London: Michael O'Mara Books, 2003); Bryan Appleyard, "The Princes' Final Farewell," *Sunday Times*, September 7, 1997; Andrew Morton, *Diana: Her True Story* (New York: Simon & Schuster, 1997); Howard Chua-Eoan, Steve Wulf, Jeffrey Kluger, Christopher Redman, and David Van

Biema, "A Death in Paris: The Passing of Diana," *Time*, September 13, 1997; Warren Hoge, "Charles Accompanies Diana Back Home to a Grieving Britain," *New York Times*, September 1, 1997; Kate Snell, *Diana: Her Last Love* (London: Granada Media, 2000); Dominick Dunne, "Diana's Secrets," *Vanity Fair*, January 2003; Jerome Dupuis, "Diana: The Unpublished Report of Witnesses at the Ritz," *L'Express*, March 12, 1998; Rosa Monckton, "Time to End False Rumors," *Newsweek*, March 2, 1998; Pascal Palmer, "I Gave Diana Last Rites," *Mirror*, October 23, 1997; "Flashback to the Accident," *Liberation*, September 2, 1997; Howard Chua-Eoan, Steve Wulf, Jeffrey Kluger, Christopher Redman, and David Van Biema, "Diana 1961–1997: Death of a Princess," *Time*, September 8, 1997; Thomas Sancton and Scott MacLeod, *Death of a Princess: The Investigation* (New York: St. Martin's Press, 1998); James Hewitt, *Love and War* (London: Blake, 1999); Warren Hoge, "Queen Breaks the Ice: Camilla's Out of the Fridge," *New York Times*, June 5, 2000; Sarah, The Duchess of York, *Finding Sarah: A Duchess's Journey to Find Herself* (New York: Atria Books, 2011); Richard Kay and Geoffrey Levy, "Camilla and the Blonde Private Secretary Who's Paid the Price for Being Too Close to Prince Charles," *Daily Mail*, June 13, 2008; Peter Foster, "Has the Puppet-Master of St. James's Palace Finally Pulled One String Too Many?," *Daily Telegraph*, December 1, 2001; P. D. Jephson, *Shadows of a Princess* (New York: HarperCollins, 2000); Robert Hardman, "Just (Call Me) William," *Daily Telegraph*, June 17, 2000; David Leppard and Christopher Morgan, "Police Fears Over William's Friends," *Sunday Times*, February 27, 2000; Claudia Joseph, *Kate: The Making of a Princess* (New York: Avon, 2009); Michelle Tauber, "Speaking His Mind," *People*, October 16, 2000; Barbara Kantrowitz, "William: The Making of a Modern King," *Newsweek*, June 26, 2000; Andrew Pierce and Simon de Bruxelles, "Our Mother Was Betrayed," *Times*, September 30, 2000; Bob Colacello, "A Court of His Own," *Vanity Fair*, October 2001; Stephen Glover, "The Royals Must Change . . . or Die," *Daily Mail*, November 11, 2003; Warren Hoge, "Charles's Response to Use of Drugs by Son Is Praised," *New York Times*, January 14, 2002; Paul Henderson, "I Was Raped by Charles's Servant," *Mail on Sunday*, November 10, 2002; Christopher Andersen, "The Divided Prince," *Vanity Fair*, September 2003; Warren Hoge, "Palace Is Roiled Again by New Round of Revelations," *New York Times*, November 11, 2002; Christopher Morgan and David Leppard, "Party Girl in William's Circle Snorted Cocaine," *Sunday Times*, February 26, 2000; J. F. O. McAllister, "Once Upon a Time, There Was a Pot-Smoking Prince," *Time*, January 28, 2002; Ben Summerskill, "The Trouble with Harry," *Observer*, January 13, 2002; Antony Barnett, "Prince Taken to Drink and Drugs Rehab Clinic," *Observer*, January 13, 2002; "Queen Mother Dies Peacefully, Aged 101," *Guardian*, March 30, 2002; Nicola Methven, "Hypno-Di-Sed," *Mirror*, September 19, 2005; Robert Hardman, *Her Majesty: Queen Elizabeth II and Her Court* (New York: Pegasus Books, 2012); Deirdre Fernand, "The Girl Who Would Be Queen," *Sunday Times*, December 31, 2006; Christopher Wilson, "Kate, the Coal Miner's Girl," *Daily Mail*, December 22, 2006; Claudia Joseph, "The Making of the Middletons," *Mail on Sunday*, December 30, 2007; Richard Kay, Geoffrey Levy, and Katie Glass, "Wild Side of Kate's Family," *Daily Mail*, August 9, 2008; Rhiannon Du Cann, "Princess Kate's Special Connection to Jordan Where She Lived as a Child and Learnt Arabic," *Express*, June 1, 2023; Mazher Mahmood and Amanda Evans, "I Called Wills a F***er," *News of the World*, July 19, 2009; Susan Schindehette and Allison Adato, "Princes in Love," *People*, August 8, 2005; Michelle Green, "Is She the One?," *People*, October 17, 2005; Alex Tresniowski and Ashley Williams, "Will & Kate: The Perfect Match," *People*, December 11, 2006; Caroline Davies, "'Blackadder' Keeps Close Ties to Camilla," *Telegraph*, January 6, 2003; Dickie

Arbiter with Lynne Barrett Lee, *On Duty with the Queen: My Time as a Buckingham Palace Press Secretary* (London: Blink, 2014); Oliver Marre, "Girl, Interrupted," *Observer*, March 18, 2007; Duncan Larcombe, "Wills & Kate Split," *Sun*, April 14, 2007; Laura Collins, Katie Nicholl, and Ian Gallagher, "Kate Was Too Middle Class," *Mail on Sunday*, April 15, 2007; David Smith, "Royal Relationships: The Breakup," *Guardian*, April 15, 2007; Zoe Griffin and Grant Hodgson, "Flatmates Who Fell in Love; Wills & Kate 2002–2007: The Fairytale's Over," *Sunday Mirror*, April 15, 2007; Rajeev Syal, "'Let Them Be, They Are Young,'" *Times*, April 16, 2007; Victoria White and Stephen White, "Life After William," *Mirror*, April 21, 2007; Laura Collins and Louise Hannah, "As Kate Re-Emerges More Tanned and Confident, a New Middleton Girl Takes a Bow," *Daily Mail*, May 27, 2007; Karen Rockett, "It's Back On," *Sunday Mirror*, June 24, 2007; Sarah Tetteh, "Thrills & Kate," *Mirror*, July 3, 2007; Sarah Knapton, "Prince Denounces 'Aggressive' Paparazzi Pursuit," *Guardian*, October 5, 2007; Richard Woods, "Leave Us Alone," *Sunday Times*, October 7, 2007; Andrew Alderson, "Prince Eyes Legal Action," *Sunday Telegraph*, October 7, 2007; Lisa Sewards, "The Day Prince William Pulled a Gun on Me," *Daily Mail*, December 28, 2007; Robert Jobson and Keith Dovkants, "Kate, the 'New Royal,' Gets Her Own Bodyguards," *Evening Standard*, January 9, 2008; Andrew Pierce, "Prince's Lawyers Warn Paparazzi Off Middleton," *Daily Telegraph*, February 23, 2008; Rebecca English, "William Landed His Air Force Helicopter in Kate's Garden," *Daily Mail*, April 21, 2008; Aislinn Simpson, "William Flies into a Storm," *Daily Telegraph*, April 21, 2008; Ben Guy, "Will Finds a Way to Get to Church on Time—in a Helicopter," Newcastle *Journal*, April 23, 2008; "William and RAF Sorry for Prince's FIVE Chinook Joyrides," BBC News, April 23, 2008; Fred Redwood, "Helicopter Stunt That Put Kate's Middleton's Home on the Map," *Telegraph*, May 20, 2008; Lucy Cockcroft, "Prince William's Chinook Flight to Stag Party Costs 8,716 Pounds," *Daily Telegraph*, June 30, 2008; Alan Hamilton, "A Feather in His Cap: Young Prince Is New Recruit to the World's Oldest Order of Chivalry," *Times*, June 17, 2008; Vicky Ward, "Will's Cup of Tea," *Vanity Fair*, November 2008; Christopher Wilson, "The Lonely Death of Charles's Other Mistress," *Daily Mail*, October 10, 2008; Richard Eden, "Kate's 'Vulnerable' Mother Speaks Out for the First Time," *Telegraph*, December 6, 2008; Geoffrey Levy and Richard Kay, "How Many More Skeletons in Kate's Closet?," *Daily Mail*, July 22, 2009; James Whitaker and David Collins, "Queen Tells Kate Middleton: It's Family ONLY at Sandringham This Christmas," *Mirror*, December 20, 2009; Nicholas Watt, "How a Hung Parliament Would Put the Queen Center Stage," *Guardian*, February 14, 2010; Liz Hoggard, "Let Them Eat Cake," *Evening Standard*, February 18, 2010; Alex Tresniowski, "A Royal Love," *People*, May 3, 2010; "Duchess of York Scandal," ABC News, May 24, 2010; David Stringer, "Prince William Makes First Royal Rescue for RAF," Associated Press, October 5, 2010.

Chapters 4 and 5

For these chapters, the author drew in part on past conversations with Peter Archer, James Whitaker, Thierry Meresse, Janet Jenkins, Alan Hamilton, Hugh Massy-Birch, Emma Sayle, Lord Mishcon, Lady Elsa Bowker, Hamish Barne, the Duchess of Alba, Alice Tomlinson, Richard Kay, Prince Rupert Loewenstein, Charles Furneaux, Jules Knight, Lady Yolanda Joseph, Tom Sykes, Fred Hauptfuhrer, Delissa Needham, Pat Charman, Jules de Rosee, Pierre Suu, Earl McGrath, Sioned Compton, Richard Greene, Guy Pelly, Geoffrey Bignell, Penny Walker,

Natalie Symonds, Kitty Carlisle Hart, Mark Butt, Barry Schenck, Tess Rock, Janet Allison, Farris Rookstool III, Wendy Leigh, Colin St. John Wilson, Evelyn Phillips, Susan Crimp, Elizabeth Widdett, and Mary Robertson.

Among the published sources consulted: Ben Summerskill, "The Trouble with Harry," *Observer*, January 13, 2002; Prince Harry, *Spare* (New York: Random House, 2023); Andrew Pierce, "'I'm Sorry for Wearing Nazi Swastika,' Says Prince Harry," *Times*, January 13, 2005; Neil Tweedie and Michael Kallenbach, "Prince Harry Faces Outcry at Nazi Outfit," *Daily Telegraph*, January 14, 2005; Janice Turner, "Harry's Choice of Costume Was Lazy," *Times*, January 15, 2005; David Leppard and Christopher Morgan, "Police Fears over William's Friends," *Sunday Times*, February 27, 2000; Andrew Pierce and Simon de Bruxelles, "Our Mother Was Betrayed," *Times*, September 30, 2000; J. F. O. McAllister, "Once Upon a Time, There Was a Pot-Smoking Prince," *Time*, January 28, 2002; Antony Barnett, "Prince Taken to Drink and Drugs Rehab Clinic," *Observer*, January 13, 2002; Corky Siemaszko and Ellen Tumposky, "Look to Put the Lid on Pot Prince," New York *Daily News*, January 15, 2002; Warren Hoge, "Charles's Response to Use of Drugs by Son Is Praised," *New York Times*, January 14, 2002; Paul Henderson, "I Was Raped by Charles' Manservant," *Mail on Sunday*, November 10, 2002; Warren Hoge, "Royal Palace Is Roiled Again by New Round of Revelations," *New York Times*, November 11, 2002; Tom Rawstorne, "William in His Own Words," *Daily Mail*, May 30, 2003; Robert Hardman, "Just (Call Me) William," *Daily Telegraph*, June 17, 2000; Richard Kay and Mike Pflanz, "Prince Harry, a Stunning Heiress and the Hewitt Connection," *Daily Mail*, February 12, 2004; "A Speech by The Queen at the Opening of a Memorial Fountain to the Late Diana, Princess of Wales," July 6, 2004, https://www.royal.uk/opening-memorial-fountain-late-diana-princess-wales-6-july-2004; Jacqueline Malley, "$75,000 Damages for Teacher Who Accused Prince Harry of Cheating," *Guardian*, February 14, 2006; Roxanne Roberts, "Fairy Tale for Grown-Ups: Charles and Camilla Once Upon a Time," *Washington Post*, February 11, 2005; Thomas Fields-Meyer and Pam Lambert, "Royal Stepmum," *People*, February 28, 2005; Patrick Jephson, "Everybody Loves a Royal Wedding . . . Usually," *Sunday Telegraph*, March 27, 2005; Hamish Bowles, "At Long Last Love," *Vogue*, April 2005; Barbara Kantrowitz, "Legal at Last," *Newsweek*, April 17, 2005; Andrew Alderson, "Husband and Wife—At Last," *Sunday Telegraph*, April 10, 2005; Simon Freeman, "The Royal Wedding Day, Minute by Minute," *Times*, April 9, 2005; Heather Timmons, "The Once and Future Camilla," *New York Times*, April 3, 2005; Live coverage by the BBC, CNN, Fox News (on which the author offered live commentary), and MSNBC on the wedding of Prince Charles and Camilla Parker Bowles; Nicola Methven, "Hyno-Di-Sed: Hewitt Put in Trance," *Mirror*, September 19, 2005; Michelle Green, "Is She the One?," *People*, October 17, 2005; Robert Stansfield, "Harry the Hangover," *Mirror*, June 16, 2006; "Queen at Harry's Army Graduation," CNN, April 12, 2006; "William Graduates from Sandhurst," BBC News, December 15, 2006; Alex Tresniowski and Ashley Williams, "Will and Kate: The Perfect Match," *People*, December 11, 2006; "The Battle to Protect Kate," *Evening Standard*, January 9, 2007; Kira Cochrane, "In Diana's Footsteps," *Guardian*, January 9, 2007; Oliver Marre, "Girl, Interrupted," *Observer*, March 18, 2007; Duncan Larcombe, "Wills & Kate Split," *Sun*, April 14, 2007; David Smith, "Royal Relationships: The Breakup," *Guardian*, April 1, 2007; Rajeev Syal, "Tony Blair: 'Let Them Be, They Are Young,'" *Times*, April 16, 2007; Victoria White and Stephen White, "Life After William," *Mirror*, April 21, 2007; Karen Rockett, "It's Back On," *Sunday Mirror*, June 24,

2007; Sarah Knapton, "Prince Denounces 'Aggressive' Paparazzi Pursuit," *Guardian*, October 6, 2007; Andrew Alderson, "Prince Eyes Legal Action," *Sunday Telegraph*, October 7, 2007; Andrew Pierce, "Prince's Lawyers Warn Paparazzi Off Middleton, *Daily Telegraph*, February 23, 2008; Aislinn Simpson, "William Flies into a Storm," *Daily Telegraph*, April 21, 2008; Rebecca English, "William Lands His Air Force Helicopter in Kate's Garden," *Daily Mail*, April 21, 2008; "William and RAF Sorry for Prince's FIVE Chinook Joyrides," BBC News, April 23, 2008; Lucy Cockcroft, "Prince William's Chinook Flight to Stag Party Costs 8,716 Pounds," *Daily Telegraph*, June 30, 2008; Richard Kay, Geoffrey Levy, and Katie Glass, "Wild Side of Kate's Family," *Daily Mail*, August 9, 2008; Paul Majendie, "Britain's Prince Harry Back from Afghan Frontline," Reuters, March 1, 2008; Robert Jobson, *Harry's War: The True Story of the Soldier Prince* (London: John Blake, 2008); Sarah Lyall, "Prince Harry Withdrawn from Afghanistan," *New York Times*, February 29, 2008; Jane Wardell, "Prince Harry Gets His Wings—and Keys to the Apache," Associated Press, May 7, 2010; Simon Perry, "Chelsy Davy Steps Out to Support Prince Harry," *People*, May 7, 2010; Amelia Hill, "Politicians Condemn Prince Harry Over 'Racist' Remark," *Guardian*, January 11, 2009; "Prince's Apology for Racist Term," BBC, January 11, 2009; Vicky Ward, "Will's Cup of Tea," *Vanity Fair*, November 2008; Geoffrey Levy and Richard Kay, "How Many More Skeletons in Kate's Closet?," *Daily Mail*, July 22, 2009; David Stringer, "Prince William Makes First Royal Rescue for RAF," Associated Press, October 5, 2010; Katie Nicholl, *William and Harry* (New York: Weinstein Books, 2010); Lee Ferran, "Prince William Proposes to Kate Middleton with Princess Diana's Engagement Ring," ABC News, November 14, 2010; Chloe Foussianes, "Prince William Talks About Proposing to Kate Middleton in a Speech at a Buckingham Palace Reception," *Town & Country*, January 21, 2020; Live coverage by the BBC, CNN, Fox News (during which the author provided live coverage), and MSNBC on the wedding of Prince William and Kate Middleton; Anthony Faiola, "William and Kate's Royal Wedding: Britain's Monarchy's New Era Sealed with a Kiss," *Washington Post*, April 29, 2011; Olivia Blair, "This Is What It's Like to Attend a Royal Wedding," *Elle*, November 1, 2017; Sarah Lyall, "A Traditional Royal Wedding, but for the 3 Billion Witnesses," *New York Times*, April 29, 2011; Katie Nicholl, "Harry Pays Tribute to William 'The Dude' . . . in Best Man Speech," *Daily Mail*, April 29, 2011; Kate Storey, "Prince William Got 'Revenge' on Prince Harry with a 'Naughty' Best Man Speech," *Town & Country*, May 20, 2018; Kayleigh Roberts, "Prince Harry's Best Man Speech Made Kate Middleton Cry During Her Royal Wedding in 2011," *Marie Claire*, March 3, 2019; Gordon Rayner, "Royal Tour: Kate Middleton and Prince William Win Over Crowds," *Telegraph*, July 1, 2011; "William Says Canada 'Far Exceeded' Expectations," CBC, July 7, 2011; Mian Ridge, "A Year After Wedding, British Monarchy Basks in 'Kate Effect,'" *Christian Science Monitor*, April 29, 2012; "'Kate Effect' Boost for East Anglia's Children's Hospices," BBC News, July 23, 2012; Robert Jobson, *The New Royal Family: Prince George, William and Kate, the Next Generation* (London: John Blake, 2013); Christopher Andersen, *William and Kate and Baby George: Royal Baby Edition* (New York: Gallery Books, 2013); "Prince Harry: Naked Pictures During Las Vegas Rager," TMZ, August 22, 2012; "Prince Harry Naked Photos Emerge After He Parties in Las Vegas," *Us*, August 22, 2012; Rebecca English, "Palace Fury at Harry Naked Photos," *Daily Mail*, August 22, 2012; Katie Kindelan, "Prince Harry Returns to England, With His Clothes On," ABC News, August 23, 2012; Catriona Harvey-Jenner, "Prince Harry Just Discussed Those 2012 Naked Las Vegas Photos and the 'Great Body He Had at the Time,'" *Cosmopolitan*, May 14, 2021; Julia Neel, "Topless Photos Cause Royal Furor," *WWD*, September 14, 2012; Nick

Hopkins and Caroline Davies, "Prince Harry: I've Killed in Afghanistan but Dad Wants Me to Act Like a Prince," *Guardian*, January 21, 2013; "Pregnant Kate Spending Second Day in Hospital," BBC News, December 4, 2012; Amy Harris, "What is Hyperemesis Gravidarum? Kate Middleton's Severe Morning Sickness Explained," *Standard*, October 18, 2017; Nicole Spector, "Kate's Hyperemesis Gravidarum: What Is It?," NBC News, September 8, 2017; "Royal Baby: Kate and William Visited by Prince Charles," BBC News, July 23, 2013; Valentine Low, "Duke and Duchess of Cambridge Formally Register Birth of Prince George," *Times*, August 3, 2013; "The Christening of Prince George of Cambridge," September 27, 2013, https://www.royal.uk/christening-prince-george-cambridge; Ben Pimlott, *The Queen: A Biography of Elizabeth II* (New York: Wiley, 1996); Sally Bedell Smith, *Elizabeth the Queen: The Life of a Modern Monarch* (New York: Random House, 2012); Lesley Messer, "Prince Harry on Being an Uncle: I'll 'Make Sure He Has Fun,' " ABC News, July 25, 2013; Maria Puente, "Prince Harry Launches 'Invictus Games' for Wounded Vets," *USA Today*, March 6, 2014; "Prince George Makes Friends on Royal Tour of New Zealand," Reuters, April 9, 2014; Nicholas Witchell, "Royal Tour: Prince George Steals the Show as Support for Monarchy Rises," BBC News, April 25, 2014; Katie Nicholl, "William and Kate Prepare for a Visit from the Queen at Their Newly Renovated Country Home," *Vanity Fair*, November 29, 2014; Maria Puente, "Prince George Makes Palace Balcony Debut," *USA Today*, June 13, 2015; James Tapper, "Prince George Makes First Appearance on Buckingham Palace Balcony," *Guardian*, June 13, 2015; Cecilia Rodriguez, "The Meaning Behind Kate Middleton's State Dinner Tiara and Red Dress," *Forbes*, October 21, 2015; Penny Junor, "Camilla Has Won Us Over and Deserves to Become Queen," *Telegraph*, April 8, 2015; Angela Levin, "Will Charles Risk Making Camilla, Duchess of Cornwall, His Queen?," *Newsweek*, December 9, 2015; Simon Perry, "A Perfect Princess! Kate and William Announce the Arrival of Their Baby Girl," *People*, May 2, 2015; Cecilia Rodriguez, "Kate Middleton Gives Birth to a Baby Girl, the New Royal Princess," *Forbes*, May 2, 2015; Tom Sykes, "William and Kate Should Stop Hiding Prince George and Princess Charlotte Away," *Daily Beast*, October 11, 2015; Lauren Moraski, "Duchess Kate Dazzles at State Dinner," CBS News, October 20, 2015; Lauren Fruen, "Up Past Bedtime: Thank You for My Rocking Horse, Mr. President!," *Sun*, April 22, 2016; Melissa Chan, "Prince Harry and Michelle Obama Discuss Queen Elizabeth's Trash Talk," *Time*, May 9, 2016; Vanessa Friedman, "The Duchess of Cambridge and Sartorial Diplomacy," *New York Times*, October 21, 2015; Minyvonne Burke, "Prince William Reveals Christmas Plans for Prince George, Princess Charlotte," *International Business Times*, December 6, 2015; Josh Duboff, "Princess Charlotte Makes Her Palace Balcony Debut at the Queen's Birthday Parade," *Vanity Fair*, June 11, 2016; "Prince William's and Kate's Royal Tour of India and Bhutan," *Time*, April 16, 2016; Erin Jensen, "Kate Middleton Packs a Mean Punch at the Launch of Heads Together," *USA Today*, May 16, 2016.

Chapters 6, 7, and 8

Information and background for these chapters was based in part on conversations with Alan Hamilton, Countess Mountbatten, Richard Kay, 8th Earl Bathurst, Oonagh Shanley-Toffolo, Lady Margaret Rhodes, Lady Yolanda Joseph, James Whitaker, Tom Sykes, Alex Kidson, Cecile Thibaud, Mark Shand, Lucia Flecha de Lima, Jules Knight, Ezra Zilkha, Robin Leach, Wendy Leigh, Janet Lizop, Harold Brooks-Baker, Elizabeth d'Erlanger, Aileen Mehle, Ron Galella,

Muriel Hartwick, Philip Higgs, Joan Rivers, Penny Russell-Smith, Gered Mankowitz, the 2nd Countess of Romanones, Liz Smith, Peter Allen, Janet Allison, Norman Parkinson, John L. Marion, and David McGough. Obviously, the wedding of Prince Harry and Meghan Markle, the births of several royal children, the deaths of Prince Philip and Queen Elizabeth II, the coronation of Charles III, Megxit, and the stunning cancer diagnoses of both the King and Kate were all major news events covered by countless news outlets across the globe.

Just a very few of the published sources consulted: Danny Boyle, "Who Is Meghan Markle? Everything We Know About Prince Harry's Girlfriend," *Daily Telegraph*, November 12, 2016; Tom Sykes, "Why Prince William and Kate Middleton Have a Work Problem," *Daily Beast*, April 11, 2017; Emmeline Saunders, "Prince Harry Admits Wanting to Punch Someone in the Wake of Mum Princess Diana's Death," *Daily Mirror*, April 17, 2017; "New Baby Prince Is Born," BBC News, April 23, 2018; Caroline Davies, "Duke and Duchess of Cambridge Name Their Baby Son Louis Arthur Charles," *Guardian*, April 27, 2018; Maria Puente, "How Does Duchess Kate Do It? From Giving Birth to Camera-Ready in Heels in Under 8 Hours," *USA Today*, April 23, 2018; Megan Fisher, "When Prince Harry Met Meghan Markle—a Royal Romance," BBC News, November 27, 2017; Tara John, "Meet Meghan Markle, Prince Harry's Fiancée and Britain's Newest Royal-to-Be," *Time*, November 27, 2017; "Prince Harry 'Thrilled' to Marry Girlfriend Meghan Markle Next Year," BBC News, November 27, 2017; Robert Booth, "Meghan Markle Could Shake Up Monarchy, Says Noam Chomsky," *Guardian*, December 1, 2017; Cecilia Rodriguez, "Kate, William, Meghan and Harry: On Stage Together for the First Time," *Forbes*, February 28, 2018; "Meghan Markle and Prince Harry: A Timeline of How Their Lives Collided," *Sunday Times*, May 20, 2018; Caroline Davies, "The Royal In-Laws: Meghan Markle's Family," *Guardian*, May 15, 2018; Elise Taylor, "How Prince Harry Met Meghan Markle," *Vogue*, May 19, 2020; Richard Palmer, "Meghan's Dad Not Going to Wedding," *Daily Express*, May 15, 2018; Live coverage by the BBC, ABC, NBC, CBS, CNN, Fox News, and MSNBC, as well as extensive coverage by all other major media outlets of the wedding of Prince Harry and Meghan Markle at Windsor Castle on May 19, 2018; Jenifer Earl, "Meghan Markle's Family Drama Pre-Royal Wedding, from Staged Paparazzi Pics to Prince Harry's Shocking Letter," Fox News, May 19, 2018; Marina Pitofsky, "Meghan Says Tabloid Reports She Made Kate Cry Were False and the 'Reverse Happened,'" *Hill*, March 7, 2021; Christopher Andersen, *Brothers and Wives: Inside the Private Lives of William, Kate, Harry, and Meghan* (New York: Gallery Books, 2021); Jill Lawless and Sylvia Hui, "Prince Charming: Kate Gives Birth to Boy, Home by Suppertime," Associated Press, April 23, 2018; Carly Ledbetter, "Thomas Markle Attacks Meghan Markle, Royal Family in Brutal Interview," *HuffPost*, July 30, 2018; Halima Sadat, *Harry & Meghan: The Royal Wedding Album* (New York: Sterling, 2018); Amy Mackelden, "Why Meghan Markle's First Solo Royal Event with the Queen Is So Significant," *Harper's Bazaar*, June 14, 2018; "Prince William Speaks About 'Traumatic' Air Ambulance Callouts," BBC News, November 20, 2018; Lisa Armstrong, "Exclusive: First-Interview with Carole Middleton: 'Life is Really Normal—Most of the Time,'" *Telegraph*, November 30, 2018; Sharnaz Shaid, "Fab Four Reunited! Prince William, Kate, Harry, Join Forces Once More," *Hello!*, October 7, 2019; Kathy Campbell, "Prince Harry Confirms Rift with Brother Prince William: 'We're Certainly on Different Paths,'" *Us*, October 20, 2019; Meadhbh McGrath, "Royal Rift: Why Are William and Harry on 'Different Paths'?," *Irish Independent*, October 27, 2019; Kate Whitfield, "Royal Rift: William and

Harry Are on Different Paths 'For One Very Good Reason,'" *Express*, October 31, 2019; Victoria Murphy, "Kate Middleton Made an 'Emotional' Visit to a Children's Hospice This Morning," *Town & Country*, November 15, 2019; Aimee Lewis, "Prince Andrew Sparks Near-Universal Condemnation with TV Interview," CNN, November 17, 2019; "Prince Andrew's Links to Jeffrey Epstein," BBC News, November 16, 2019; Camilla Tominey and Victoria Ward, "Queen Did Not Approve Prince Andrew's Excruciating *Newsnight* Interview," *Sunday Telegraph*, November 18, 2019; Jack Royston, "Prince Andrew Should Lose Royal Titles, Face Extradition Over Epstein: Poll," *Newsweek*, June 26, 2020; Rosemary Feitelberg, "Harry and Meghan Withdraw 'Sussex Royal' Trademark Applications," *WWD*, February 21, 2020; "Harry and Meghan to End Use of 'SussexRoyal' Brand," BBC News, February 22, 2020; Ryan Parry, Ruth Styles, and Cheyenne Roundtree, "Meghan and Harry Are Living in This $18 Million Beverly Hills Mansion of Mega-Rich Hollywood Actor/Producer Tyler Perry and Arranged by Mutual Friend Oprah," *Daily Mail*, May 7, 2020; Caitlin O'Kane, "Tyler Perry Let Harry and Meghan Stay in His Home and Use His Security When the Royal Family Stripped Theirs Away," CBS News, March 8, 2021; James McClain, "Meghan Markle, Prince Harry Buy $14.7 Million Montecito Compound," *Variety*, August 12, 2020; Brooks Barnes, "Prince Harry and Meghan Sign Megawatt Netflix Deal," *New York Times*, September 2, 2020; Erin Vanderhoof, "Meghan and Harry Win a Battle in Their War Against Paparazzi," *Vanity Fair*, October 9, 2020; "Harry and Meghan Not Returning as Working Members of Royal Family," BBC News, February 19, 2021; Mark Landler, "Harry and Meghan Going Public at a Tough Time for the Royals," *New York Times*, February 26, 2021; "Buckingham Palace to Investigate Claims Meghan Bullied Staff," BBC News, March 3, 2021; *Oprah, with Meghan and Harry: A CBS Primetime Special*, directed by Leon Knoles, CBS, March 7, 2021; Danica Kirka and Jill Lawless, "Global Reaction to Harry and Meghan Interview Pours In," Associated Press, March 9, 2021; Caroline Linton, "Harry and Meghan Detail Royal Struggles in Bombshell Oprah Interview," CBS News, March 8, 2021; Jennifer Hassan, "'What Have They Done?' Britain's Media Reacts in Horror to Meghan and Harry Interview," *Washington Post*, March 9, 2021; "Meghan and Harry Interview: Urgent Palace Talks Over Claims," BBC News, March 9, 2021; Megan Specia, "In Britain, Meghan and Harry Talk Stirs Debate on Entrenched Racism," *New York Times*, March 9, 2021; Tom Sykes, "Prince William: My Family Is Not Racist, and No, I Haven't Spoken to Harry Yet," *Daily Beast*, March 11, 2021; Benjamin Mueller, "Royal Rift Reveals Britain's Underbelly: 'A Very Big Silence Around Race,'" *New York Times*, March 12, 2021; Rob Picheta, "Meghan Reveals 'Concerns' Within Royal Family About Her Baby's Skin Color," CNN, March 8, 2021; Leah Asmelash, "Michelle Obama Says It 'Wasn't a Complete Surprise' to Hear Meghan Talk of Racism in the Royal Family," CNN, March 16, 2021; "Prince Philip Has Died Aged 99, Buckingham Palace Announces," BBC, April 9, 2021; Marilyn Berger, "Prince Philip Died at 99 at His Home in Windsor Castle," *New York Times*, April 9, 2021; Anna Schaverien, "Two Tributes to Prince Philip, a.k.a. 'Grandpa,'" *New York Times*, April 11, 2021; Robert Lacey, *Battle of Brothers: William and Harry—the Inside Story of a Family in Tumult* (New York: HarperCollins, 2020); Rachel Elbaum, "All Eyes on Prince Harry, and Royal Rift, After His Return to U.K. for Prince Philip's Funeral," NBC News, April 16, 2021; Eliza Thompson, "Prince William, Prince Harry's Reunion at Philip's Funeral Was a 'Baby Step' in Healing Their Relationship," *Us*, May 7, 2021; Elise Taylor, "Is Kate Middleton Now the Firm's Greatest Asset?," *Vogue*, May 11, 2021; Elizabeth Paton, "Losing Meghan, Prince Harry—and Potentially Billions of Pounds," *New York Times*,

October 12, 2021; "Kate Middleton and Her Family Business," CNN Money, September 15, 2021; Quinci LeGardye, "Kate Middleton Gives a Surprise Piano Performance for Christmas Eve," *Harper's Bazaar*, December 25, 2021; Associated Press, "Singer Praises Middleton's Piano Skills After Surprise Performance," December 28, 2021; Doug Faulkner and Daniela Relph, "George, Charlotte and Louis Have First Day at Lambrook School," BBC News, September 7, 2022; Mark Landler, "Queen Elizabeth II Dies at 96," *New York Times*, September 8, 2022; Hannah Furness, "'Fab Four' Reunite in Sorrow for Surprise Windsor Walkabout," *Telegraph*, September 10, 2022; Ben Macintyre, "The Queen's Funeral Was the Grandest the World Has Seen," *Times*, September 19, 2022; "The State Funeral for Her Majesty The Queen," Queen Elizabeth II, Royal Family, September 19, 2022, https://www.royal.uk/news-and-activity/2022-09-19/the-state-funeral-for-her-majesty-the-queen; "Queen Elizabeth II's Funeral, As It Happened," *Times*, September 19, 2022; Rhonda Garelick, "The State of Kate," *New York Times*, January 13, 2023; James Crawford-Smith, "How Princess Kate Mastered Coronation Style," *Newsweek*, May 4, 2023; Michael M. Grynbaum, "Were Will and Kate Late to the Coronation? The News Media Wonders," *New York Times*, May 6, 2023; Mark Kleinman, "Princess of Wales's Parents' Party Supplies Firm Sold After Brush with Insolvency," Sky News, May 18, 2023; Kase Wickman, "Rose Hanbury Sends Legal Notice to Stephen Colbert After His Affair Joke," *Vanity Fair*, March 22, 2024; Tina Brown, "Heavy Lies the Crown," *New York Times*, March 25, 2024; Danielle Stacey, "The Special Meaning Behind Princess Kate's Incredible New Honor from King Charles," *Hello!*, April 23, 2024; "Princess Gives Cancer Fight Update," NBC News, June 14, 2024; Mark Duell, "Kate Middleton Is Seen in Public for First Time Since Cancer Diagnosis," *Daily Mail*, June 15, 2024; Mark Landler, "'Good Days and Bad Days': The Princess of Wales Gives Update on Cancer," *New York Times*, June 14, 2024; Holly Evans and Barney Davis, "Kate Middleton's Triumphant Return to Public Life at Trooping the Colour after Six Months Fighting Cancer," *Independent*, June 17, 2024; "Kate Middleton Receives Standing Ovation Upon Arriving at Wimbledon," TMZ, July 14, 2024; Matthew Young and Zahra Khaliq, "Emotional Moment Kate Middleton Gets Standing Ovation from Wimbledon's Centre Court," *Mirror*, July 14, 2024; James Middleton, *Meet Ella: The Dog Who Saved My Life* (New York: Pegasus Books, 2024); Karla Adam, "Princess Kate Says She Has Finished Cancer Chemo Treatment," *Washington Post*, September 9, 2024; Matt Rudd, "James Middleton: Kate, William and the Dog That Saved My Life," *Times*, September 23, 2024; James Crawford-Smith, "Princess Kate's Unexpected Fashion Moment Goes Viral," *Newsweek*, September 25, 2024; Max Colchester, "Kate Middleton Returns with a New Royal Role," *Wall Street Journal*, October 12, 2024; Starr Bowenbank, "Prince William 'Makes Excuses' to Avoid Kate Middleton's Family for This Relatable Reason," *InStyle*, November 27, 2024; Simmone Shah, "Kate Middleton Says Her Cancer Is in Remission," *Time*, January 14, 2025; Mehera Bonner, "Kate Middleton Visits Her Cancer Treatment Hospital for First Time Not Arriving Via a Secret Back Entrance," *Cosmopolitan*, January 14, 2025; Kristin Contino, "Former Royal Aide Says Prince William Will Exude This Quality When He Becomes King," *Marie Claire*, February 21, 2025; Ben Jureidini, "Already 'Hugely Influential' Behind the Scenes, Insiders Reveal What Kind of Queen Kate Middleton Will Be," *Tatler*, April 25, 2025; Katie Kindelan, "Kate Middleton Describes Cancer Journey as a 'Roller Coaster,'" ABC News, July 2, 2025; Emily Ferguson and Alicia Liberty, "Princess Kate Dazzles in Red as She Attends First State Banquet in Two Years," *Express*, July 8, 2025; Janine Henni, "Kate Middleton Caught Off Guard by Emotional Standing Ovation at Wimbledon,"

People, July 12, 2025; Daniela Relph and Galya Dimitrova, "'A Fresh Start': William and Kate to Move to New Windsor Home," BBC News, August 16, 2025; "Photos of Donald Trump and Jeffrey Epstein Projected onto Windsor Castle," *Vanity Fair*, September 18, 2025; Michael D. Shear, "Red Carpet Rolled Out for Trump in Britain," *New York Times*, September 18, 2024; Tom McArthur, "Sweet Treats for Kate and Melania as They Host Scouts," BBC, September 18, 2025; Simon Perry and Janine Henni, "Kate Middleton Was 'Aware' of Pressure of Trump State Visit: 'All Eyes Were on Her'," *People*, September 22, 2025; Mark Landler, "Holding Back Tears, Prince William Shows a New Side of a Future King," *New York Times*, October 10, 2025.

Bibliography

Allison, Ronald, and Sarah Riddell, eds. *The Royal Encyclopedia*. London: Macmillan, 1991.

Andersen, Christopher. *After Diana: William, Harry, Charles, and the Royal House of Windsor*. New York: Hyperion, 2007.

———. *Brothers and Wives: Inside the Private Lives of William, Kate, Harry, and Meghan*. New York: Gallery Books, 2021.

———. *The Day Diana Died*. New York: William Morrow, 1998.

———. *The Day John Died*. New York: William Morrow, 2000.

———. *Diana's Boys: William and Harry and the Mother They Loved*. New York: William Morrow, 2001.

———. *Game of Crowns: Elizabeth, Camilla, Kate, and the Throne*. New York: Gallery Books, 2016.

———. *The King: The Life of Charles III*. New York: Gallery Books, 2022.

———. *William and Kate: Royal Baby Edition*. New York: Gallery Books, 2013.

———. *William and Kate: A Royal Love Story*. New York: Gallery Books, 2011.

———. *William and Kate: Special Wedding Edition*. New York: Gallery Books, 2011.

Anne the Princess Royal, with Ivor Herbert. *Riding Through My Life*. London: Pelham, 1991.

Arbiter, Dickie, with Lynne Barrett-Lee. *On Duty with the Queen: My Time as a Buckingham Palace Press Secretary*. Dorking: Blink Publishing, 2014.

Aronson, Theo. *Royal Family: Years of Transition*. London: Thistle Publishing, 2014. First published 1983 by Murray (London).

Barry, Stephen P. *Royal Service: My Twelve Years as Valet to Prince Charles*. New York: Macmillan, 1983.

Beaton, Cecil. *Beaton in the Sixties: More Unexpurgated Diaries*. London: Weidenfeld & Nicolson, 2003.

Berry, Wendy. *The Housekeeper's Diary: Charles and Diana Before the Breakup*. New York: Barricade Books, 1995.

Blair, Tony. *A Journey: My Political Life*. New York: Alfred A. Knopf, 2010.

Bocca, Geoffrey. *Elizabeth and Philip*. New York: Holt, 1953.

Botham, Noel. *The Murder of Princess Diana*. New York: Pinnacle, 2004.

Bower, Tom. *Revenge: Meghan, Harry and the War Between the Windsors*. London: Blink Publishing, 2022.

Bradford, Sarah. *Diana*. New York: Viking, 2006.

———. *Elizabeth: A Biography of Britain's Queen*. New York: Farrar, Straus, and Giroux, 1996.

Brander, Michael. *The Making of the Highlands*. London: Constable, 1980.

Bryan, J., III, and Charles J. V. Murphy. *The Windsor Story*. New York: William Morrow, 1979.

Burrell, Paul. *A Royal Duty*. New York: Signet, 2004. First published 2003 by G. P. Putnam's Sons (New York).

———. *The Way We Were: Remembering Diana*. New York: William Morrow, 2006.

Campbell, Lady Colin. *Diana in Private: The Princess Nobody Knows*. London: Smith Gryphon, 1992.

Cannadine, David. *The Decline and Fall of the British Aristocracy*. New Haven: Yale University Press, 1990.

Cannon, John, and Ralph Griffiths. *The Oxford Illustrated History of the British Monarchy*. Oxford: Oxford University Press, 1992.

Cathcart, Helen. *The Queen Herself*. London: W. H. Allen, 1982.

———. *The Queen and Prince Philip: Forty Years of Happiness*. London: Coronet Books, 1987.

Clarke, Mary. *Diana Once Upon a Time*. London: Sidgwick & Jackson, 1994.

Clifford, Max, and Angela Levin. *Max Clifford: Read All About It*. London: Virgin Books, 2005.

Davies, Nicholas. *Diana: The Lonely Princess*. New York: Birch Lane, 1996.

———. *Queen Elizabeth II: A Woman Who Is Not Amused*. New York: Birch Lane, 1996.

———. *William: The Inside Story of the Man Who Will Be King*. New York: St. Martin's Griffin: 1999.

Delderfield, Eric R. *Kings and Queens of England and Great Britain*. 3rd ed. Newton Abbot: David & Charles, 1990.

Delorm, Rene, with Barry Fox and Nadine Taylor. *Diana and Dodi: A Love Story*. Los Angeles: Tallfellow Press, 1998.

Dempster, Nigel, and Peter Evans. *Behind Palace Doors: Marriage and Divorce in the House of Windsor*. New York: Putnam, 1993.

Dimbleby, Jonathan. *The Prince of Wales: A Biography*. New York: William Morrow, 1994.

Dolby, Karen, ed. *The Wicked Wit of Queen Elizabeth II*. London: Michael O'Mara Books, 2015.

Edwards, Anne. *Diana and the Rise of the House of Spencer*. London: Hodder & Stoughton, 1999.

Ferguson, Ronald. *The Galloping Major: My Life and Singular Times*. London: Macmillan, 1994.

Fisher, Graham, and Heather Fisher. *Elizabeth: Queen & Mother*. New York: Hawthorn Books, 1964.

Foreman, J. B., ed. *Scotland's Splendour*. Glasgow: Collins, 1961.

Fox, Mary Virginia. *Princess Diana*. Hillside, NJ: Enslow, 1986.

Goldsmith, Lady Annabel. *Annabel: An Unconventional Life*. London: Phoenix, 2005.

Goodall, Sarah, and Nicholas Monson. *The Palace Diaries: A Story Inspired by Twelve Years of Life Behind Palace Gates*. London: Mainstream, 2006.

Graham, Caroline. *Camilla and Charles: The Love Story*. London: John Blake, 2005.

———. *Camilla: The King's Mistress*. London: John Blake, 1994.

Graham, Tim. *Diana: HRH The Princess of Wales*. New York: Summit, 1988.

———. *The Royal Year 1993*. London: Michael O'Mara, 1993.

Gregory, Martyn. *The Diana Conspiracy Exposed*. New York: Moyer Bell, 2000.

Hardman, Robert. *Her Majesty: Queen Elizabeth II and Her Court*. New York: Pegasus Books, 2012.

Hewitt, James. *Love and War*. London: John Blake, 1999.

Hill, Duncan, Alison Guantlett, Sarah Rickayzen, and Gareth Thomas, eds. *The Royal Family: A Year by Year Chronicle of the House of Windsor*. Bath: Parragon, 2012.

Hoey, Brian. *All the Queen's Men: Inside the Royal Household*. London: HarperCollins, 1992.

Holden, Anthony. *Charles: A Biography*. London: Weidenfeld & Nicolson, 1988.

———. *The Tarnished Crown: Princess Diana and the House of Windsor*. New York: Random House, 1993.

Hough, Richard. *Born Royal: The Lives and Loves of the Young Windsors*. New York: Bantam Books, 1988.

HRH The Prince of Wales. *Charles in His Own Words*. Rosemary York, ed. London: W. H. Allen, 1981.

———. *Harmony: A New Way of Looking at Our World*. New York: HarperCollins, 2010.

———. *The Old Man of Lochnagar*. London: Hamish Hamilton Children's Books, 1980.

———. *A Vision of Britain: A Personal View of Architecture*. London: Doubleday, 1989.

———. *Watercolours*. London: Little, Brown, 1991.

HRH The Prince of Wales and Charles Clover. *Highgrove: Portrait of an Estate*. London: Chapmans, 1993.

HRH The Prince of Wales and Candida Lycett Green. *The Garden at Highgrove*. London: Weidenfeld & Nicholson, 2000.

Hutchins, Chris, and Peter Thompson. *Sarah's Story: The Duchess Who Defied the Royal House of Windsor*. London: Smith Gryphon, 1992.

Jephson, P. D. *Shadows of a Princess: Diana, Princess of Wales, an Intimate Account by Her Private Secretary*. New York: HarperCollins, 2000.

Jobson, Robert. *Catherine, the Princess of Wales: A Biography of the Future Queen*. New York: Pegasus Books, 2024.

———. *The New Royal Family: Prince George, William and Kate, the Next Generation*. London: John Blake, 2013.

———. *William's Princess*. London: John Blake, 2006.

Joseph, Claudia. *Kate: The Making of a Princess*. New York: Avon, 2010.

Junor, Penny. *Charles*. New York: St. Martin's Press, 1987.

———. *The Firm: The Troubled Life of the House of Windsor*. New York: Thomas Dunne Books, 2005.

———. *Prince William: The Man Who Will Be King*. New York: Pegasus Books, 2012.

Knatchbull, Timothy. *From a Clear Blue Sky*. London: Hutchinson, 2009.

Lacey, Robert. *Battle of Brothers: William and Harry—the Inside Story of a Family in Tumult*. New York: HarperCollins, 2020.

———. *Majesty: Elizabeth II and the House of Windsor*. New York: Harcourt Brace Jovanovich, 1977.

———. *Queen Mother*. Boston: Little, Brown, 1987.

Lloyd, Ian. *William & Catherine's New Royal Family: Celebrating the Arrival of Princess Charlotte*. London: Carlton Books, 2015.

Lorimer, David. *Radical Prince: The Practical Vision of the Prince of Wales*. Edinburgh: Floris Books, 2003.

Maclean, Veronica. *Crowned Heads: Kings, Sultans and Emperors: A Royal Quest*. London: Hodder & Stoughton, 1993.

Marr, Andrew. *The Real Elizabeth: An Intimate Portrait of Queen Elizabeth II*. New York: Henry Holt, 2012.

Martin, Ralph G. *Charles & Diana*. New York: Putnam, 1985.

Mayer, Catherine. *Born to Be King: Prince Charles on Planet Windsor*. New York: Henry Holt, 2015.

Montgomery-Massingberd, Hugh, ed. *Burke's Guide to the British Monarchy*. London: Burke's Peerage New English Library, 1977.

Morrah, Dermot. *To Be a King: A Privileged Account of the Early Life and Education of H.R.H. the Prince of Wales Written with the Approval of H.M. The Queen*. London: Hutchinson, 1968.

Morrow, Ann. *The Queen*. London: Granada, 1983.

Morton, Andrew. *Diana: Her True Story—in Her Own Words*. New York: Simon & Schuster, 1997.

———. *Diana: In Pursuit of Love*. London: Michael O'Mara, 2004.

———. *Inside Buckingham Palace*. London: Michael O'Mara, 1991.

Nicholl, Katie. *Kate: The Future Queen*. New York: Weinstein Books, 2013.

Pasternak, Anna. *Princess in Love*. London: Bloomsbury, 1994.

Pimlott, Ben. *The Queen: A Biography of Elizabeth II*. New York: Wiley, 1996.

Prince Harry. *Spare*. New York: Random House, 2023.

Reese-Jones, Trevor, with Moira Johnston. *The Bodyguard's Story: Diana, the Crash, and the Sole Survivor*. New York: Warner Books, 2000.

Rhodes, Margaret. *The Final Curtsey: The Autobiography of Margaret Rhodes, First Cousin of the Queen and Niece of the Late Queen Elizabeth the Queen Mother*. London: Umbria, 2011.

Sakol, Jeannie, and Caroline Lathan. *The Royals*. New York: Congdon & Weed, 1987.

Sancton, Thomas, and Scott Macleod. *Death of a Princess: The Investigation*. New York: St. Martin's Press, 1998.

Sarah, The Duchess of York, with Jeff Coplon. *My Story*. New York: Atria Books, 1996.

Scobie, Omid. *Endgame: Inside the Royal Family and the Monarchy's Fight for Survival*. New York: Dey Street, 2023.

Scobie, Omid, and Carolyn Durand. *Finding Freedom: Harry and Meghan*. New York: Dey Street, 2020.

Seward, Ingrid. *The Queen and Di*. New York: HarperCollins, 2000.

———. *William & Harry: The People's Princes*. London: Carlton Books, 2008.

Simmons, Simone, with Susan Hill. *Diana: The Secret Years*. London: Michael O'Mara, 1998.

Simmons, Simone, with Ingrid Seward. *Diana: The Last Word*. New York: St. Martin's Press, 2005.

Smith, Sally Bedell. *Diana in Search of Herself: Portrait of a Troubled Princess*. New York: Times Books, 1999.

———. *Elizabeth the Queen: The Life of a Modern Monarch*. New York: Random House, 2012.

———. *Prince Charles: The Passions and Paradoxes of an Improbable Life*. New York: Random House, 2017.

Snell, Kate. *Diana: Her Last Love*. London: Granada Media, 2000.

Spencer, Charles. *The Spencers: A Personal History of an English Family*. New York: St. Martin's Press, 2000.

Spoto, Donald. *The Decline and Fall of the House of Windsor*. New York: Simon & Schuster, 1995.

———. *Diana: The Last Year*. New York: Harmony Books, 1997.

Lord Stevens of Kirkwhelpington. *The Operation Paget Inquiry Report into the Allegation of Conspiracy to Murder Diana, Princess of Wales, and Emad El-Din Mohamed Abdel Moneim Fayed*. London, December 14, 2006.

Thornton, Michael. *Royal Feud: The Queen Mother and the Duchess of Windsor*. London: Michael Joseph, 1985.

Thornton, Penny. *With Love from Diana*. New York: Pocket Books, 1995.

Vickers, Hugo. *Alice: Princess Andrew of Greece*. New York: St. Martin's Press, 2002.

———. *Elizabeth the Queen Mother*. London: Arrow, 2006. First published 2005 by Hutchinson (London).

Wade, Judy. *The Truth*. London: John Blake, 2001.

Warwick, Christopher. *Princess Margaret: A Life of Contrasts*. London: André Deutsch, 2000. First published 1983 Weidenfeld & Nicholson (London).

Wharfe, Ken, with Robert Jobson, *Diana: Closely Guarded Secret*. London: Michael O'Mara Books, 2003.

Whitaker, James. *Diana v. Charles*. London: Signet, 1993.

Wilson, Christopher. *A Greater Love: Prince Charles's Twenty-Year Affair with Camilla Parker Bowles*. New York: William Morrow, 1994.

———. *The Windsor Knot*. New York: Citadel Press, 2003.

Ziegler, Philip. *Queen Elizabeth II: A Photographic Portrait*. London: Thames & Hudson, 2010.

Index